Consumed!

A Passion for the Great Commission

Thomas P. Johnston

Dedication

This book is dedicated to my love, Raschelle, without whom the writing of this book would not have been possible.

Thanks

A special thanks to Wendy Chorot for her tireless and detailed editorial work.

And a very special thanks to President of Midwestern Baptist Theological Seminary, Dr. Jason Allen, to Dr. Jason Duesing, Provost of Midwestern, and to the Midwestern Board of Trustees for their generosity in granting me a sabbatical to write this book during the Spring Semester, 2017. I am humbled and grateful for the privilege that they have afforded me.

Consumed!

A Passion for the Great Commission

Thomas P. Johnston

www.evangelizology.com

Evangelism Unlimited, Inc.

Liberty, Missouri

2017

Consumed!—A Passion for the Great Commission

Table of Contents

Foreword

Some of the most important words ever spoken on this earth were those uttered by the Lord Jesus after His death and resurrection when He communicated to His disciples His will for them and His church to carry on His work of reaching the lost with the Gospel. Those words uttered during several post-resurrection appearances of Jesus prior to His ascension have been known to believers through the centuries as the Great Commission. When most Christians hear the term the Great Commission, they immediately think of the Great Commission passage in Matthew's Gospel account. However, Jesus in actuality commissioned His disciples to evangelize the world recorded in five different passages of Scripture in each of the four Gospels and the book of Acts. These words of Jesus that He delivered to His disciples before departing this world have been considered His "marching orders" for the true Christian church for over two millennia. If these are some of the most important words to come from the lips of the Lord Jesus which indicate His purpose for His church for all time, knowing their precise meaning and their practical implications should prove to be highly significant for the Body of Christ.

Words convey meaning and verbs are considered the most important part of speech in any language. In this book *Consumed!-A Passion for the Great Commission*, Dr. Tom Johnston, Evangelism Professor at Midwestern Baptist Theological Seminary, has taken the actual words of the Great Commission passages in the New Testament and significant words, in particular the verbs, related to the fulfillment of and response to the Great Commission to provide both a theological and practical analysis of the meaning and implications of the Great Commission for the church today. Through his scholarly research and writing, Dr. Johnston brings both clarity to the meaning and application of the Great Commission and correction to prevailing erroneous notions concerning the Great Commission. The linguistic giftedness, scholarly abilities, and passionate heart for the Great Commission with which the Lord has blessed Dr. Tom Johnston qualify him to be able to produce such an important and timely work in the field of evangelism.

I know first-hand that Dr. Tom Johnston possesses a personal passion for the Great Commission which will become evident to anyone reading this book. One of my first encounters with Dr. Johnston was at a meeting of the Southern Baptist Convention in San Antonio, Texas. Both of us had students with us who we were taking out to do street witnessing near the Alamo. For several years since then we have taught evangelism classes together and been on the streets and in neighborhoods together in cities across America taking students from our respective seminaries sharing the Gospel through Crossover. Crossover is an evangelistic outreach effort sponsored by the North American Mission Board conducted the week prior to the Southern Baptist Convention in the city in which the Convention is held each year. Dr. Johnston has brought students to my "home turf" of New Orleans where I serve as an Evangelism Professor at New Orleans Baptist Theological Seminary and helped us evangelize in our city during the celebration of Mardi Gras. I have heard him teach about the Gospel equipping students to share their faith, preach the Gospel publically, and share the Gospel personally with conviction and passion. The Great Commission is not simply a theological concept for Dr. Johnston. The Great Commission is an intentional lifestyle for him.

This book is a comprehensive examination and critical analysis of the Great Commission as revealed through the words of the New Testament. Although scholarly and theological, the book also is practical and motivational. Professors and students, pastors and church members all will benefit from the reading of this book. My hope is that the Spirit of the Lord will use the words of this book about the Great Commission analyzing God's words in His Book about the Great Commission to light a fire that will consume hearts with a renewed passion for the Great Commission and will culminate in a renewed commitment to the fulfillment of the Great Commission through the church in this generation!

Preston L. Nix, Ph.D.
Professor of Evangelism and Evangelistic Preaching
Occupying the Roland Q. Leavell Chair of Evangelism
Director, Leavell Center for Evangelism and Church Health
Chairman, Pastoral Ministries Division
New Orleans Baptist Theological Seminary, New Orleans, Louisiana
August 2017

CHAPTER ONE

GOD'S WORDS AT WORK
—ἐνεργέω—

The Great Commission represents God at work. It is God extending His creative power into the souls of men. In His Great Commission Jesus Christ invites mankind to participate in His creative power in this world. Let's begin by considering God's creative power.

God created the world from nothing. He spoke and His first creation was light. Two Hebrew words brought something out of nothing: יְהִי אוֹר—"Let light be." The result? "And there was light" (Genesis 1:3). God, introducing Himself to man, explained His creative energy captured in the power of His words. He spoke and it came to be. For each of the first six days of creation God merely uttered a different set of words, and these words unleashed a whirlwind of creative activity within that which had not previously existed!

This chapter will consider the preeminence of God's word on mission. Beginning with the words of God, it will move to the power of the words of Christ—who was God became flesh. It will move to how Christ invites men to use these same words, extending God's creative activity into world history. By working through Christ's followers, God continues to extend the power of His mighty words to fulfill His work on this earth.

The Word of God

The Song of Moses, found in Deuteronomy 32, gives a beautiful picture of God operating through His words. Moses began this song with a summons to listen to his human words, as he transcribed divine words from God:

"Give ear, O heavens, and I will speak, and let the earth hear the words of my mouth. May my teaching drop as the rain, my

speech distill as the dew, like gentle rain upon the tender grass, and like showers upon the herb" (Deuteronomy 32:1-2 ESV).

Moses called every angelic host in heaven and every future human being on earth to stop and pay attention to the words of his mouth. The scope of this summons is overwhelming. He called every person in human history to listen to his words. Yet even more important was that the transcendent God chose to use Moses as a human intermediary to communicate His words to the world!

These words of God transcribed by the hand of Moses (contained in the Torah or the five books of Moses) were to have an amazing impact wherever they soaked the soil. The words of Moses were to resemble rain, dew, raindrops, and showers. The fourfold repetition is unambiguous. God chose to use His words to accomplish His supernatural work in the natural realm, much like rain, dew, raindrops, and showers water the ground and cause it to sprout and bear fruit. Isaiah elaborated on this same idea in Isaiah 55:

> *"For my thoughts are not your thoughts, neither are your ways my ways, declares the LORD. For as the heavens are higher than the earth, so are my ways higher than your ways and my thoughts than your thoughts. For as the rain and the snow come down from heaven and do not return there but water the earth, making it bring forth and sprout, giving seed to the sower and bread to the eater, so shall my word be that goes out from my mouth; it shall not return to me empty, but it shall accomplish that which I purpose, and shall succeed in the thing for which I sent it"* (Isaiah 55:8-11 ESV).

As Isaiah transcribed the words of God, he rekindled language from Deuteronomy 32. Isaiah described the work of God as similar to the transforming impact of rain upon the earth. This God, who transforms this world by His words, would continue to do so wherever He was to send them out. God promised that His word would always accomplish His ends, and never return to Him empty.

The words of man fly away, but the word of God remains forever.

Anticipating the doubts of ever-questioning men, God prepped

His readers with the idea that His thoughts are not man's thoughts, and that His ways are not man's ways. Likewise, a battle has raged ever since the release of Holy Scriptures into world history. It is a battle of man's will against God's will. Within this raging battle, God has chosen to contain all the energies of His creative powers in His word.

The Words of Christ

When Jesus was on earth, He made three radical declarations related to His words:

> "Everyone then who hears these words of mine and does them will be like a wise man who built his house on the rock. And the rain fell, and the floods came, and the winds blew and beat on that house, but it did not fall, because it had been founded on the rock" (Matthew 7:24-25 ESV).

Notice that the word "rock" is in the singular. Jesus communicated that His words, and only His words, functioned as the solid foundation for all of life. Quite an astounding statement. Later in His ministry He made another radical declaration related to His words:

> "Heaven and earth will pass away, but my words will not pass away" (Matthew 24:35 ESV).

In saying this, Jesus differentiated His words from all other human words. Whereas the rest of mankind's words come and go, the words of Jesus will remain forever. His words are more stable and sure than the ground upon which men take their stand!

In the Great Commission in Matthew, Jesus made a third radical statement. He commanded His disciples that they should follow-up future disciples who had believed in Him and been baptized, teaching them to observe only what He commanded:

> "Go therefore and make disciples of all nations, baptizing them in the name of the Father and of the Son and of the Holy Spirit, teaching them to observe all that I have commanded you. And behold, I am with you always, to the end of the age" (Matthew 28:19-20 ESV).

It is certainly significant and not by chance that Jesus focused the

3

entire content of all future discipleship training upon a subsection of His words, that is, His commands. Two chapters of this book will be devoted to considering the commands of Christ. It was Christ who affirmed the rest of Scripture by the words of His mouth. Likewise, Jesus Christ extended His divine authority to the apostolic writings based on the following texts:

> "But the Helper, the Holy Spirit, whom the Father will send in my name, he will teach you all things and bring to your remembrance all that I have said to you" (John 14:26 ESV).

> "When the Spirit of truth comes, he will guide you into all the truth, for he will not speak on his own authority, but whatever he hears he will speak, and he will declare to you the things that are to come. He will glorify me, for he will take what is mine and declare it to you" (John 16:13-14 ESV).

Jesus conveyed His divine authority to the writings of the apostles in three directions:

1. To the four Gospels, being that they were written with apostolic provenance

2. Jesus also conferred divine authority to the books of the Old Testament by speaking of them in the Gospels

3. He gave His divine authority to the Book of Acts and the New Testament Epistles.

All these books combined have become the foundation upon which is established every believer in the history of the churches. Christians are established on the words of the Bible, as upon the rock of Jesus' words.

Jesus Christ chose His words to be the method by which He would reveal Himself to every future living human. Amazingly, though Jesus never wrote a book, the Son of God relied upon His Apostles to be the authors by which He would relay these eternal words. But that is exactly how He chose to operate. At Christ's bidding—by their writings—the Apostles became the primary teachers of the Church. "And He Himself gave some *to be* apostles" (Ephesians 4:11). These apostles not only gave us the four Gospels, but they also gave us further explanation in the Book of Acts and the Epistles. These apostles explained the continuing power of the

Word of God in evangelism.

Work (ἐνεργέω)

The Apostle Paul chose a powerful verb when he remembered back to his days of evangelizing among the Thessalonians. The verb that came to his mind was to "work," "energize," or "excite." The verb in the Greek is ἐνεργέω (to work in). Paul used this verb when he spoke of the impact of his words upon the minds and hearts of the Thessalonian believers, which led them to receive the gospel:

> And we also thank God constantly for this, that when you received the word of God, which you heard from us, you accepted it not as the word of men but as what it really is, the word of God, which is at work [ἐνεργέω] in you believers (1 Thessalonians 2:13 ESV).

The power behind Paul's preaching did not consist of the words of men, but rather the power resided in the word of God, "which is at work in you believers." The Greek word behind the English word "work" is the verb ἐνεργέω (to work in). This active energy was the spark, before, behind, in, and around the words of Paul when he shared the gospel with the Thessalonians. His were not the mere words of a man. There was divine power infusing the words of Paul—he was sharing God's words.

Paul used this verb ἐνεργέω (to work in) to describe God's work in other places. In Ephesians 1:11, Paul focused on God's effectual working according to His sovereign will. The entirety of His mighty work in this world was completed and fully accomplished in Jesus Christ (Ephesians 1:20).

In Galatians 2:8, Paul called God, "He who worked effectively" through Peter and "worked effectively in me [Paul]." Likewise, using a related noun, Paul described his ministry as "the effective working [ἡ ἐνέργεια] of His power" (Ephesians 3:7). God determined that His words would operate as spiritual dynamite in this world to change lives and give eternal life!

Paul came to a crescendo of the work of God by using the verb ἐνεργέω with its related noun, ἡ ἐνέργεια:

> Him we proclaim, warning everyone and teaching everyone with all wisdom, that we may present everyone mature in Christ. For

> this I toil, struggling with all his energy [ἡ ἐνέργεια] that he
> powerfully [ἡ δύναμις] works [ἐνεργέω] within me
> (Colossians 1:28-29 ESV).

Just as God works mightily through His words, this same God has chosen to operate mightily through His people. As Paul labored as an evangelist, God worked through him mightily as he proclaimed Christ. So also, this gospel worked in Paul "mightily" (ἡ δύναμις)—this identical word is used of the "power" of the gospel in Romans 1:16.

The same effectual working is available to everyone who is a part of the body of Christ (Ephesians 4:16). And in Ephesians 3:20 Paul affirmed that God "is able to do exceedingly abundantly above all that we ask or think, according to the power that works [ἐνεργέω] in us." Indeed, it is this God "who works [ἐνεργέω] in you both to will and to do [ἐνεργέω] for *His* good pleasure" (Philippians 2:13). The evangelist is not left to his own insignificant power as he goes out with the gospel of Christ. All the saving energy of God's word is available to him to accomplish God's work.

Meanwhile, another spiritual being effectually works among men—none other than the "prince of the power of the air, the spirit who now works [ἐνεργέω] in the sons of disobedience" (Ephesians 2:2). Paul described this geo-political rival as the "mystery of lawlessness" whose deceitful scheming was already at work in his day:

> For the mystery of lawlessness is already at work [ἐνεργέω]. Only
> he who now restrains it will do so until he is out of the way
> (2 Thessalonians 2:7 ESV).

Satan himself works to lead people astray in every culture and generation. In synchronous interrelationship with the sinister work of the Evil One, man's lusts ooze forth from within his own heart. These lusts work (ἐνεργέω) in combination with the Law to bear the fruit of sin which leads to death (Romans 7:5). So, against the dungeon of these destructive powers strikes the only hammer of hope—the word of God.

Paul explained that instead of being held captive by the workings of the world, the flesh, and the Devil, man can become captive to the effectual workings of the gospel. How are the effectual workings of God acquired through the gospel of Christ? It is through properly "receiving" the word of the gospel. Receiving this gospel not as the mere words of men, but as it really is, the word of God (cf. 1 Thessalonians 2:13). The humble reception of this gospel initiates its effectual working in the soul of man.

Paul expanded on this idea by using the phrase, "hearing of faith"—a whole chapter is given over to this important concept. In Galatians 3 Paul asked two rhetorical questions:

> This only I want to learn from you: Did you receive the Spirit by the works of the law, or by the hearing of faith? (Galatians 3:2).

> Therefore He who supplies the Spirit to you and works miracles among you, does He do it by the works of the law, or by the hearing of faith? (Galatians 3:5).

Closely connected to the divine power of the word of God, Paul argued for a "hearing of faith" that unlocks the effectual working of God in and through God's word. This hearing precedes and follows saving faith. And this "hearing" unlocks God's continued work in the soul of man according to His mighty power:

> And what is the exceeding greatness of His power [ἡ δύναμις] toward us who believe, according to the working [ἐνεργέω] of His mighty [τὸ κράτος] power [ἡ ἰσχύς] which He worked [ἐνεργέω] in Christ when He raised Him from the dead and seated Him at His right hand in the heavenly places (Ephesians 1:19-20).

Paul multiplied the words he used in Ephesians 1 to describe the powerful working of God—as he wrote of God's undiminished dominion—even though he often found himself closed behind the doors of the Roman prison system!

Paul later punctuated this point when he affirmed that Christ works effectually through faith alone and by love alone:

> You have become estranged from Christ, you who attempt to be justified by law; you have fallen from grace. For we through the Spirit eagerly wait for the hope of righteousness by faith. For in Christ Jesus neither circumcision nor uncircumcision avails anything, but faith working [ἐνεργέω] through love (Galatians 5:4-6).

Two additional words link the verb "working" (ἐνεργέω)

7

directly to the Great Commission. The first word interlocking the energy or working of God and the Great Commission is the adjective ἐνεργής (meaning effective, active, powerful). This word was used by Paul of God opening an effective door of ministry for him in Ephesus:

> But I will tarry in Ephesus until Pentecost. For a great and effective [ἐνεργής] door has opened to me, and there are many adversaries (1 Corinthians 16:8-9).

This mighty door stood open to the Apostle Paul, although there were many adversaries. Using the same word, the author of Hebrews explained the penetrating power of God's living word:

> For the word of God is living and powerful [ἐνεργής], and sharper than any two-edged sword, piercing even to the division of soul and spirit, and of joints and marrow, and is a discerner of the thoughts and intents of the heart (Hebrews 4:12).

The effectiveness of open doors to the gospel is unequivocally linked to the effective working of God's mighty word. Both are necessary simultaneously. Neither is independent of the other.

A second verbal Great Commission link interlocks the working of God with the gospel of Christ. Paul introduced his theme for the Book of Romans—the power of justification by grace alone through faith alone.

> For I am not ashamed of the gospel of Christ, for it is the power [ἡ δύναμις] of God to salvation for everyone who believes, for the Jew first and also for the Greek (Romans 1:16).

Paul affirmed that the "effectual spark" of faith found its combustible agent in the gospel of Christ—spiritual dynamite indeed! Paul used the same word for the power of the gospel (ἡ δύναμις) as he did in Colossians 1:29 for God's power working through his proclamation (ἡ δύναμις). Oh, the mighty word we have received! Oh, this mighty working! What a powerful weapon at our disposal.

God's Word Is Alive!

Living and Active

As much as any living creature, the word of God is living (ζάω) and as noted above, it is active:

> For the word of God is living [ζάω] and powerful [ἐνεργής], and sharper than any two-edged sword, piercing even to the division of soul and spirit, and of joints and marrow, and is a discerner of the thoughts and intents of the heart. And there is no creature hidden from His sight, but all things are naked and open to the eyes of Him to whom we must give account (Hebrews 4:12-13).

As much as we are alive, the word of God is alive. Surely if God could make stones into sons of Abraham (Matthew 3:9), then likewise He is able to breathe life into His words. Likewise, Stephen described the words of Moses as "living words":

> "He was in the assembly in the wilderness, with the angel who spoke to him on Mount Sinai, and with our ancestors; and he received living words to pass on to us" (Acts 7:38 NIV).

Exhaled by God

Paul explained that the word of God was literally exhaled by God:

> All Scripture is breathed out by God and profitable for teaching, for reproof, for correction, and for training in righteousness, that the man of God may be complete, equipped for every good work (2 Timothy 3:16-17 ESV).

The words on the pages of Scripture are so close to God's heart and mouth, that they are described as having been breathed out by Him—just as the words "Let there be light" were breathed out on the day He created the world.

Life-Giving

God's words are the only source of spiritual life on earth. Moses began his song with the spiritual effectiveness of his words, "May my teaching drop as the rain, my speech distill as the dew" (Deuteronomy 32:2 ESV). Moses then continued, after completing his song, to discuss the life-giving function of his words:

> And when Moses had finished speaking all these words to all Israel, he said to them, "Take to heart all the words by which I am warning you today, that you may command them to your children, that they may be careful to do all the words of this law.

9

> For it is no empty word for you, but your very life, and by this word you shall live long in the land that you are going over the Jordan to possess" (Deuteronomy 32:45-47 ESV).

These words were not spoken by God in vain. These words contain life. These words are "your very life"!

Nourishment

The Apostle Peter explained the life-giving characteristic of the words of God, by calling them "milk" to the soul of man:

> Therefore, laying aside all malice, all deceit, hypocrisy, envy, and all evil speaking, as newborn babes, desire the pure milk of the word, that you may grow thereby, if indeed you have tasted that the Lord is gracious (1 Peter 2:1-3).

Peter admonished all followers of Jesus to long for the spiritual nourishment that only God's words can and do provide. Because God's words are alive, they provide true spiritual nourishment. They nourish us, as well as those under our charge. God's words are the only source of life-changing activity in the world.

God's Word Is Active!

Just as the word of God is "living and active," so also within the pages of Scripture we read of its activity. As a living being God's word runs, it spreads, it multiplies, it grows mightily, it prevails, and it bears fruit! These concepts are used in Scripture to portray God's word as a living being!

It Comes!

> In the fifteenth year of the reign of Tiberius Caesar, while Pontius Pilate was governor of Judea, Herod was tetrarch of Galilee, his brother Philip tetrarch of the region of Iturea and Trachonitis, and Lysanias tetrarch of Abilene, during the high priesthood of Annas and Caiaphas, God's word [τὸ ῥῆμα] came [γίνομαι] to John the son of Zechariah in the wilderness (Luke 3:1-2 HCSB).

God Himself transpierced human affairs and penetrated this world "in the sight of all nations" (Isaiah 52:10 NASB)—sending His word through John the Baptist. It is noteworthy that "word of God" was the subject of the action. This living "word of God" visited John the

Baptist, and through John its promised blessings began unfolding upon world history.

It Runs!

> *Finally, brethren, pray for us, that the word of the Lord may run [τρέχω] swiftly and be glorified, just as it is with you, and that we may be delivered from unreasonable and wicked men; for not all have faith* (2 Thessalonians 3:1-2).

Paul described the word of God as an athlete running in full stride, picking up a very human analogy and applying it to the word. The Greek verb for *running* is τρέχω. Just as the Psalmist affirmed that he would run in obedience to the word of God, "I will run in the way of your commandments when you enlarge my heart!" (Psalm 119:32 ESV). Likewise, Philip ran when the Holy Spirit beckoned him to overtake a certain chariot, "So Philip ran to him, and heard him reading the prophet Isaiah, and said, 'Do you understand what you are reading?'" (Acts 8:30). So also, the word of God runs throughout the world.

It Spreads!

> *And the word of the Lord was being spread [διαφέρω] throughout all the region* (Acts 13:49).

The verb to "spread abroad" is διαφέρω. Like the luxuriant tree spreading forth, used to describe King Nebuchadnezzar in Daniel 4, the word of God, like a living thing, grows and multiplies. It adds shoots, branches, and leaves. It ever expands its reach within the world of men.

It Multiplies and It Grows!

> *But the word of God grew [αὐξάνω] and multiplied [πληθύνω]* (Acts 12:24).

This living and active word is alive and well. Elsewhere it is described as an inanimate object, a double-edged sword (Hebrews 4:12). Yet the word of God is more than an inanimate weapon, it is a living organism. This word multiplies (πληθύνω) in strength and grows (αὐξάνω) in its reach.

The verb for "grow" is found numerous times in the New Testament related to growing in the Christian faith. For example,

Peter encouraged his readers to "grow in the grace and knowledge of our Lord and Savior Jesus Christ" (2 Peter 3:18). Paul encouraged the Colossian believers to grow in the knowledge of God (Colossians 1:10). For it is God who gives the growth (1 Corinthians 3:6-7).

This word multiplies. The Greek verb πληθύνω has the implication of increasing in size, to multiply, increase, make full. When the word of God kept on spreading (αὐξάνω), the result was a great multiplication (πληθύνω) in the number of disciples:

> And the word of God continued to increase [αὐξάνω], and the number of the disciples multiplied [πληθύνω] greatly in Jerusalem, and a great many of the priests became obedient to the faith (Acts 6:7 ESV).

So also, not long after the conversion of Saul of Tarsus (later to be known as the Apostle Paul), we read:

> Then the churches throughout all Judea, Galilee, and Samaria had peace and were edified. And walking in the fear of the Lord and in the comfort of the Holy Spirit, they were multiplied [πληθύνω] (Acts 9:31).

It Grows Mightily and It Prevails!

> So the word of the Lord grew [αὐξάνω] mightily [κράτος] and prevailed [ἰσχύω] (Acts 19:20).

Building on the idea of the word of God growing (αὐξάνω), during the revival in Ephesus, Luke used another verb to explain the level of this growth—that verb was "to prevail" (ἰσχύω). So powerful was the growth and might of this word going forth that it actually became preeminent in the lives and hearts of men and women in Ephesus.

It Bears Fruit!

> Because of the hope laid up for you in heaven, of which you previously heard in the word of truth, the gospel which has come to you, just as in all the world also it is constantly bearing fruit [καρποφορέω] and increasing [αὐξάνω], even as it has been doing in you also since the day you heard of it and understood the grace of God in truth (Colossians 1:5-6 NASB).

Just as the word of God prevails, neither is it sterile! God has given seed that germinates (καρποφορέω). It is fruitful seed. It will produce the results God predetermines for it (Isaiah 55:10-11). This word has power to and will fructify.

It Always Accomplishes Its Work!

God's word always accomplishes the will of God—it never falls short of fulfilling His predetermined purposes!

> *"So shall my word be that goes out from my mouth; it shall not return to me empty, but it shall accomplish [συντελέω] that which I purpose, and shall succeed [εὐοδόω] in the thing for which I sent it"* (Isaiah 55:11 ESV).

Isaiah used three phrases to summarize the divine activity of the word which proceeds from God's mouth. First, it shall not return to Him in vain. Second, enshrined in the verb συντελέω, God's word will complete, accomplish, and finish the good pleasure of God. Third, His words will thrive to good success (εὐοδόω) in its purposes. The child of God can rest assured, that when he has humbly and boldly shared the word of God as best he knows how, that God consubstantiates (abides within) through His words to fulfill His eternal purposes.

So much more could be said about the characteristics of God's eternal words. May these suffice as an introduction to the topic. In concluding this chapter, let us consider three practical categories related to the Bible in evangelism and Christian ministry.

Making It Practical

Recognizing the Battle Against the Word of God

In Jesus' Parable of the Sower, Satan was depicted by the "birds of the air" that come and pluck the seed from the ground before it is established in the soil:

> *"Now the parable is this: The seed is the word of God. The ones along the path are those who have heard; then the devil comes and takes away the word from their hearts, so that they may not believe and be saved"* (Luke 8:11-12 ESV).

Simultaneous to the sowing of the word, the Evil One, here called the Devil, assaults the hearer's heart, plucking the eternal seed from ever taking root. His only tactic is to go after the seed, which is the word of God. The location of his sordid assault is within the recesses of man's soul. It is clear that this depicts a spiritual battle. Jesus explained that the central element of this battle culminated in different receptions of the word of God sown.

Understanding the Varieties of Responses to the Word of God

The Parable of the Sower, cited above, includes three other receptions of the word of God. The Devil's frontal attack is to remove the seed as it is being sown. As the person hears the life-saving gospel message of Jesus Christ, Satan simultaneously plucks that seed from man's heart. But this is not the only response in this parable. Two other responses display the flank and rear attacks of Satan. In His second explanation, Jesus described the shallow soil in which the word of God was not immediately snatched by Satan. Rather this rocky soil receives the word with joy, but it never succeeds in dropping down a root:

> "But the ones on the rock are those who, when they hear, receive the word with joy; and these have no root, who believe for a while and in time of temptation fall away" (Luke 8:13).

As the heat of the sun rises on it, the same day it receives the word with joy, it immediately begins to wither and waste away. Temptations or trials overwhelm this sprouted seed and it dries up.

The third seed sample goes one step farther. It is sown in the heart. Satan does not snatch it away. Early trials and tribulations come. It weathers those storms. But it brings forth no fruit to maturity:

> "Now the ones that fell among thorns are those who, when they have heard, go out and are choked with cares, riches, and pleasures of life, and bring no fruit to maturity" (Luke 8:14).

Here we find a plant buffeted by sin and selfish pursuits. All its strength is so wasted in worthless activities that it brings no fruit to maturity. The Devil dangles selfishness before some Christians and they fall for it. Inward-focused Christianity prowls in every church and selfishness tempts every Christian heart.

The last soil noted by Jesus is the good soil. This soil hears the word, receives it with joy, grows to maturity, and bears fruit with perseverance:

> *"But the ones that fell on the good ground are those who, having heard the word with a noble and good heart, keep it and bear fruit with patience"* (Luke 8:15).

Christ would have His disciples press on toward the fourth soil. In another place, Christ encouraged His followers to hear His words and put them into practice (Luke 6:47-48). So the Christian should strive to please his Master.

In Acts, we find a similar array of responses to the proclamation of the gospel:

- Saul of Tarsus responded violently against Stephen's sermon in Acts 7-8
- Ananias and Sapphira sinned while being a part of the church in Acts 5
- Simon the Sorcerer believed and was baptized, then he offered the apostles money to receive the power to give the Holy Spirit in Acts 8
- The Ethiopian Eunuch heard the gospel, requested baptism, and went on his way rejoicing in Acts 8.

Undoubtedly, wherever and whenever the word of God is proclaimed it elicits a variety of responses. In the Parable of the Sower, these differences were not attributed to the evangelist, nor to a difference in message, nor to a different manner of sharing that message. The difference lodged within the hearer's reception of the word of God.

Noting Even that False Teachers Fight Over God's Words

False teachers are found within and outside of the church. In the case of Jeremiah 23, he prophesied God's condemnation on false teachers who stole the words of God from one another:

> *"Therefore, behold, I am against the prophets, declares the LORD, who steal my words from one another. Behold, I am against the prophets, declares the LORD, who use their tongues and declare, 'declares the LORD.' Behold, I am against those who prophesy lying dreams, declares the LORD, and who tell them and lead my people astray by their lies and their recklessness, when I did not*

THOMAS P. JOHNSTON

send them or charge them. So they do not profit this people at all, declares the LORD" (Jeremiah 23:30-32 ESV).

By the time of Jeremiah, God's words were a commodity to these false prophets. They stole their reinterpretations of God's words from one another. Even though they used God's words, they did not feed the people of God, but led them astray.

Rightly Wielding the Word of God

In juxtaposition to the false wielding of God's sword by the false shepherds in Jeremiah 23, the man of God is to rightly handle the "word of truth":

Do your best to present yourself to God as one approved, a worker who has no need to be ashamed, rightly handling [ὀρθοτομέω] the word of truth (2 Timothy 2:15 ESV).

The verb ὀρθοτομέω is translated "right handling." It may be noted that there are examples of Jesus "rightly handling" the Old Testament Scriptures. Right handling of the word of truth is exemplified throughout the Book of Acts. There are 65 uses of the noun ὁ λόγος ("word") in Acts. Of these 65 uses, it is used 55 times to describe the message proclaimed in Acts:[1]

- "Word" (17 times): Acts 1:1; 2:41; 6:4, 5; 8:4, 21; 10:29, 36, 44; 11:19; 14:25; 15:6; 16:6; 17:11; 20:7, 38; 22:22

- "Words" (9 times): Acts 2:22, 40; 4:4, 29; 5:5; 7:22; 14:12; 15:32; 20:2

- "Word of God" (12 times): Acts 4:31; 6:2, 7; 8:14; 11:1; 12:24; 13:5, 7, 44, 46; 17:13; 18:11

- "Word of the Lord" (7 times): Acts 8:25; 13:48, 49; 15:35, 36; 16:32; 19:20

- "Word of His grace" (twice): Acts 14:3; 20:32

- "Reported word" (once): Acts 15:27

- "Word of exhortation" (once): Acts 13:15

- "Word of the gospel" (once): Acts 15:7

---

[1]Textual differences follow Ἡ Ἁγία Γραφή (Athens, 2004).

- "Word of this salvation" (once): Acts 13:26

- "Living word" (once): Acts 7:38

- "Word of the Lord Jesus" (once): Acts 19:10

- "Words of the Lord Jesus" (once): Acts 20:35

- "Words of the prophets" (once): Acts 15:15.

Further, there are 12 uses of the noun τὸ ῥῆμα ("word") for apostolic preaching in the Book of Acts:

- "Words" (5 times): Acts 2:14; 10:22, 44; 11:14; 13:42

- "Word" (twice): Acts 10:37; 28:25

- "Blasphemous words" (twice): Acts 6:11, 13

- "Word of the Lord" (once): Acts 11:16

- "The words of this life" (once): Acts 5:20

- "Words of truth and reason" (once): Acts 26:25

The uses of ὁ λόγος and τὸ ῥῆμα combine to a total of 67 uses of "word" or "words" for the message of the disciples in the Book of Acts. By comparison the noun "gospel" (τὸ εὐαγγέλιον) is found a total of two times in Acts (15:7; 20:24). The comparison of 67-to-2 is incredibly lopsided. This usage does not imply that the gospel was not important to the apostolic church. Rather it confirms the symbiotic relationship between the gospel of Jesus and the living word of God. Each contains and confirms the other. This usage also clarifies that the gospel is a verbally communicated message.

Here are several examples of the uses of these words. The first use of "word [ὁ λόγος] of God" in Acts is in 4:31:

> And when they had prayed, the place where they were assembled together was shaken; and they were all filled with the Holy Spirit, and they spoke the word of God [τὸν λόγον τοῦ Θεοῦ] with boldness (Acts 4:31).

The first use of τὸ ῥῆμα in Acts is in 2:14:

> But Peter, standing up with the eleven, raised his voice and said to them, "Men of Judea and all who dwell in Jerusalem, let this be known to you, and heed my words [τὰ ῥήματά μου] (Acts 2:14).

Acts 10:44 uses both words for "word"—ὁ λόγος and τὸ ῥῆμα:

> While Peter was still speaking these words [τὰ ῥήματα ταῦτα],
> the Holy Spirit fell upon all those who heard the word [τὸν λόγον]
> (Acts 10:44).

ὁ λόγος and τὸ ῥῆμα are sometimes used for the words of the Bible (word of God), the words of Jesus (word of the Lord), or the words spoken by the apostles. While there is a distinction between the "Word of God" and the "word of men" in evangelizing, these overlap in meaning as noted in Luke 10:16 and 1 Thessalonians 2:13.

By biblical teaching and by biblical example the very words of the word of God are infused with His supernatural life-saving and life-changing power. The full potentiality of God's omnipotent tongue has been recorded for personal use, corporate exhortation, and powerful evangelism. As He created the heavens and the earth, it is indeed through His word that God recreates His people.

Just as God spoke the world into existence with the words "Let there be light," the same power continues to operate in, with, by, and through the words of God. There is hidden power within the words of God. It is only through the proclamation of these words that the light of the gospel of Jesus shines into darkened minds and hearts of men and women to enlighten them and transform them into sons and daughters of God:

> But even if our gospel is veiled, it is veiled to those who are
> perishing, whose minds the god of this age has blinded, who do
> not believe, lest the light of the gospel of the glory of Christ, who
> is the image of God, should shine on them (2 Corinthians 4:3-4).

CHAPTER TWO

CALLED TO GO
—πορεύομαι—

Evangelical Christianity has always hinged on born-again Christians taking initiative. With the energizing Holy Spirit resident in their souls, and being led by the light of Scripture, followers of Jesus pulsate with an eager desire to obey their Master. In fact, the synergy is so tight between being born again and being taught in God's word, that it may appear at first glance that the initiative being taken by the new believer originates from within himself. It is easy for the new or young Christian to misconstrue that this urging, prodding, and guiding of the Holy Spirit to be of his own making. The cooperative inter-working of the Holy Spirit's energy within him can lead the new Christian to take credit for it—even to pride himself in his accomplishments for the Lord. Paul warned Timothy against laying hands too quickly upon a new Christian, "Lest he fall into reproach and the snare of the Devil" (1 Timothy 3:7). Even so, once the Holy Spirit enters a soul through the new birth, something happens within that soul. Rather than spiritual death there is spiritual life pumping through their veins. And along with that spiritual life comes the urging to obey the Great Commission.

This chapter considers the call of God on Christians to be involved in the Great Commission. There is also the call to salvation, which will be considered in another chapter. This chapter does not deal with the specific call to be a pastor or missionary. Rather the purpose of this chapter is to discern what is meant by the general "Go" in the Great Commission.

Setting for the Great Commission

As Christ was approaching His death and resurrection, He continued to reveal Himself more fully to His disciples. Even though they did not understand it, He sought to prepare them for His death and resurrection:

> And all were astonished at the majesty of God. But while they were all marveling at everything he was doing, Jesus said to his disciples, "Let these words sink into your ears: The Son of Man is about to be delivered into the hands of men." But they did not understand this saying, and it was concealed from them, so that they might not perceive it. And they were afraid to ask him about this saying (Luke 9:43-45 ESV).

Over and over Jesus prepared them for His death and resurrection, and even after the fact they still did not believe it to be true.

> Afterward he appeared to the eleven themselves as they were reclining at table, and he rebuked them for their unbelief and hardness of heart, because they had not believed those who saw him after he had risen (Mark 16:14 ESV).

Likewise, there were some things that Jesus waited to tell them until the night before He died. In John 16:4 Jesus said, "And these things I did not say to you at the beginning, because I was with you" (NASB). There were even some further things that would need to wait until after His death and resurrection. In verse 12, Jesus said, "I still have many things to say to you, but you cannot bear them now." So, the Bible clearly reveals stages of revelation of certain truths at specific times.

Meanwhile, Jesus took on a whole different agenda in preaching to the multitudes. He spoke to them in parables so that they would not understand the application of what He was saying. This point was explained in Matthew 13, Mark 4, and Luke 8, between the Parable of the Sower and its application.

> And when he was alone, those around him with the twelve asked him about the parables. And he said to them, "To you has been given the secret of the kingdom of God, but for those outside everything is in parables, so that 'they may indeed see but not perceive, and may indeed hear but not understand, lest they should turn and be forgiven.'" And he said to them, "Do you not understand this parable? How then will you understand all the parables?" (Mark 4:10-13 ESV).

> With many such parables he spoke the word to them, as they

were able to hear it. He did not speak to them without a parable, but privately to his own disciples he explained everything (Mark 4:33-34 ESV).

Although it might sound unfair at first glance, Jesus spoke to the crowds in parables to hide the truth from them. He then explained the parables in private to His disciples. So, Jesus had a general message—consisting primarily of the need for morality—for the crowds of people. These teachings were meant to draw them to see their need for a Savior. And to those who did seek Him as Savior and follow Him, He continued to reveal Himself with greater and greater depth.

Two milestones changed the content of His teaching to His disciples. The first milestone was crossed at the death of Christ. At this point the new way of salvation was opened as prophesied in Jeremiah 31, Ezekiel 36, and Joel 2. Jesus called it the "New Covenant in My blood" (Luke 22:20). The supernatural demonstration delineating that the New Covenant now replaced the Old Covenant took place when God tore the curtain separating the Holy of Holies from the Holy Place at the Jerusalem Temple:

And Jesus cried out again with a loud voice and yielded up his spirit. And behold, the curtain of the temple was torn in two, from top to bottom. And the earth shook, and the rocks were split (Matthew 27:50-51 ESV).

And Jesus uttered a loud cry and breathed his last. And the curtain of the temple was torn in two, from top to bottom (Mark 15:37-38 ESV).

It was now about the sixth hour, and there was darkness over the whole land until the ninth hour, while the sun's light failed. And the curtain of the temple was torn in two. Then Jesus, calling out with a loud voice, said, "Father, into your hands I commit my spirit!" And having said this he breathed his last (Luke 23:44-46 ESV).

Salvation was purchased "by His blood." "It is finished" was recorded in John 19:30. The milestone was reached. The Old Covenant became "obsolete" (Hebrews 8:13), replaced by the New Covenant. This first milestone had an impact on the content of the preaching of Jesus to His disciples.

A second milestone, which marks a significant distinction between the Old and New Covenants, was the baptism of the Holy Spirit within the disciples. At one point within the Resurrection Preaching of Jesus, He breathed on His disciples to demonstrate His yet future gift of the Holy Spirit.

> And when he had said this, he breathed on them and said to them, "Receive the Holy Spirit" (John 20:22 ESV).

This gift was definitively bestowed at Pentecost as recorded in Acts 2. The Holy Spirit fell upon the disciples of Christ in fulfillment of His promise to them as given in Luke's Great Commission:

> "Behold, I send the Promise of My Father upon you; but tarry in the city of Jerusalem until you are endued with power from on high" (Luke 24:49).

In the interim time between His death and the sending of the Holy Spirit at Pentecost, Jesus revealed Himself and taught the disciples for a period of forty days. Jesus' preaching during these forty days is called His "Resurrection Preaching." Jesus never addressed the crowds of unbelievers during this time, but only His disciples. And it was during these forty days that He commissioned His disciples, giving them the Great Commission, recorded for us in five passages of Scripture.

Calls to Go in the Great Commission

The verb "Go" is found in two of the five Great Commission passages. Matthew 28:19 reads, "Go [πορεύομαι] therefore and make disciples of all nations." Mark 16:15: "And He said to them, 'Go [πορεύομαι] into all the world and preach the gospel to every creature.'" Neither author stated that Jesus' words were limited to what they wrote in their Gospel. Rather, each Gospel writer chose to emphasize different hues of God's mandate for His followers until He returns. Both Matthew and Mark use the same word "Go." Mark then picked up "and preach the gospel"—which is assumed in Matthew, thus being an ellipsis. Jesus linked "Go" and "preach" in Matthew 10:7. However, whereas the Commissions in Matthew and Mark were succinct, Luke's Commission took on a didactic role. Luke 24 explained the message of the gospel and the content of preaching. The geographic displacement commanded in the word "Go" was depicted by its centrifugal extent, "to all nations," beginning from its centripetal point, "Jerusalem" (Luke 24:47).

The Book of Acts is understandably linked to the Great Commission in Luke, being that Luke was also the author of Acts. Jesus repeated His admonition regarding the reception of the Holy Spirit. In Luke 24:49 they were commanded to wait in Jerusalem until they were "endued with power from on high." In Acts 1:8 that command was restated as follows, "But you shall receive power when the Holy Spirit has come upon you." It appears that the centrifugal action of going into all the world would result from the power of the Holy Spirit coming upon the disciples, and sending them from Jerusalem to Judea, Samaria, and to the ends of the earth.

In Jesus' Resurrection Preaching in John, we read this command to His disciples, "As the Father has sent [ἀποστέλλω] Me, I also send [πέμπω] you" (John 20:21).

All five of these Great Commission passages include the need for a geographic displacement of some kind. The word "Go" is the first command in the Great Commission. This verb calls all Christians to get up and get out into the world. Theirs is to take the initiative based on:

1. The supreme authority of Christ (Matthew 28:18)

2. The promised power from on high (Luke 24:49; Acts 1:8).

The church did send out Saul and Barnabas in Acts 13. However, the outreach described in Acts 8:1-4 was spontaneous, as was the evangelism in Antioch in Acts 11:19-21. The Holy Spirit works in the heart of the newly born believers, giving them the desire to share the gospel with others. His presence in someone's heart should propel them to "Go."

To Whom Is the Great Commission Addressed?

All the Great Commission commands were communicated to the disciples. In Matthew 28:16 and Mark 16:14 the audience is delineated as "the eleven." When Jesus appeared to the disciples at the end of Luke 24, there included the eleven, "those who were with them," and the two disciples from the Road to Emmaus who came to report to them (Luke 24:13, 33). In John 20:19 we read that the disciples were assembled. Acts did not introduce Jesus' audience directly. Luke wrote in Acts that Jesus gave "commandment to the apostles whom He had chosen" (Acts 1:2). Later, in Acts 1:15, the group is said to include 120 names.

From this we can deduce that the initial recipients of Christ's Great Commission appear to be the eleven. In Luke, John, and Acts it is less clear how many were assembled. Paul mentioned that Jesus addressed over 500 at one time after His resurrection from the dead (1 Corinthians 15:6). Therefore, the exact number to hear Jesus give the Great Commission is unclear. Additionally, as mentioned above, the command was likely repeated in different ways throughout the days of Jesus' Resurrection Preaching. It makes sense that if Jesus appeared to them at different times and in different places for forty days that each account of the life of Christ highlights different vignettes of what He said, including different aspects of Christ's Great Commission.

Another verse of interest to the question of recipients of the Great Commission includes the New Testament terminology *followers of Jesus*. In Acts 11 we read the first use of the word "Christian" for a follower of Christ:

> And in Antioch the disciples were first called Christians (Acts 11:26 ESV).

Several deductions can be made from the variations in terminology. First, the common name for "followers of Jesus" was *disciples*. Second, Jesus had Himself named the original twelve as *apostles* in Luke 6:13. And they are cited in Scripture as "twelve apostles" in Matthew 10:2, Luke 22:14, and Revelation 21:14. We find "eleven apostles" in Acts 1:26. Third, the term *Christian* in Acts 11:26 was used as a synonym for *disciple*. Fourth, the term *believer* can also be added into this mix. In several passages in Acts, Luke used the participle of the Greek verb "believe" (πιστεύω) to describe those who were coming to Christ (Acts 2:44; 4:32; 5:14; 19:18; 21:20, 25; 22:19). The concept of "believing ones" is often translated *believers* in our English texts:

> And believers were increasingly added to the Lord, multitudes of

both men and women (Acts 5:14).

In three other places the term "believer" is derived from a Greek adjective (πιστός), used 67 times in the New Testament.

So, to whom is Christ's Great Commission addressed? Is it only the eleven? The 120 or the 500? Was the command to be passed on to every follower of Christ, who may be called a Christian, a disciple, or a believer? Surely, Jesus gave commandments to His followers.

If you love Me, keep My commandments (John 14:15).

If you keep My commandments, you will abide in My love, just as I have kept My Father's commandments and abide in His love (John 15:10).

It might be startling for New Testament Christians to think that Christ gave commandments that we are called to obey. One of these "commandments" of Jesus is the Great Commission. Therefore, the Great Commission is a command of Christ to all His followers.

Calls to Go in the Old Testament

The Old Testament has commands to go forth with a message that parallel the Great Commission in the New Testament. Many of these parallels are found in the Psalms and some in the Prophets. Some are general and others are specific—as when God was calling a prophet to do His will. Because there are so many of each, only several examples will be noted.

Sing to the LORD, bless his name; tell of his salvation from day to day. Declare his glory among the nations, his marvelous works among all the peoples! (Psalm 96:2-3 ESV).

Oh give thanks to the LORD; call upon his name; make known his deeds among the peoples! Sing to him, sing praises to him; tell of all his wondrous works! (Psalm 105:1-2 ESV).

Notice the resulting recipients of these admonitions—the nations and the peoples. God's people were commanded through these Psalms to declare His salvation or His glory to the nations around

25

them. Likewise, Isaiah wrote two general admonitions that parallel Christ's Great Commission:

> Go on up to a high mountain, O Zion, herald of good news; lift up your voice with strength, O Jerusalem, herald of good news; lift it up, fear not; say to the cities of Judah, "Behold your God!" (Isaiah 40:9 ESV).

> How beautiful upon the mountains are the feet of him who brings good news, who publishes peace, who brings good news of happiness, who publishes salvation, who says to Zion, "Your God reigns" (Isaiah 52:7 ESV).

In these Isaiah prophesies the recipients of obedience to these admonitions were not the nations or peoples, but rather Jerusalem, Judah, and Zion. Could these prophesies be the precedent for the words of Jesus to His disciples?

> "When they persecute you in this city, flee to another. For assuredly, I say to you, you will not have gone through the cities of Israel before the Son of Man comes" (Matthew 10:23).

Just as there are calls to "Go!" in the Old Testament, so there are other calls to "Go!" in the New Testament.

Other Calls to Go in the New Testament

There are many calls to "Go!" in the New Testament. Many of these parallel the Great Commission and apply its emphasis to one person. Hence the former demoniac from Gerasenes was commanded by Jesus to return to his hometown and tell his townspeople what great things that the Lord had done for him:

> However, Jesus did not permit him, but said to him, "Go home to your friends, and tell them what great things the Lord has done for you, and how He has had compassion on you" (Mark 5:19).

Rather than follow up and disciple this newly delivered demoniac, surprisingly, Jesus gave him an immediate ministry assignment. It was a specific commissioning for him.

One of the central persons in the New Testament who received a series of other commands to "Go!" was the Apostle Paul. The commands start with Ananias being sent to Paul with a command to "Go!"

But the Lord said to him, "Go, for he is a chosen instrument of mine to carry my name before the Gentiles and kings and the children of Israel. For I will show him how much he must suffer for the sake of my name" (Acts 9:15-16 ESV).

Here are several of the callings of Paul:

As they ministered to the Lord and fasted, the Holy Spirit said, "Now separate to Me Barnabas and Saul for the work to which I have called them" (Acts 13:2).

And a vision appeared to Paul in the night. A man of Macedonia stood and pleaded with him, saying, "Come over to Macedonia and help us." Now after he had seen the vision, immediately we sought to go to Macedonia, concluding that the Lord had called us to preach the gospel to them (Acts 16:9-10).

"Then He said to me, 'Depart, for I will send you far from here to the Gentiles'" (Acts 22:21).

But the following night the Lord stood by him and said, "Be of good cheer, Paul; for as you have testified for Me in Jerusalem, so you must also bear witness at Rome" (Acts 23:11).

Therefore, King Agrippa, I was not disobedient to the heavenly vision, but declared first to those in Damascus and in Jerusalem, and throughout all the region of Judea, and then to the Gentiles, that they should repent, turn to God, and do works befitting repentance (Acts 26:19-20).

Paul had many calls to "Go!" and to "Stay!" He exemplifies the need to properly hear and discern God's call. Sometimes God has reasons for sending that we do not understand.

God's Reasons for Sending

Interestingly, God sometimes reveals what is going on in the lives of others that triggered Him to call an obedient believer into action. Three reasons are made manifest and show the importance of spiritual sensitivity in the work of personal evangelism. God knows what is going on in the lives of others that we do not know. And sometimes His mysterious calling relates to those things that He is supernaturally preparing in the lives of others.

First, the Ethiopian Eunuch was struggling to understand the Scriptures that he was reading while he was traveling. God had placed in his heart an urgent desire to understand what he was reading. His earnest quest was demonstrated by the fact that he was reading aloud while bouncing down a desert road in a chariot—consider the dust on the Great Isaiah Scroll!

> So he arose and went. And behold, a man of Ethiopia, a eunuch of great authority under Candace the queen of the Ethiopians, who had charge of all her treasury, and had come to Jerusalem to worship, was returning. And sitting in his chariot, he was reading Isaiah the prophet. Then the Spirit said to Philip, "Go near and overtake this chariot." So Philip ran to him, and heard him reading the prophet Isaiah, and said, "Do you understand what you are reading?" And he said, "How can I, unless someone guides me?" And he asked Philip to come up and sit with him. The place in the Scripture which he read was this: "He was led as a sheep to the slaughter; and as a lamb before its shearer is silent, so He opened not His mouth. In His humiliation His justice was taken away, and who will declare His generation? For His life is taken from the earth." So the eunuch answered Philip and said, "I ask you, of whom does the prophet say this, of himself or of some other man?" Then Philip opened his mouth, and beginning at this Scripture, preached Jesus to him (Acts 8:27-35).

Consider how Luke emphasized the fact that the unnamed Ethiopian Eunuch was reading Scripture:

- *He was reading Isaiah the prophet* (v. 28).

- *And heard him reading the prophet Isaiah* (v. 30).

- *Do you understand what you are reading?* (v. 30).

- *The place in Scripture which he read was this* (v. 32).

- *Of whom does the prophet say this?* (v. 34).

Luke pressed several points:

1. The Ethiopian Eunuch was reading aloud.

2. He was reading Holy Scripture.

3. The eunuch was reading from the prophet Isaiah.

4. He did not understand what he was reading.

This man of prominence, by divine design, invited a complete stranger to help him interpret Scripture. For this reason, Philip had been sent to the eunuch—because, un-foreknown to Philip, this man was reading Scripture with a desire to understand its meaning.

Second, in the next chapter Ananias was sent to Saul, because Saul was praying:

> And the Lord said to him, "Rise and go to the street called Straight, and at the house of Judas look for a man of Tarsus named Saul, for behold, he is praying, and he has seen in a vision a man named Ananias come in and lay his hands on him so that he might regain his sight" (Acts 9:11-12 ESV).

In this case, Ananias was being sent by God to share the gospel and baptize Saul—because Saul was praying. God was simultaneously leading Saul to pray and leading Ananias to go and evangelize him.

Third, in the following chapter of Acts, evangelism was preceded by a series of visions. Here we find God sovereignly calling out His elect, as well as God's guiding in the life of Peter to prepare him with doctrinal insights. Cornelius received a visitation from God asking him to go and invite Peter to share the gospel with him. Peter, for his part, received a series of visions to prepare him to evangelize among the Gentiles. God was at work in the inner hearts and minds of both the evangelist and the recipient of the gospel—evangelism is no mere carnal work.

The result of this encounter was that Cornelius and all those who were with him were baptized with the Holy Spirit, merely on hearing the word of the gospel proclaimed. This event was used to prepare Peter for his important speech in Acts 15:7-11, a speech in which he expounded salvation by hearing alone, by Scriptures alone, by faith alone, by grace alone, and by Christ alone. Do these points sound familiar? So, God had a magnificent plan. His purposes were often unclear to those fulfilling them—as Paul understood when he wrote some of his letters from a prison cell.

Listening for God's Call

There is the general command and there are also specific or particular callings that are different for each individual. This is where it becomes important to learn to listen for the voice of God.

29

Consider five examples of God's calling in the Old Testament. First, there was God's audible call of Samuel when he was the High Priest Eli's assistant in the Tabernacle in Shiloh. First Samuel 3:4 reads that the Lord called to Samuel in the night. The young Samuel eagerly answered, "Here I am!" thinking that the voice he heard was that of Eli the priest. After his third visit to Eli, the old High Priest recognized that the Lord God was calling Samuel. Yes, even as God called back in those days, He is still calling—it's one of His revealed methods.

Second, centuries later the prophet Elijah was running from the wicked Queen Jezebel. He feared for his life. He had been faithful to God on Mount Carmel, and now his life was at risk. God spoke to Elijah as he hid himself in a cave and asked him, "What are you doing here?" Elijah stated his case to the Lord. Then God answered him with three signs. The first sign was an earthquake and wind. But God wasn't in the earthquake. The second sign was fire. But God wasn't in the fire either. Then after the fire came a "still small voice." The Lord God was in the *still small voice*—and then God spoke to Elijah and encouraged him (1 Kings 19:9-12).

Third, in Job 33 the friend of Job, Elihu, stated that God spoke to men in dreams, in order to keep them from eternal death—the Pit. These nocturnal warnings were given to man to turn him from his evil deeds:

> For God speaks in one way, and in two, though man does not perceive it. In a dream, in a vision of the night, when deep sleep falls on men, while they slumber on their beds, then he opens the ears of men and terrifies them with warnings, that he may turn man aside from his deed and conceal pride from a man; he keeps back his soul from the pit, his life from perishing by the sword (Job 33:14-18 ESV).

In the dead of night, while men are sleeping, God is at work. He sometimes warns through dreams, to turn man from his pride. The same Hebrew word for "turn" (*shub*) in Job 33 is also used of the word of God "turning the soul" in Psalm 19:7 and of the Lord "restoring the soul" in Psalm 23:3. God is in the business of turning, restoring, and leading His people. He uses dreams to warn mankind, to keep him humble, and to cause him to consider eternal things.

Fourth, the prophet Isaiah wrote of God speaking in the ear of His people—most often by the direct application of His word in some way. When the follower of Jesus strays to the right or to the left, here comes the promised voice whispering in his ear, "This is the way, walk in it!"

> *And your ears shall hear a word behind you, saying, "This is the way, walk in it," when you turn to the right or when you turn to the left* (Isaiah 30:21 ESV).

God promised that He would guide His people, even to the point of speaking to them in their ear when they turn to the right or to the left of God's will.

Fifth, Moses wrote in Deuteronomy 18 the example of a Levite priest feeling compelled in his mind to minister to the Lord in "the place which the Lord your God chooses" (code words for the forthcoming Temple in Jerusalem, not yet chosen by King David). In three verses God gave regulations concerning such a priest:

> *"And if a Levite comes from any of your towns out of all Israel, where he lives—and he may come when he desires—to the place that the LORD will choose, and ministers in the name of the LORD his God, like all his fellow Levites who stand to minister there before the LORD, then he may have equal portions to eat, besides what he receives from the sale of his patrimony"* (Deuteronomy 18:6-8 ESV).

Understanding that the Levitical priesthood is an Old Testament leadership position, and understanding that the Levites were a tribe of Israel, it is interesting to note that if a Levite were to come to Jerusalem "with all the desire of his mind" that they were commanded to take him in and care for him. God would work within the Levite by giving him godly desires. God's calling can include the work He does in His people's hearts through inner promptings of the Holy Spirit.

Therefore, the voice of the Lord comes to man in a variety of ways. Meanwhile, Evangelical Christianity hinges on born-again Christians taking initiative in obeying the voice of the Lord. Because Evangelicalism does not accept a fully authoritative hierarchy, it is reliant on Christ Himself moving among His people to build His Church and accomplish His work.

The Link of Go with Preach

There is a clear pattern of dual verbs in Christ commissioning His people. One verb encourages geographic movement, Go!" and the second verb explains what was to be done after the geographic displacement has taken place, "Preach!" In the next chapter we will consider the methodological verbs linked to the command to "Go!"

The Link of Go with Examples of Going

So also, in further chapters, it is discerned that the calls to "Go!" did not fall on deaf ears. The Bible gives examples of obedience to the call to "Go!" These examples explain how the contemporaries of Jesus interpreted His call to "Go!" as well as also providing divinely authoritative texts describing their obedience.

CHAPTER THREE

AND PREACH
—κηρύσσω—

Once the disciples went out, what did Jesus send them out to do? This is the great question of this chapter, following closely on the heels of the former chapter. For without a clear understanding of mission, the Christian life is reduced to unfettered activism. Perhaps one of the greatest difficulties in the church stems from disagreements over views of mission. Could it be that Jesus Christ allowed this most important topic to be intentionally clouded for future generations of Christians? Or did Jesus communicate with crystalline clarity something that man has clouded with schism and controversy? This chapter seeks to objectify this most important topic by applying the lens of the study of Great Commission verbs. Properly interpreting the Great Commission casts the objective for the entire operation of what is called "The Church."

Very early in the history of the churches there were disagreements as to how and what the Great Commission entailed. Among the many first century house churches in Corinth there ran an undercurrent of division and divisiveness. Apparently concerned Christians from Chloe's house church explained the problem to Paul. They saw four different factions developing among these first generation Christians. The first faction identified with Paul who had evangelized them and planted the church movement in Corinth, ministering among them for a year and a half. He had planted an assembly in the synagogue that moved to the home of Justus. Paul then took leave of them, beginning to make his way to Jerusalem. The second faction identified around Apollos (1 Corinthians 1:12). He came and "watered" the ministry that Paul had "planted." Hence, working with the same group of people. Apparently, Apollos was more eloquent a speaker than Paul. Perhaps his Alexandrian accent and tutelage gave him greater academic stature in the minds of some. The Paul and Apollos factions appear to be the most prominent ones (1 Corinthians 3:4).

A third faction titled itself by Cephas (aka. Peter). Matthew positioned Peter's prominence in his listing of the Apostles: "first, Simon, who is called Peter" (Matthew 10:2). Paul called him by his original name, Cephas, which he did four times in 1 Corinthians: 1:12; 3:22; 9:5; and 15:5. This faction may have been more Judaic, since Peter, along with James and John, segmented his ministry to those of the circumcision (Galatians 2:9). A fourth faction had also developed, affiliating their allegiance to Christ. There was no way to out-do that association! In Corinth, these four factions—Paul, Apollos, Cephas, and Christ—were in rivalry and not walking in unity.

Further consideration suggests that these factions differed on their view of the Great Commission. We learn from 1 Corinthians 3 that the source of disagreement between the Paul and Apollos factions was *how* Paul planted, as opposed to *how* Apollos watered. There was a missional differentiation. This missional differentiation continues within churches today. These differences include:

- Whether conversion is necessary or not
- When and in what way conversion takes place
- The role of a Sinner's Prayer
- How and when one is to be baptized
- The similarities, differences, and results of Spirit baptism and water baptism
- If initiative evangelism is necessary or not
- The role of preparations for evangelism (lifestyle, acts of mercy, or apologetics)
- How one is to be discipled
- If obedience in discipleship effectuates their salvation.

How much wiggle room did Jesus leave in His Great Commission—that groups could seize upon one of its emphases to divide from other followers of Christ? With what kind of clarity did

Jesus speak His desire for His followers? Did He give specificity as to what His disciples were to accomplish and how they were to accomplish it? This chapter will focus on the verbs that Jesus used in His Great Commission passages to describe the specific activities that He had in mind. Building from this foundation, the remainder of the chapter will consider other commands that follow the verb "Go!" in the New Testament.

Great Commission Verbs

Perhaps the reader will agree with me that the entire New Testament is "God-breathed" and that therefore—by the mouths of multiple authors and persons—the Holy Spirit speaks with one common voice. The presupposition of this section is that the Great Commission passages are not in opposition to each other, nor are they in contra-distinction to one another. Rather, the supposition is that God in His infinite insight and foresight inspired four authors to write down five different Great Commission passages for His perfect revelatory purposes. Our challenge, like that of the Ethiopian Eunuch, is to determine inter-connectedness and commonality of focus.

It appears that a chronological approach allows all the Great Commission verses to inter-connect in marvelous simplicity and clarity. In the first place, as has been noted in the prior chapter, two Great Commission passages include the command to "Go!" (πορεύομαι) (Matthew 28:19 and Mark 16:15). The others merely imply the command by using other verbs, such as "send" (πέμπω) (John 20:21). In order to properly organize the Great Commission verbs, it is necessary to move back before the "Go!" This is where Jesus sent His disciples in John 20:21.

The Great Commission began with Christ's example, "As the Father has sent Me." Jesus, by this statement, laid out all the recorded information about His life and ministry as an example to His future disciples. There are clearly parts of His ministry which were not meant to be repeated, such as His Virgin Birth. Clearly His crucifixion and resurrection were not meant to be mimicked, as His atoning sacrifice was accomplished "once and for all" (Hebrews 9:27-28; 10:10, 12, 14). But there are other aspects of the life of Jesus in which He provided His followers an example:

- His submission to His parents
- His growth in wisdom and stature
- His going out
- His sending others out
- His evangelizing
- His discipling relationships
- His many other relationships (with government officials, religious figures, tax gatherers, etc.)
- His preaching and teaching content and style
- His commands.

The statement "as the Father has sent Me" alludes to the example of Jesus in His 36 personal evangelism conversations. These witnessing encounters provide insight for consideration in the "How To" of fulfilling the Great Commission. Jesus Himself commanded His disciples that they ought to follow His example.

Therefore, the chronological analysis of the Great Commission begins with the example of Jesus. It continues up to the giving of the Great Commission with its command to "Go!" It is here where the Great Commission can appear to become a puzzle of complexity.

Using the Great Commission in Matthew as a guide, the other commissions of Jesus fit right into place. Beginning with Matthew 28:19-20, the Great Commission included five verbs, four related to the apostles and one related to Christ:

1. "Go!" [πορεύομαι]
2. "Win disciples!" [μαθητεύω]
3. "Baptizing!" [βαπτίζω]
4. "Teaching to observe!" [διδάσκω + τηρέω]
5. "I am with you!" [εἰμί]

Of these five verbs, the first four verbs relate to the mission upon which Christ was sending His disciples. The fifth verb was used to explain the promise of Christ's presence accompanying His disciples in their obedience of this mission. At first glance these verbs appear to be the complete package of what is entailed in Christ's Great Commission. However, further scrutiny divulges that the main concept in Christ's Great Commissions in Mark, Luke, and Acts is missing in Matthew. What is missing in this sequence of verbs is the proclamational imperative.

There are at least four ways of approaching the missing proclamational imperatives in Matthew. First, by considering the idea of proclamation as secondary to the Great Commission. Hence, Jesus' Great Commission in Matthew would trump the other Great Commissions and render them secondary to the Church's mission. Second, by not looking at Matthew's Great Commission chronologically. Hence, the proclamational element would be included in the fourth command, "teaching them to observe." Third, by presuming the proclamational element to be included as part of μαθητεύω ("win disciples"). This interpretation follows that μαθητεύω in Matthew 13:52 is translated "fully instructed." Hence, again, the church is all about discipleship and not about evangelism. Fourth, presuming that the proclamational element is an ellipsis in Matthew 28:19. Since the need to "Go and preach" had already been communicated in Matthew 10:7, it can be assumed as obviously necessary to "make a disciple." Hence, the example of Joseph of Arimathea "having been won as a disciple" in Matthew 27:57 speaks not of the proclamation or the process of discipling, but of the result of a disciple being won over.

Church history has adopted the second view of Matthew's Great Commission. When infant baptism was codified in the third and fourth centuries of the Western Church, Matthew's Great Commission could not be read chronologically, since baptism was made prerequisite to becoming a disciple. Further, the verb "Go!" could not be applied to all disciples of Christ due to the clergy-laity distinction necessary in a state-church model. Only chosen and trained clergy have permission to "Go!" One should not expect mainstream lexicons and commentaries to properly deal with Matthew's Great Commission due to the massive historic and ecclesiastical weight involved in the proper interpretation of this passage.

In order to sort out and cross-pollinate the methodological implications of the five Great Commission passages, the proposed approach will be contextual in several ways. First, the Great Commission passages will be considered from the point-of-view of Old Testament prophesies. Second, the five Great Commissions will be considered as a telescoping theme in each Gospel, beginning from the first calls of Jesus, moving to specific sending passages, and climaxing with each Great Commission. Third, the Great Commission passages will be aligned with other commissionings in the New Testament. Finally, with all these as background, the goal will be to superimpose the puzzle pieces of each Great Commission passage upon their place within the portrait of Christ's will for His people.

Select Old Testament Prophesies

The Great Commission in the New Testament was not new in Scripture. Its emphases had been foretold and exemplified within the writings of the Old Testament. While there was the centripetal emphasis of mission in the Old Testament—moving from the periphery into the center—there were also the centrifugal aspects—moving in the opposite direction, from a central point outwardly. One aspect of "mission" in the Old Testament was for the nations of the world to come to Jerusalem to worship in Solomon's Temple. Another element in the Old Testament related to Israel going out to the nations and proclaiming salvation to them. Jesus amplified this second approach when He sent out His disciples to proclaim the gospel throughout the world.

Consider for example these passages from the Psalms:

Sing to the LORD, bless his name; tell of his salvation from day to day. Declare his glory among the nations, his marvelous works among all the peoples! (Psalm 96:2-3 ESV).

Oh give thanks to the LORD; call upon his name; make known his deeds among the peoples! Sing to him, sing praises to him; tell of all his wondrous works! (Psalm 105:1-2 ESV).

Consider, for example, the plural use of the word for "nation" (τὸ ἔθνος) is found 70 times in the Psalms. The plural use of the word for "people" (ὁ λαός) is found 37 times. These show up in 97 verses in the Psalms. Not all of these are in missional passage, but some are (see Psalm 67). In each of these verses there is the need for displacement to the nations and peoples of the earth. But there is also the method and message to be told once before the universal audience. Because this is a book on verbs, we will deal with the message under the rubric of verbs: repent, believe, persuade, confess. Consider the method and message encouraged by these sets of verbs (giving the Septuagint Greek of each verb):

- Method:
  Psalm 96:2-3: Sing [ᾄδω], bless [εὐλογέω], tell [εὐαγγελίζω], declare [ἀναγγέλλω]
  Psalm 105:1-2: Give thanks [ἐξομολογέω], call upon [ἐπικαλέω], make known [ἀπαγγέλλω], sing [ᾄδω], sing praises [ψάλλω], tell [διηγέομαι].

- Message:
  Psalm 96:2-3: The LORD, His name, His salvation, His glory, His marvelous works
  Psalm 105:1-2: The LORD, His name, His deeds, His wondrous works.

- Audience:
  Psalm 96:2-3: among the nations, among all the peoples
  Psalm 105:1-2: among the peoples.

- Duration:
  Psalm 96:2-3: from day to day.

The discerning reader may note that there is a slight variance between the Greek verbs and their English counterparts (translated from the Hebrew). Yet the basic gist of the prophetic call of these Psalms is communicated. God commands in these Psalms a triumphant, outward, verbal communication of His magnificent works. From a New Testament perspective, the most magnificent work of God is His having sent Jesus Christ into the world to live a sinless life, to die a substitutionary death for our sins, and to be raised from the dead on the third day.

Just as there are Great Commission admonitions in the Book of Psalms, so there are Great Commission admonitions in the Book of Isaiah:

Go on up to a high mountain, O Zion, herald of good news; lift up

> *your voice with strength, O Jerusalem, herald of good news; lift it up, fear not; say to the cities of Judah, "Behold your God!"* (Isaiah 40:9 ESV).

> *How beautiful upon the mountains are the feet of him who brings good news, who publishes peace, who brings good news of happiness, who publishes salvation, who says to Zion, "Your God reigns"* (Isaiah 52:7 ESV).

Let us consider these Isaiah prophecies using the same rubric that was used for the commands in the Book of Psalms. (Again the English will be accompanied by the Septuagint Greek.):

- Method:
  Isaiah 40:9: Herald good news [εὐαγγελίζω], herald good news [εὐαγγελίζω], say [λέγω]
  Isaiah 52:7: Brings good news [εὐαγγελίζω], publishes [ἀκοή], brings good news [εὐαγγελίζω], publishes [ἀκουστός + ποιέω], says [λέγω].

- Message:
  Isaiah 40:9: Good news, good news, "Behold your God"
  Isaiah 52:7: Good news, peace, good news of happiness, salvation, "Your God reigns."

- Messenger:
  Isaiah 40:9: O Zion, O Jerusalem.

- Audience:
  Isaiah 40:9: The cities of Judah
  Isaiah 52:7: To Zion.

- Confidence:
  Isaiah 40:9: Up on a high mountain, lift up your voice with strength, lift it up, be not afraid
  Isaiah 52:7: Upon a mountain.

The cogent reader will note that the Hebrew verbs were not always translated into English in the same way as found in the Septuagint Greek. Nevertheless, the concepts and ideas remain. In both of these passages God, through Isaiah, gathered a thick series of verbs. The Hebrew verbs in Isaiah 40:9 include two duplicates, one negation, and a sixth verb: *basar* (twice), *ruwm* (twice), *lo yare'* (once), and *'amar* (once). Isaiah 52:7 gives us two Hebrew duplicate verbs and a fifth verb: *basar* (twice), *shama'* (twice), and *'amar* (once).

These are examples of the general call of God to evangelize in the Book of Isaiah. There are also examples of individual or particular calls to speak forth God's words. One such example is found in Jeremiah 26:

> In the beginning of the reign of Jehoiakim the son of Josiah, king of Judah, this word came from the LORD: "Thus says the LORD: Stand in the court of the LORD's house, and speak to all the cities of Judah that come to worship in the house of the LORD all the words that I command you to speak to them; do not hold back a word. It may be they will listen, and every one turn from his evil way, that I may relent of the disaster that I intend to do to them because of their evil deeds. You shall say to them, 'Thus says the LORD: If you will not listen to me, to walk in my law that I have set before you, and to listen to the words of my servants the prophets whom I send to you urgently, though you have not listened, then I will make this house like Shiloh, and I will make this city a curse for all the nations of the earth'" (Jeremiah 26:1-6 ESV).

In this command to Jeremiah, God was very clear. He sent him to go to a certain location. It was the same location where he had been arrested and placed in the stocks in Jeremiah 20:1-2. God told him to "stand." (We will see more of this verb in future chapters.) Then He commanded Jeremiah to "speak" (Hebrew: *dabar*; Greek: χρηματίζω). Then God gave him a message. And, even though Jeremiah may have been tempted to do so, God specifically reminded him "not to diminish a word" of His message to them.

The Old Testament has teaching that parallels the Great Commission, and it has examples of individual calls, similar to what is found in the New Testament. All these texts provide context to what Christ meant when He gave His disciples the Great Commission.

Early Callings of Jesus

Even as God called His prophets and people in the Old Testament to bear testimony of His name, so in the Gospels, Christ was training His disciples to be His missionaries once He left the earth. Therefore, in one sense, the Gospel books parallel the verbs

41

"teaching them to observe all that I have commanded you." The Gospels provide Christ's methodology of "teaching them to observe." Hence, as we can expect in training, Christ manifested a sequence of training both in His explanation of His purposes, as well as in developing the disciples to be missionaries.

Two of these stages of formation will be highlighted. First, His calling of His disciples. Second, the sending passages that are found in the Gospels of Matthew, Mark, and Luke. As to Christ calling His disciples, Matthew and Mark are quite similar. Luke and John provide different contexts for their purposes.

> From that time Jesus began to preach, saying, "Repent, for the kingdom of heaven is at hand." While walking by the Sea of Galilee, he saw two brothers, Simon (who is called Peter) and Andrew his brother, casting a net into the sea, for they were fishermen. And he said to them, "Follow me, and I will make you fishers of men." Immediately they left their nets and followed him. And going on from there he saw two other brothers, James the son of Zebedee and John his brother, in the boat with Zebedee their father, mending their nets, and he called them. Immediately they left the boat and their father and followed him. And he went throughout all Galilee, teaching in their synagogues and proclaiming the gospel of the kingdom and healing every disease and every affliction among the people (Matthew 4:17-23 ESV).

As always, Jesus did not call His disciples to do something that He was not already doing, both as a way of life and as an example. He was preaching before He called His disciples and He preached after He called His disciples. They knew what they were getting into—no "bait and switch" here. Likewise, we have two separate calls of two sets of brothers. Consider how Matthew did not cite the words of the call of Jesus to James and John. The reason for this omission is that it was already stated in the prior account of His calling Peter and Andrew. There was no need for repetition, as it was already made clear how Jesus called His disciples.

In His discipleship training, Jesus began by asking those who were open to His message (we learn from John 1), to go deeper in their relationship with Him. Jesus did not haphazardly call out to the crowds. We will learn later that He hand-picked the twelve to be His Apostles. The disciples were to help Him fish for men.

Therefore, later we read that His disciples were baptizing people in John 3-4. We will also read when and how Jesus specifically sent them out.

The one difference of interest between the calls of Jesus as inscribed in Matthew and Mark is the addition of one word in Mark—the verb "become":

> And Jesus said to them, "Follow me, and I will make you become fishers of men" (Mark 1:17 ESV).

With that one verb, Mark moved the emphasis from the "making" process in the focus on Matthew to the end of the process, which was becoming a "fisherman of men." By the end of Mark, this is exactly what Christ had accomplished. In the last verse in Mark we read that Jesus accomplished His end with His disciples:

> And they went out [ἐξέρχομαι] and preached [κηρύσσω] everywhere, the Lord working with them and confirming the word through the accompanying signs. Amen (Mark 16:20).

Luke chose to emphasize a different one of Jesus' callings to His disciples. The context is different, and so is the content. In Luke, we find Jesus' individual call to Simon. The context is right after the miraculous catch of fish:

> But when Simon Peter saw it, he fell down at Jesus' knees, saying, "Depart from me, for I am a sinful man, O Lord." For he and all who were with him were astonished at the catch of fish that they had taken, and so also were James and John, sons of Zebedee, who were partners with Simon. And Jesus said to Simon, "Do not be afraid; from now on you will be catching men" (Luke 5:8-10 ESV).

Assuming Jesus was speaking to His disciples in Greek, it is amazing that He used the final verb in this citation to describe Peter's mission. First, this individual call was meant to be generalized to apply to all subsequent disciples. Second, the verb used was the Greek ζωγρέω, to "capture men alive." Although it is translated "catching" in this version, it is actually a military term used twice in the New Testament and eight times in the Old Testament. While Christians are seeking to "capture men alive," the same verb is found of the work of the Devil, "having been taken captive by him to do his will" (2 Timothy 2:26).

The term ζωγρέω (to capture men alive) takes on a different twist from the "fish for men" of Matthew and Mark. With "make you" and "become" Matthew and Mark emphasized the act of catching persons. Luke emphasized the end result of the fishing, that is, the live capture of men. It is, in fact, the end result that Matthew's Great Commission also emphasizes, as we will see below. Matthew 28:19 emphasized the "winning of a disciple," as can be proven by the fact that only won disciples are baptized.

John's calling of the disciples continued telescopically. We find the early calls of Jesus, "Follow Me," in John 1:43, and "Come and see," in John 1:39. But in John 4 Jesus began to call His disciples to look on the harvest fields of human hearts:

> *"Do you not say, 'There are still four months and* then *comes the harvest'? Behold, I say to you, lift up your eyes and look at the fields, for they are already white for harvest!"* (John 4:35).

Using the example of the Woman at the Well and the receptivity of her Samaritan village, Jesus impressed on the disciples to consider the urgency of a ready harvest. Three verses later Jesus tells these same disciples, "I sent you to reap" (John 4:38). The verb for "send" is ἀποστέλλω, and the verb for "reap" is θερίζω.

In agricultural parlance, one sows and another reaps. Reaping takes place at harvest-time when the grain is fully mature. After cutting the stalk in reaping, then there is the process of threshing the grain—separating it from the stalk. Likewise, in another context, Paul spoke of the ministry as plowing and threshing (1 Corinthians 9:10). Again sowing and reaping are agricultural terms describing evangelism. Jesus applied the words of Psalm 126 to the call of His disciples:

> *Those who sow in tears shall reap with shouts of joy! He who goes out weeping, bearing the seed for sowing, shall come home with shouts of joy, bringing his sheaves with him* (Psalm 126:5-6 ESV).

Therefore, Christ was calling His disciples to send them out to fish for men, to capture men alive, and to reap a harvest of souls. While this was His end goal, stated from the beginning, we read of Jesus actually sending His disciples out on mission trips about midway through His ministry.

Sending Passages of Jesus

There are four places in Matthew, Mark, and Luke where Jesus sent out His disciples. The pattern of these sending passages is this:

- Context of sending portion
- Calling the disciples to Himself
- Training sermon
- Send off
- Debriefing time.

Here are the four passages listed from longest to shortest:

- Matthew 9:35-11:1 (47 verses)
- Luke 10:1-24 (24 verses)
- Mark 6:6-13 (7 verses)
- Luke 9:1-6 (6 verses).

Each of these portions is quite interesting, and much of the material is repeated. For the purposes of a quick overview, we will summarize Luke 9.

The sending passage in Luke 9 focuses on Jesus sending His twelve disciples. First of all, He called them together. Their names are listed in Matthew 10. Luke mentions the level of authority given to them. Then He mentioned what they were sent to accomplish. They were given "power and authority." Jesus vested His disciples with an abundance of spiritual power and authority to accomplish the work to which He was calling them. The extent of this power was made evident (1) using the ministry of Jesus as an example; and (2) being that the spiritual realm and natural realms overlap, e.g. exorcizing demons, healing diseases, and evangelizing lost souls. The miraculous is here used by way of an "Ad Extremum" argument to show that the disciples were literally given all the spiritual authority that they would need to accomplish their work; spiritual authority was not to be their weakest link! Next, Jesus sent them out for two reasons: (1) to preach (κηρύσσω) the kingdom or rule of God; and (2) to heal (ἰάομαι) the sick. Although the last could be applied to building hospitals, this was not the implication of Jesus. He was literally giving them power to perform acts of healing. But the order of the verbs is important. Wherever "preaching" and "healing" are used in a listing, preaching *always* comes first:

> *And he went throughout all Galilee, teaching in their synagogues and proclaiming the gospel of the kingdom and healing every disease and every affliction among the people* (Matthew 4:23 ESV).

> *And Jesus went throughout all the cities and villages, teaching in their synagogues and proclaiming the gospel of the kingdom and healing every disease and every affliction* (Matthew 9:35 ESV).

> *"And as you go, preach, saying, 'The kingdom of heaven is at hand.' Heal the sick, cleanse the lepers, raise the dead, cast out demons. Freely you have received, freely give"* (Matthew 10:7-8).

> *Then He appointed twelve, that they might be with Him and that He might send them out to preach, and to have power to heal sicknesses and to cast out demons* (Mark 3:14-15).

> *So they went out and preached that people should repent. And they cast out many demons, and anointed with oil many who were sick, and healed* them (Mark 6:12-13).

> *And they went out and preached everywhere, the Lord working with* them *and confirming the word through the accompanying signs. Amen* (Mark 16:20).

> *But now even more the report about him went abroad, and great crowds gathered to hear him and to be healed of their infirmities* (Luke 5:15 ESV).

> *And he came down with them and stood on a level place, with a great crowd of his disciples and a great multitude of people from all Judea and Jerusalem and the seacoast of Tyre and Sidon, who came to hear him and to be healed of their diseases. And those who were troubled with unclean spirits were cured* (Luke 6:17-18 ESV).

> *And he sent them out to proclaim the kingdom of God and to heal* (Luke 9:2 ESV).

> *And they departed and went through the villages, preaching the gospel and healing everywhere* (Luke 9:6 ESV).

> *And the crowds with one accord paid attention to what was*

being said by Philip when they heard him and saw the signs that he did (Acts 8:6 ESV).

In the case of the disciples of John the Baptist reporting back to him, this order is reversed (e.g. Luke 7:22). Jesus used a crescendo approach emphasizing the point of stumbling over His words, as elaborated in verse 23. The disconnect between receiving the miracles of Jesus while stumbling over His teaching is discussed in John 6, 10, and 12.

Jesus sent them with no money in Luke 9:3. He later reversed that command just before His death in Luke 22:35-36. Jesus then taught His disciples to find a receptive home and to stay there—in other words take a receptive home as a work of God by remaining there. He taught dealing with an unreceptive city, and then He sent them out. The two verbs used to explain what they were to do after being sent out were to "preach the gospel" (εὐαγγελίζω) and to "heal" (θεραπεύω) everywhere.

The focus of the ministry which Jesus called His disciples to accomplish was spiritual. Primarily, it was proclamational, preaching, teaching, and evangelizing. Secondarily, it involved a supernatural element, such as healing or casting out of demons. Jesus limited His call to His disciples to these elements. It makes sense that He was training His disciples for what He was going to commission them to do in His Resurrection Preaching.

The Chronological Interpretation of the Great Commission

We are now ready to provide an analysis of the chronological interpretation of the Great Commission. The first four verbs in Matthew's Great Commission establish a foundation for the proper understanding of the Great Commission. The verb "Go!" as has already been considered is found replete throughout a variety of commands in the New Testament. It therefore retains first place in the chain of human commandments.

The missing element is the verb "preach," "proclaim," "declare," or "bear witness." Yet the proclamational command is present in the Great Commissions of Mark, Luke, and Acts. It can be shown to be omitted because of lack of need for repetition, much like the call "Follow Me and I will make you fishers of men" was summarized in Matthew 4:21, "He called them." There are several examples of calls to displacement and preaching already in Matthew, for example:

> *In those days John the Baptist came preaching in the wilderness of Judea* (Matthew 3:1).

> *And he went throughout all Galilee, teaching in their synagogues and proclaiming the gospel of the kingdom and healing every disease and every affliction among the people* (Matthew 4:23 ESV).

> *And Jesus went throughout all the cities and villages, teaching in their synagogues and proclaiming the gospel of the kingdom and healing every disease and every affliction* (Matthew 9:35 ESV).

> *"And as you go, preach, saying, 'The kingdom of heaven is at hand'"* (Matthew 10:7).

> *When Jesus had finished instructing his twelve disciples, he went on from there to teach and preach in their cities* (Matthew 11:1 ESV).

Therefore, to understand why the proclamational aspect appears missing in Matthew, and to seek to synchronize it with Mark, Luke, and Acts, it follows that the missing command to preach must be an ellipsis.

Likewise, the content of the message preached was an ellipsis. It is found in multiple places in Scripture that it is the message of the gospel which converts the human soul. Further, the word "gospel" is found in Mark's Great Commission as the object of what is to be preached. In Luke's Great Commission the message is further delineated by Jesus:

> *Then He said to them, "Thus it is written, and thus it was necessary for the Christ to suffer and to rise from the dead the third day, and that repentance and remission of sins should be preached in His name to all nations, beginning at Jerusalem. And you are witnesses of these things. Behold, I send the Promise of My Father upon you; but tarry in the city of Jerusalem until you are endued with power from on high"* (Luke 24:46-49).

Jesus described the message He commissioned His disciples to preach in precise detail:

- The suffering of Christ

- The resurrection of Christ on the third day

- The call to and response of repentance

- The opportunity for remission of sins

- All preach in the name of Christ.

Christ's disciples were to "bear witness" of this message to all nations. Therefore, while the message of the gospel was not included in Matthew's Great Commission, its exclusion there does not eliminate the authority of Christ's Great Commission in Luke. So also, the lack of a message is another ellipsis in Matthew's Great Commission.

Of interest is what Matthew did include in Christ's Great Commission. He included the result of a person hearing and believing the gospel, that is, the making of a disciple. Three points here. First, the word "them" (αὐτός) as the object of the action baptizing is in the masculine plural. It cannot be referencing "the nations," being it is a neuter noun in Greek. It must be referencing the baptizing of a "won disciple" based on the verb μαθητεύω (to win or make disciples). In this sense, Matthew's Great Commission coincides with John 4:38, "I sent you to reap." The disciple must be "won" before he is baptized, based on the masculine plural of "them" (αὐτός). Second, the verb μαθητεύω (to win or make disciples) was translated as "won … disciples" in the 1984 New International Version of Acts 14:21:

> They preached the gospel in that city and won [μαθητεύω] a large number of disciples. Then they returned to Lystra, Iconium and Antioch (Acts 14:21 NIV).

The translators chose to shorten the concept of long-term "discipleship" to the immediate fruits of evangelism, to "win a disciple." Research shows that Paul was in Lystra for only a short time. Thus, he could not have entered into a long-term training and mentoring program. Third, the use of the verb μαθητεύω (to win or make disciples) closest to Matthew's Great Commission is found toward the end of Matthew 27:

> Now when evening had come, there came a rich man from

> *Arimathea, named Joseph, who himself had also become a*
> *disciple [μαϑητεύω] of Jesus* (Matthew 27:57).

We learn from John 19:38 that Joseph of Arimathea was a disciple (εἰμί + μαθητής) of Jesus, but "secretly, for fear of the Jews." Therefore, prior to and during the crucifixion, Joseph was already considered to "have been won as a disciple" (μαθητεύω), even though he was not an open disciple, but a secret one. Surely the verb μαθητεύω (to win or make disciples) cannot refer to an open disciple. Rather this verb points to the very early stages of just becoming a new disciple of Jesus by hearing and believing—before going public through baptism.

Whereas Matthew 27:57 and Acts 14:21 address the chronological point at the beginning of the life of the disciple, even to a point prior to public profession, Matthew 13:52 points to the individual spiritual vitality operating within the heart of the disciple:

> *And he said to them, For this reason every scribe discipled to the*
> *kingdom of the heavens is like a man [that is] a householder who*
> *brings out of his treasure things new and old*
> (Matthew 13:52 DARBY).

The new disciple becomes like a homeowner. Immediately at conversion the Holy Spirit brings to his heart both new concepts and old truths. He has a new spiritual discernment that he did not have before.

So, as it stands the Great Commission of Christ includes:

1. Going

2. Preaching

3. Preaching the gospel

4. Winning disciples to Christ.

These four commands are followed by three further verbal components:

5. Baptizing them

6. Teaching them to obey

7. Teaching them to obey "all that I have commanded you."

Whole chapters of this book are given to these last three points.

In summary, the focus of the Great Commission shifts:

- From the disciples who go
- To the nations to whom they go to win disciples
- To ministry to the new disciples that are made.

The term "them" is found after both verbs in steps 5 and 6 above. The action shifts from the generalized *nations* to the particularized *disciples*. Once a disciple is "won" or "made" then he becomes a new priority in the fulfillment of Christ's Great Commission. In this way, following Christ's example, the newly made disciple is mentored ("taught to observe") how to "Follow Christ" so that Christ can make him become a "fisher of men."

CHAPTER FOUR

AND THEY WENT
—ἔρχομαι—

There are two steps to being "sent out" in the Bible. One step, as considered previously, is the many passages wherein Christ commissioned His followers to "Go!" There are numerous verbs, descriptions, and examples related to this part of the Great Commission. Nevertheless, fully understanding "Go!" is not complete without considering how the disciples obeyed this command to "Go!"

Acts 13, Mission Trip Verbs (Part 1)

One of the greatest examples of obedience to the command to "Go!" is found in Barnabas and Saul being sent out on a mission trip in Acts 13:

> Then after fasting and praying they laid their hands on them and sent them off [ἀπολύω]. So, being sent out [ἐκπέμπω] by the Holy Spirit, they went down [κατέρχομαι] to Seleucia, and from there they sailed to Cyprus. When they arrived at Salamis, they proclaimed the word of God in the synagogues of the Jews. And they had John to assist them. When they had gone through the whole island as far as Paphos, they came upon a certain magician, a Jewish false prophet named Bar-Jesus (Acts 13:3-6 ESV).

Being "sent off" (ἀπολύω) and "sent out" (ἐκπέμπω), the disciples "went down" (κατέρχομαι) (Acts 13:3-4). Their obedience was codified in Scripture by the use of active verbs. This chapter will overview the various uses of "going" verbs as displayed through several key texts of Scripture.

Not only were the disciples "called" and "sent," they went a step further by obeying the commission to "go forth." The obedience of the apostles and disciples is best studied by considering the various series of active verbs in Acts. In Acts 13,

Barnabas and Saul were "sent out" (ἀπολύω) by the church, as well as "sent out" (ἐκπέμπω) by the Holy Spirit. Then, as we follow the next steps of these missionaries, we encounter our first series of active verbs:

- They went down [κατέρχομαι] to Seleucia
- They sailed [ἀποπλέω] to Cyprus
- They arrived [γίνομαι] in Salamis
- They preached [καταγγέλλω] the word of God in the synagogue
- They had gone through [διέρχομαι] the island of Paphos
- They found [εὑρίσκω] a sorcerer (Acts 13:4-6).

These six verbs provide the bridge between the sending in Antioch and the incident in Paphos that occasioned Saul receiving the name Paul. If we consider these six verbs we find that four of them relate to travel, one to ministry (preaching), and one to spiritual discernment in traveling. It is very clear, therefore, that obedience to Christ's command to "Go and preach the gospel" includes actual "going"—that is, travel.

As on any mission trip, there is the urging of the Holy Spirit to participate. There is the sending off by the church. And then there is often quite a bit of travel to get to the proper destination for ministry. Such was also the recorded experience of Paul and Barnabas.

Acts 13, Mission Trip Verbs (Part 2)

After Luke recorded the experience that led Saul to receive the name Paul, he included another significant sequence of travel verbs. These verbs related to Paul's travels from Paphos to Antioch of Pisidia:

- Paul and his party set sail [ἀνάγω] from Paphos
- They came [ἔρχομαι] to Perga in Pamphylia
- When they departed [διέρχομαι] from Perga

- They came to [παραγίνομαι] Antioch of Pisidia
  (Acts 13:13-14).

This entire series of verbs consists uniquely of travel verbs. Once Paul arrived at Antioch of Pisidia, Luke was then prepared to describe the setting for his first recorded sermon in Acts. As far as the second list of travel verbs, they seem to validate two things:

- "Go" in the Great Commission includes "Go," and not merely "As you go."

- "Going on a mission trip" to preach the gospel is valid as part of obeying Christ's Great Commission.

The student of the Bible will also note that Paul's travels included many cities and stops that are not included in Luke's narrative. Under the inspiration of the Holy Spirit, Luke chose and described only those events which would allow the Book of Acts to become henceforth the primary guidebook for the entire missionary activity of New Testament churches.

Acts 8, Citywide Evangelism Verbs

In Acts 8 Luke introduced the only named "evangelist" in the New Testament, Philip. Philip's ministry included both citywide evangelism and personal evangelism. In his citywide evangelism, Philip's travels are explained in several key traveling verbs:

> And Saul approved of his execution. And there arose on that day a great persecution against the church in Jerusalem, and they were all scattered throughout the regions of Judea and Samaria, except the apostles. Devout men buried Stephen and made great lamentation over him. But Saul was ravaging the church, and entering house after house, he dragged off men and women and committed them to prison. Now those who were scattered went about preaching the word. Philip went down to the city of Samaria and proclaimed to them the Christ (Acts 8:1-5 ESV).

Philip's travels began when persecution arose for the church in Jerusalem, persecution instigated by Saul, who was to become the Apostle Paul. This persecution led to the spread of the gospel of Jesus Christ to regions 2 and 3 (Jerusalem, Judea, Samaria, end of the earth), as listed in Acts 1:8.

- They were all scattered [διασπείρω] throughout the regions of Judea and Samaria (Acts 8:1 ESV)

- Now those who were scattered [διασπείρω] went about [διέρχομαι] preaching the word (Acts 8:4 ESV)

- Philip went down [κατέρχομαι] to the city of Samaria and proclaimed to them the Christ (Acts 8:5 ESV).

Here Luke shifted his use of multiple travel verbs, using one verb for geographic movement, one word for ministry methodology, and one word for the message:

- v. 4: were scattered [διασπείρω]; preaching [εὐαγγελίζω]; the word [ὁ λόγος]

- v. 5: went down [κατέρχομαι]; proclaimed [κηρύσσω]; the Christ [ὁ Χριστός].

In this way, the obedience of the scattered disciples is showcased. They are fulfilling Christ's Great Commission verb-for-verb, noun-for-noun.

Acts 8, Personal Evangelism Verbs

This methodological pattern of command and obedience can be assumed when reading the New Testament. Barnabas and Saul were sent, so they went. Philip was told "to arise and go" to the desert road in Acts 8, "So he arose and went." The pattern is so predictable that it can be overlooked. Yet common experience shows that this type of obedience is not commonplace.

This passage describing Philip's conversation with the Ethiopian Eunuch combines numerous points of interest. For the purposes of this chapter, we will focus on God's call and Philip's obedience.

Now an angel of the Lord spoke to Philip, saying, "Arise [ἀνίστημι] and go [πορεύομαι] toward the south along the road which goes down from Jerusalem to Gaza." This is desert. So he arose [ἀνίστημι] and went [πορεύομαι]. And behold, a man of Ethiopia, a eunuch of great authority under Candace the queen of the Ethiopians, who had charge of all her treasury, and had come to Jerusalem to worship, was returning. And sitting in his chariot, he was reading Isaiah the prophet. Then the Spirit said to Philip, "Go near [προσέρχομαι] and overtake [κολλάω] this chariot." So

Philip ran to him, and heard him reading the prophet Isaiah, and said, "Do you understand what you are reading?" And he said, "How can I, unless someone guides me?" And he asked Philip to come up and sit with him (Acts 8:26-31).

A look at a map of Palestine shows that Philip had to travel at least 50-65 kilometers, just to get from Samaria to Jerusalem, not considering how far he had to travel on the desert road before he met the eunuch, nor the many twists and turns in the roads in those days. Luke's narrative is not exhaustive, but crisply descriptive. After 50-65 kilometers of travel Philip came across one unnamed man in a chariot, reading. It is highly likely that he was not driving the chariot, since he was reading aloud. So, there had to be another driver. Also, since he was a high, cabinet-level official of Ethiopian Queen Candace, it is highly likely that he had an entourage of bodyguards. Philip, however, was told by the Holy Spirit to "Go near and overtake the chariot." So "Philip ran up to him" closely enough to hear him reading and to recognize what he was reading.

We find in the missionary trip of Philip the evangelist, a summary of his gospel conversation all the way to the point of baptism. While the preaching and baptism portions of the dialogue will be considered in future chapters, with the Ethiopian Eunuch, we have an example of God leading to a spiritually-inquisitive individual prepared to hear the gospel by reading the Scriptures.

Arise (ἀνίστημι) and Go (πορεύομαι)

Luke used an interesting strategy when he transcribed this incident. He used the exact same verbs for the command of the angel (v. 26) and to describe Philip's obedience (v. 27). The angel said arise (ἀνίστημι) and go (πορεύομαι). So Philip arose (ἀνίστημι) and went (πορεύομαι). Under the inspiration of the Holy Spirit, Luke wanted to display the exacting obedience of Philip, as he obeyed the prompting of the Lord.

Go Up (προσέρχομαι) and Join (κολλάω)

In the second set of commands, we read that the Spirit told Philip to "go up" (προσέρχομαι) and overtake—or "cling to" (κολλάω)—this chariot. In other words, get right next to it. This time Luke used a different verb to describe the action of Philip. Luke wrote that Philip ran up (προστρέχω) to the chariot.

Ran up (προστρέχω) and heard (ἀκούω)

As Philip obeyed the Spirit's prompting, he drew close enough to the chariot to (1) hear that the eunuch was reading Scripture—likely in Hebrew or perhaps Greek; and (2) recognize that he was reading from the prophet Isaiah, from what we now consider to be Isaiah 53. Consider the split-second decisions of Philip to allow the eunuch's current spiritual condition and questions to shape the conversation. Further, the eunuch, a man of stature and importance, reached out to a complete stranger by asking for his assistance in interpreting a portion of Scripture with which he was having difficulty. God has an amazing way of coordinating events and timing conversations. This example of Philip should motivate all Christians through the ages to be attuned to the voice of the Holy Spirit calling them to share the Good News of Jesus to those around them.

Jesus' Obedience

As we have noted there are numerous examples of the methodological rhythm of command and obedience. Followers of Jesus instinctively (it would seem) know to obey the voice of God in evangelism. It is, in fact, the same pattern which was noted in the obedience of Jesus to His Father's will. So important to Jesus was His absolute obedience of His Father's will, that He called it His food:

> Jesus said to them, "My food is to do the will of him who sent me and to accomplish his work" (John 4:34 ESV).

Jesus ate and drank obedience of His Father's will. It was absolutely necessary for His spiritual survival and it nurtured Him spiritually. He fully obeyed His Father, even as was stated in Psalm 119:

> The LORD is my portion; I promise to keep your words. I entreat your favor with all my heart; be gracious to me according to your promise. When I think on my ways, I turn my feet to your testimonies; I hasten and do not delay to keep your

commandments (Psalm 119:57-60 ESV).

These verses reverberate with the truth expressed in Psalm 119:4, "You have commanded your precepts to be kept diligently" (ESV). Christ, the word became flesh, diligently obeyed the voice of His Father. He did not need a warning from God nor even to be commanded twice. Christ diligently obeyed the first time. He fully obeyed the voice of His Father.

It is not surprising, then, that the followers of Christ also obey the voice of God. God speaks through His word, Christ's disciples hear, and they follow the example of Jesus who obeyed to the end. God calls to Christians, they hear His voice, and they follow.

On Hesitation and Disobedience

Yet there are some examples of hesitation in Scripture, but these are more exceptional than normal. Yes, there are times when we see hesitation. Lot, who was later called "the righteous Lot" by Peter in 2 Peter 2:7, lingered when the angels clearly told him to leave Sodom:

> As morning dawned, the angels urged Lot, saying, "Up! Take your wife and your two daughters who are here, lest you be swept away in the punishment of the city." But he lingered. So the men seized him and his wife and his two daughters by the hand, the LORD being merciful to him, and they brought him out and set him outside the city (Genesis 19:15-16 ESV).

Lot lingered. His spirit appeared willing but his flesh was weak. The men mercifully "pulled Lot out of the fire" as it were (Jude 23). We can be grateful that in those instances, we have a gracious Lord and Master who takes us by the hand, and compels us on the right path. Perhaps Peter had the example of Lot etched in his mind because of his own sinfulness in denying the Lord Jesus Christ three times, while He was being beaten and tortured?

Peter even denied Christ with an oath:

> Now Peter was sitting outside in the courtyard. And a servant girl came up to him and said, "You also were with Jesus the Galilean." But he denied it before them all, saying, "I do not know what you mean." And when he went out to the entrance, another servant girl saw him, and she said to the bystanders, "This man was with

> *Jesus of Nazareth." And again he denied it with an oath: "I do not know the man." After a little while the bystanders came up and said to Peter, "Certainly you too are one of them, for your accent betrays you." Then he began to invoke a curse on himself and to swear, "I do not know the man." And immediately the rooster crowed. And Peter remembered the saying of Jesus, "Before the rooster crows, you will deny me three times." And he went out and wept bitterly* (Matthew 26:69-75 ESV).

It must be remembered that this Peter had the same human nature that we all have. Were it not for the grace of God we would do much worse than Peter! And yet Peter was lovingly confronted by Jesus in John 21. Jesus led Peter to repent and turn from his sin by giving him the opportunity to verbally affirm—three times—his love for Him. And we, who have denied Christ both verbally and by our silence, can take heart in Jesus' loving confrontation of Peter.

In Acts 9, Ananias hesitated when he was asked to go share the gospel with Saul of Tarsus:

> *Now there was a disciple at Damascus named Ananias. The Lord said to him in a vision, "Ananias." And he said, "Here I am, Lord." And the Lord said to him, "Rise [ἀνίστημι] and go [πορεύομαι] to the street called Straight, and at the house of Judas look for a man of Tarsus named Saul, for behold, he is praying, and he has seen in a vision a man named Ananias come in and lay his hands on him so that he might regain his sight." But Ananias answered, "Lord, I have heard from many about this man, how much evil he has done to your saints at Jerusalem. And here he has authority from the chief priests to bind all who call on your name." But the Lord said to him, "Go [πορεύομαι], for he is a chosen instrument of mine to carry my name before the Gentiles and kings and the children of Israel. For I will show him how much he must suffer for the sake of my name." So Ananias departed [ἀπέρχομαι] and entered [εἰσέρχομαι] the house* (Acts 9:10-17 ESV).

The same verbs used for Philip in Acts 8:26, "arise (ἀνίστημι) and go (πορεύομαι)," were also used for Ananias. But Ananias was reluctant to go. God repeated His command to go (πορεύομαι). Ananias went (ἀπέρχομαι) all the way, including entering into (εἰσέρχομαι) the house where Paul was being kept. And thereafter we read of the conversion of the one who was to become the primary protagonist of the remainder of the Book of Acts, and the author of 14 books of the New Testament.

God knows the weakness of our flesh. He tells us that the spirit is willing, but our flesh is weak. So, God gave enough examples of disobedience and restoration to give us hope, and enough examples of obedience to show us what is the proper way. So, while there was some hesitation noted in the New Testament, the overwhelming examples in Acts show a pattern of obedience to God's call. In the Book of Acts, we also find an example of struggling to discern God's leading.

Struggling to Find God's Leading

In Acts 16, Paul and Silas were struggling to know God's plan for their missionary journey. As they headed out on what is considered Paul's second missionary journey, they began by visiting the churches that Paul had helped establish—not too far from Paul's hometown of Tarsus. After visiting the Pisidian churches planted during the first missionary journey, Paul and Silas then struggled to discern God's will for their next phase in missionary service. Their struggle was explained by a series of verbs and counter-verbs. While the reader may read these five verses in two minutes, the events related in these verses include travel on today's roads of about 771 kilometers—assuming a direct route. If Paul and his companions walked 40 kilometers (24 miles) a day, the distance between Iconium and Troas would take them 20 days of non-stop walking. If one accounts for (1) time sharing the gospel, (2) the dead-ends they took, and (3) the revised leadings of God indicated in the text, it seems reasonable to assume that the timeline involved in the locations mentioned in Acts 16 up to the Macedonian call included several months of seeking God's guiding!

- They had gone through [διέρχομαι] Phrygian and the region of Galatia

  o Forbidden [κωλύω] by the Holy Spirit to speak the word in Asia

- They came [ἔρχομαι] to Mysia

- And tried to go [πειράζω + πορεύομαι] to Bithynia

- o   But the Spirit did not permit [οὐ ἐάω] them

- They by-passed [παρέρχομαι] Mysia

- They came down [καταβαίνω] to Troas (Acts 16:6-8).

There is probably over 1,000 kilometers (600 miles) of travel contained in these three verses. Discerning God's guiding was far more complex and time consuming than it would at first appear.

Two thoughts emanate from this list of verbs. First, just because Jesus sends us out in His Great Commission does not mean that we will know how it will play out for each one of us. It takes trial and error. It takes tenacity to know how to fulfill His commission for each one of us. Second, it pleases God for us to diligently seek and search out His will. For example, consider Jeremiah 29:13 found after the great promise of verse 11:

> For I know the plans I have for you, declares the LORD, plans for welfare and not for evil, to give you a future and a hope. Then you will call upon me and come and pray to me, and I will hear you. You will seek me and find me, when you seek me with all your heart (Jeremiah 29:11-13 ESV).

God is pleased that we seek Him "with all of our heart." And included within this idea of seeking Him is seeking His will. God promises that He will allow Himself to be found by us. And yet we are required to seek Him with all our heart.

Meanwhile, after Paul and Silas had wandered through Bithynia, Galatia, and Phrygia, God brought the vision of the man from Macedonia. "Come over and help us!" (Acts 16:9). Paul had grown in his perceptiveness of God's calling. He conjectured to his team "concluding that God had called us to evangelize them" (Acts 16:10 HCSB). Now Paul had a plan for his missionary team. God had called them to "evangelize [εὐαγγελίζω] them."

Acts 27, God's Watch-care As We Go

Paul's voyage from Caesarea to Rome is described in significant detail. In Matthew's Great Commission Jesus promised, "Behold, I am with you always, to the end of the age." As we go, Jesus promises to join with us in our travels in obedience to His Great

Commission. One of the awesome examples of God's watch-care in travel is found in the travels of Paul as described in Acts 27.

One of the longest travel passages in the Book of Acts comes in the second to last chapter of that book. The account almost comes as a metaphor for the ministry of Paul, and by analogy, a metaphor of the ministry of all who would follow Christ. This trip includes some unique features:

- Paul was a prisoner
- Paul underwent one of the three shipwrecks he experienced (cf. 2 Corinthians 11:25)
- Paul's presence led to the supernatural saving of all the passengers in the ship.

This portion will only consider the first leg of the journey from Caesarea to Fair Havens on the Island of Crete:

> And when it was decided that we should sail for Italy, they delivered Paul and some other prisoners to a centurion of the Augustan Cohort named Julius. And embarking in a ship of Adramyttium, which was about to sail to the ports along the coast of Asia, we put to sea, accompanied by Aristarchus, a Macedonian from Thessalonica. The next day we put in at Sidon. And Julius treated Paul kindly and gave him leave to go to his friends and be cared for. And putting out to sea from there we sailed under the lee of Cyprus, because the winds were against us. And when we had sailed across the open sea along the coast of Cilicia and Pamphylia, we came to Myra in Lycia. There the centurion found a ship of Alexandria sailing for Italy and put us on board. We sailed slowly for a number of days and arrived with difficulty off Cnidus, and as the wind did not allow us to go farther, we sailed under the lee of Crete off Salmone. Coasting along it with difficulty, we came to a place called Fair Havens, near which was the city of Lasea (Acts 27:1-8 ESV).

Now why was Paul undertaking this voyage?

1. He had purposed in his heart to see Rome (Acts 19:21)
2. He was encouraged by God that he would bear witness in Rome (Acts 23:11)
3. He had appealed his imprisonment to Caesar (Acts 25:11).

Likewise, God promised Paul during the shipwreck that he would be brought before Caesar, and that all those in the ship would be spared (Acts 27:24). So, Paul's journey to Rome was a missional journey ordained of God. It only follows, then, that all these travel verbs were part of Paul obeying Christ's command to "Go into all the world."

Consider then the lengths of God's providential care for us to be brought to the right place at the right time. Through storms, imprisonment, and snakebites, God led the Apostle Paul to arrive at his proper destination, so that he could bear witness of Jesus Christ to the Emperor of Rome. So God works through the pains and challenges of life to bring us right where He wants us, so that we can bear testimony to His name.

Proposed Lessons from Going and Went

Several lessons may be gleaned from the content of this chapter. The first take-away is that Christ's Great Commission presupposes obedience. It is the duty of those purchased by the blood of Jesus to obey their Savior.

Second, the command "to go" implies that "we do go." Not only is obedience implied in the command, but obedience is exemplified on the pages of the New Testament. What Christ meant by "Go!" is not an abstract concept. It has been communicated very concretely by command and example.

Third, there is travel required in "going." "As you go"—as found in Matthew 10:7—is only part of the picture. The emphasis in that passage is: while going, preach as you go. "Go" in the Great Commission commands geographic displacement. We may need to cross the street, go across town, or cross the world. But we must "Go!"

Fourth, Paul and Silas struggled to know God's direction. God chose to close one door after another. Likewise, we ought to avoid being hasty to "evangelize" or "minister" our way. Ezekiel waited seven days before God gave him a word for the captives at Tel Abib (Ezekiel 3:15-16). God may guide us to a new or different approach in a new location.

Fifth, "going" might necessitate waiting and praying. Just as Paul remained in Philippi for a time before he was led to go out to the place of prayer, so also we need to consider the need to wait on the Lord for Him to provide clear direction.

Sixth, God predicates His saving work on His people "going." If Paul and Silas had not gone to Philippi, then they would not have encountered Lydia at the place of prayer. God foreordained in His sovereign plan that "going" was necessary to reach Lydia.

Seventh, Jesus promised to accompany His children as they go out. Just as Christ was with Paul leading, guiding, and encouraging in the midst of imprisonment and shipwreck, so Christ will be with His followers. He will not leave us or forsake us.

CHAPTER FIVE

AND PREACHED
—καταγγέλλω—

Just as the disciples and followers of Jesus obeyed the command to "Go!" so when they "Went!" they did something. Not having something concrete to do when going turns the Great Commission into mere "activism." Rather there were two main verbal groupings in Christ's Great Commission to His followers. One was "Go!" and the other was "Preach!" The best and clearest way to understand what is meant by the second imperative in this pair is to consider what the disciples of Jesus did after they "Went!" in the Book of Acts.

Jesus sent out His disciples to "Go!" and "Preach!" Further, there are ample examples of Jesus, the disciples, the Apostles, and others going, so there are numerous examples of the followers of Jesus preaching. This chapter will consider the series of verbs that delineate the processes used by the followers of Christ as they proceeded to preach the gospel. Several of these examples are arranged according to category to provide the best opportunity for application and emulation.

Two main sections organize this chapter. The first section addresses the means by which a pattern of ministry can be developed. The second section focuses on examples of verbs used in five ministry situations. We begin by answering the question: "After we go, then what?"

Developing a Pattern of Ministry

Going is great. But knowing what to do when we get there is even better. In this section, we will consider when Peter did not know why he was divinely led to the house of Cornelius. Likewise, Paul—searching for God's will—heard the call of God when he went to go to Philippi to speak with Lydia. Lastly, Paul in his years of missionary activity, developed a pattern of ministry. These three examples exemplify how Christ leads His people into His harvest fields.

Acts 10, Determining What to Do After Going

A somewhat humorous example of going somewhere and not knowing what to say is found in the example of Peter speaking to the gathered household and friends of Cornelius in Acts 10. When Jesus sent His disciples to "Go" He also wanted them to "Preach." Because the message preached will be considered by way of verbs (repent, believe, and receive), we will focus here on the methodology of passing on that message. The New Testament methodology is described as "preaching."

Here is the slightly humorous question of Peter:

> And he said to them, "You yourselves know how unlawful it is for a Jew to associate with or to visit anyone of another nation, but God has shown me that I should not call any person common or unclean. So when I was sent for, I came without objection. I ask then why you sent for me" (Acts 10:28-29 ESV).

It appears, from this question, that Peter did not know why he was called to speak to Cornelius and the crowd. Here is an example of "Go!" without a clear understanding of "Preach!" nor of what to preach. Cornelius ended his gracious response to Peter as follows:

> "So I sent for you at once, and you have been kind enough to come. Now therefore we are all here in the presence of God to hear all that you have been commanded by the Lord" (Acts 10:33 ESV).

Hearing the words "commanded by the Lord" seemed to jolt Peter's mind to thinking, "the Great Commission of Jesus!" It was like those very words shined a light in Peter's mind, and he understood that his purpose was (1) to preach and (2) to preach the gospel. Which he did!

By the way, Peter was still in the midst of preaching this message when the Holy Spirit came down on the group. This manifestation of the Holy Spirit coming down was a sign to Peter that this group had in fact believed in Jesus, and that they needed to be baptized. The incident set up what is perhaps the most important five verses in Acts from a doctrinal point-of-view. From Acts 15:7-11 we learn that salvation is:

1. Communicated with words out of the mouth alone

2. By the power of the Scriptures alone

3. By believing alone

4. By grace alone

5. Through Christ alone.

Consider some of the verbs leading up to this preaching opportunity for Peter:

> *So he invited them in to be his guests. The next day he rose and went away with them, and some of the brothers from Joppa accompanied him. And on the following day they entered Caesarea. Cornelius was expecting them and had called together his relatives and close friends. When Peter entered, Cornelius met him and fell down at his feet and worshiped him. But Peter lifted him up, saying, "Stand up; I too am a man." And as he talked with him, he went in and found many persons gathered (Acts 10:23-27 ESV).*

After Peter invited the men from Cornelius to spend the night with him (thereby breaking the Old Testament law of non-association), then he went away with them.

- He rose [ἀνίστημι] and went away [ἐξέρχομαι] with them
  - And some brothers from Joppa accompanied [συνέρχομαι] him
- The following day they entered [εἰσέρχομαι] Caesarea
- Cornelius was expecting [προσδοκάω] them
  - And had called together [συγκαλέω] his relatives and close friends
- When Peter entered [εἰσέρχομαι]
  - Cornelius met him and fell down at his feet and worshiped him
  - Peter lifted him up

- And as he talked [συνομιλέω] with him, he went in [εἰσέρχομαι] and found many persons gathered [συνέρχομαι].

It is interesting that Luke used three cognates of the verb ἔρχομαι (to come, go), including three uses of "go in" (εἰσέρχομαι)—the action that was disallowed of Jews to "go in" and commune with Gentiles. Peter knew that he contradicted laws against association with Gentiles, such as Deuteronomy 7:3, "Nor shall you make marriages with them. You shall not give your daughter to their son, nor take their daughter for your son." He was still ministering according to the pre-crucifixion teaching of Jesus:

> These twelve Jesus sent out, instructing them, "Go nowhere among the Gentiles [τὸ ἔθνος] and enter no town of the Samaritans, but go rather to the lost sheep of the house of Israel" (Matthew 10:5-6 ESV).

However, later Jesus revised the limitation against going to the Gentiles [τὸ ἔθνος]. In Matthew 28:19 Jesus clearly said, "Make disciples of all nations [τὸ ἔθνος]." Peter and the Judaizers still clung to the pre-Resurrection Preaching of Jesus.

Nevertheless, after a long litany of traveling verbs, Luke used only one simple preaching verb:

- Then he said [φημί] to them.

With that simple verb, Peter began to speak the simple gospel. And it was not long before there was a response to that message.

Peter was uncertain what to do after he "Went!" This perplexity warns the reader of Acts of the Apostles that "Go!" is only the beginning of the Great Commission. After the missionary goes, he must be clear about why he went. The early disciples evangelized wherever they went.

> Now those who were scattered went about evangelizing [εὐαγγελίζω] the word (Acts 8:4, translation mine).

Lest the Great Commission only be considered "Christian Activism," the obedient follower of Christ must remember that after he goes, he is to preach Jesus.

Acts 16, Responding to God's Specific Guiding

We saw in our last chapter that Paul and Silas had wandered through Bithynia, Galatia, and Phrygia, seeking to understand God's plan for them. After several months of seeking, God brought the vision of the man from Macedonia. "Come over and help us!" (Acts 16:9). Paul was spiritually perceptive enough to understand this dream as a divine call to action. He explained this call to his team: "concluding that God had called us to evangelize them" (Acts 16:10 HCSB). The main verb used by Paul to explain what they were to do in Macedonia was to "evangelize [εὐαγγελίζω] them." And this conclusion led to another series of travel verbs. The first series related to travel to Macedonia:

- They set sail [ἀνάγω] from Troas

- They ran a straight course [εὐθυδρομέω] to Samothrace

- They came [ἐπιοῦσα] to Neapolis the next day

- From there to Philippi (Acts 16:11-12).

Once again we discern that there was significant travel involved. On the trip mentioned in those two verses, the gospel was carried for the first time from Asia to Europe!

The second series of verbs related to their life and ministry once they had arrived at their destination city, Philippi:

- They found a place to stay [διατρίβω]

  o They stayed [διατρίβω] there several days

- On the Sabbath we went out [ἐξέρχομαι] of the city to the riverside

  o Where we supposed [νομίζω]

  o That prayer was made [προσευχή + εἰμί]

- They sat down [καθίζω]

  o And spoke to the women who had gathered [συνέρχομαι] there

- And began to speak [λαλέω] to the women who had assembled there (Acts 16:12-13).

We find a parallel account in Ezekiel, where Ezekiel stayed seven days before speaking to the exiles what the Lord had told him to say. In fact, the text twice repeats the words "seven days" (Ezekiel 3:15-16) emphasizing the length of time. Also, Ezekiel 3:16 emphatically states "at the end of seven days the word of the LORD came to me saying." Ezekiel needed the seven days to get his bearings, and to hear a specific call from the Lord.

For Paul, the specific call after spending several days in Philippi was to seek out a possible "place of prayer" on the riverside. They were acting on inference and supposition. This is all that is available to the missionary or church planter when he lacks specific direction. Do something! And he did, and God had prepared someone with a hearing of faith!

Consider the third series of verbs relates to the salvation process in the life of Lydia:

- A certain woman, a seller of purple from the city of Thyatira was listening [ἀκούω]

- The Lord opened [διανοίγω] her heart

- To give heed [προσέχω]

- To what Paul was saying [λαλέω] (Acts 16:14).

In a masterfully interwoven pattern, the symbiotic relationship between God, the evangelist, and the person saved was clarified in this verse. This interrelationship will be considered more closely in Chapter 7.

It must be remembered that without the first two series of verbs, the third series of verbs does not exist. In other words, the travel to the destination and the specific leading at that destination are both important precursors to be in proximity where God can allow divine appointments for salvation.

Acts 17, Paul Settled on a Pattern of Missionary Ministry

Well into his third missionary journey, Paul began to settle on a pattern of ministry with which he became comfortable. This pattern is important for several reasons. First, it shows that Paul needed to develop patterns of ministry. A pattern gave him a mental picture of what needed to a done and in what order. Second, a pattern helped him train new co-laborers, whose names we read in the Book of Acts, as well as in other of his epistles. Third, a pattern provides us an example in order to obey Paul's command in 1 Corinthians 11:1, "Imitate me, just as I also *imitate* Christ." Fourth and perhaps most importantly for Bible interpretation, because Luke codified Paul's customary practice, the reader of the Book of Acts can deduce when he changed his customary practice. For example, in some cases a city had no synagogue, as in Philippi (Acts 16:13). In another case, God promised that Paul would not to be harmed in Corinth (Acts 18:9-10). Or consider the time Paul paid for ceremonial head-shaves in Jerusalem (Acts 21:24, 26).

In his customary practice, Luke gave us another pattern of verbs:

> Now when they had passed through Amphipolis and Apollonia, they came to Thessalonica, where there was a synagogue of the Jews. Then Paul, as his custom was, went in to them, and for three Sabbaths reasoned with them from the Scriptures, explaining and demonstrating that the Christ had to suffer and rise again from the dead, and saying, "This Jesus whom I preach to you is the Christ." And some of them were persuaded; and a great multitude of the devout Greeks, and not a few of the leading women, joined Paul and Silas. But the Jews who were not persuaded, becoming envious, took some of the evil men from the marketplace, and gathering a mob, set all the city in an uproar (Acts 17:1-5).

In his travels, Paul was passing through Amphipolis and Apollonia, and he came on Thessalonica. Here Luke expounded Paul's "customary method" in a city where there was a synagogue:

- Paul went in [εἰσέρχομαι] to the synagogue
- Paul reasoned [διαλέγομαι] with them
  - From the Scriptures
- He explaining [διανοίγω] and demonstrating [παρατίθημι]
  - Concerning Christ—His death and resurrection
- It was this message that he was preaching [καταγγέλλω]

73

The English Geneva translated the verb διαλέγομαι as "disputed." Likewise, διανοίγω could be translated as "opening" and παρατίθημι as "alleging" or "establishing." So also, καταγγέλλω can be translated "declaring." Clearly Paul was setting up a disputation as described in Deuteronomy 25:1-4, which concludes with the verse, "You shall not muzzle the ox while it threshes out the grain" (1 Corinthians 9:9). The Scriptures were to be "the court" through which every matter was arbitrated.

We would be remiss if we did not include expected results of Paul's customary practice. Again, there are several verbs involved:

- Some of them were persuaded [πείθω]

- And joined [προσκληρόω] Paul and Silas

- But the Jews who were not persuaded [ἀπειθέω]

- Gathered [προσλαμβάνω] evil men (Acts 17:4-5).

Jesus once again divided people. This response was exactly according to His sermon to train the disciples for evangelism. "Do not think that I came to bring peace on earth. I did not come to bring peace but a sword" (Matthew 10:34). In the context of evangelism, people are divided. This Paul knew. It was part of Jesus' teaching, it was a part of Paul's custom, and it was part of his expectation.

Paul's pattern was therefore:

- To go where people were, particularly if possible those who were seeking spiritual meaning in life

- Reasoning with those people about spiritual things, by opening up the Scriptures and explaining its meaning to them

- Challenging them with the gospel of Christ, both the death and resurrection of Jesus, and its implication to their lives.

Paul developed this pattern of ministry—a pattern that became normative to all Christians who wanted to properly follow Christ on mission, because of (1) Paul's place in the Book of Acts; and (2) Paul's commands to follow his example:

Therefore I urge you, imitate me (1 Corinthians 4:16).

Imitate me, just as I also imitate *Christ* (1 Corinthians 11:1).

There are several errors that may take place related to imitating Christ:

- To have no care to imitate at all

- To rationalize away necessary aspects of imitation, thereby not following them

- To imitate by going through the motions without knowing the purpose behind those actions

- To imitate particularities not meant to be imitated.

In this last category we may be seeking to minister in the actual cities where Paul was called to minister, or to recreate his voyages as a fulfillment of imitation. The lucid reader of the Bible will be guided by the Holy Spirit to properly imitate the principles in the practices of Paul.

God allowed Paul to develop a ministry pattern, custom, or habit. Likewise, Christ will lead His followers to develop godly ministry patterns after the manner of Paul. When a believer goes out into the harvest, he should roll up his sleeves and "go to it." The Holy Spirit will then guide him specifically, just as He did with Philip and the Ethiopian Eunuch.

Five Ministry Situations

While fleshing out examples of obeying the Great Commission, the Book of Acts provides different verbal groupings related to individual ministry settings. This next section addresses five different types of contexts for evangelism in Acts. Principles may be drawn from these narratives and applied to contemporary ministry opportunities.

Street Preaching (Acts 2)

The reader of the Book of Acts quickly notices that God foreordained Peter—forgiven for denying Christ just weeks before—to take a stand for Jesus in Jerusalem and preach the Pentecost Sermon. It was this sermon that sparked the fulfilment of the Great Commission in Acts, "You will be my witnesses in

Jerusalem and in all Judea and Samaria, and to the end of the earth" (Acts 1:8 ESV).

Before this important sermon, Luke addressed the human side of the "preaching." In Acts 2 we find a beautiful series of verbs:

- Peter, standing up [ἵστημι] with the eleven

- Raised [ἐπαίρω] his voice

- And said [ἀποφθέγγομαι] (Acts 2:14).

Perhaps the most difficult elements in street preaching are

- Standing up to speak

- Raising your voice to be heard

- Beginning to speak!

Peter overcame these three hurdles. In Acts 2, with three verbs, Doctor Luke described the actions of Peter on Pentecost. Peter took a stand. As Martin Luther who said, "Here I stand, and I can do no other," so Peter stood. But then he raised or lifted up his voice. He had to project his voice because of the crowds of people. A whisper would not have been enough. Peter had to raise his voice to draw attention to himself and to be heard over the noise of the street.

Then words or utterances came through his lips. The verb ἀποφθέγγομαι is derived from the preposition ἀπὸ, meaning "from" and the noun φθέγμα which means "a sound," "a saying," or "a word." Φθέγμα refers to words that come out of the mouth. Just as the tongues of fire earlier in the chapter were truly miraculous, the sermon of Peter was very much a Spirit-filled and truly human experience:

- Peter had to stand up

- He had to think about his first words, his introductory sentence

- Peter had to choose the proper pitch, intonation, emotion, and volume necessary for the occasion

- He then needed to take a breath and release the air out of his lungs to get those first words out.

Herein Peter provided a great example of obedience. The general command to preach the gospel was given by Jesus. But at Pentecost, Peter ascertained a unique occasion—orchestrated by the Holy Spirit—which he considered an opportunity from the Lord. His grasp of the situation led him to the conviction that the miracle provided an opportunity for an explanation. All the apostles had already been sharing the "wonderful works of God" in various languages. Meanwhile, the Holy Spirit must have brought the Joel 2 passage to his mind as he considered the miracle that they were experiencing at Pentecost. He then needed to act on this growing conviction—having ascertained that it must be from the Lord. Scripture confirms that this entire cerebral process was a spiritual process by stating in Acts 2:4 that all who were gathered were "filled with the Holy Spirit."

Notice also, that the 120 gathered in the upper room spoke the praises of God in many different languages in verse 4. And yet it appears that Peter's sermon was given in only one language through his one set of lips. Although that one language is not listed in the text, it is likely to be the same language that Paul spoke in his Acts 22 testimony to the Jews in Jerusalem (i.e. "Hebrew," Acts 21:40). Later Paul made it clear that only known languages edify the hearer (1 Corinthians 14:4-5, 19). So Peter spoke using his own mouth in a common language by which all his hearers could be edified.

In Acts 15 Peter reminded the Jerusalem church council that the Acts 10 sermon was "by my [his] mouth":

> And after there had been much debate, Peter stood up [ἀνίστημι] and said [λέγω] to them, "Brothers, you know that in the early days God made a choice among you, that by my mouth [διὰ τοῦ στόματός μου] the Gentiles should hear the word of the gospel and believe" (Acts 15:7 ESV).

In fact, the Jews in Jerusalem were so moved by his Pentecost message that 3,000 repented, believed, and were baptized.

Synagogue Preaching (Acts 13)

Paul's first major sermon continues a pattern of verbs similar to Peter's Pentecost Sermon. Paul's sermon was not a spontaneous street preaching event, like that of Peter at Pentecost, rather it was within the walls of a synagogue. After a long sequence of verbs related to Paul's travels to Antioch of Pisidia, Paul arrived in Pisidian Antioch, where he found a synagogue. Explaining events at this synagogue, Luke used another string of verbs that set up Paul's first recorded major sermon:

- They went into [εἰσέρχομαι] the synagogue on the Sabbath

- They sat down [καθίζω]

- *There was the reading of the Law, and the rulers of the synagogue invited them to speak*

- Paul stood up [ἀνίστημι]

- He motioned [κατασείω] with his hand

- And he spoke [λέγω] (Acts 13:14-16).

Once Paul entered the synagogue, and once he was invited to speak, the first verb used was that he stood up. He raised himself out of the sitting position and stood before the people to speak. Standing up was Paul's first act of faith that God would give him the words to speak to those in attendance at the meeting. It is reminiscent of Christ's words in Matthew:

> "When they deliver you over, do not be anxious how you are to speak or what you are to say, for what you are to say will be given to you in that hour" (Matthew 10:19 ESV).

Jesus stated this promise in the context of persecution. If there would be an opportunity to speak, those words would be given by divine assistance. The same idea can also be transferred to a spontaneous public evangelism opportunity or to personal evangelism. God gives the proper words at the proper time to accomplish His will!

So then, Paul stood up and motioned with his hand. We also find Paul motioning with his hand in Acts 21:40 and in Acts 26:1. In so doing, Paul drew the attention to himself, indicating that he was planning to address the gathering.

Then he opened his mouth and began to speak. In preaching we find a wonderful interrelationship between the preacher, God who calls and teaches the preacher, God's divine purposes for each individual listener, and all the combined knowledge and experience of the preacher coalescing and coming to bear upon the message that God gives His servants. It all begins by getting to the location of ministry (Go!), and standing up to speak when the opportunity presents itself (Preach!)!

Personal Evangelism (Acts 8)

In our last chapter we saw how Philip showed exemplary obedience in following God's directives to speak to the Ethiopian Eunuch. This conversation with the eunuch proves important, because it explains how God used Scripture to prepare the heart and to provide the context and content of the message about Christ. It also explains the use of questions to initiate spiritual conversations. The dialogue described begins with Philip overhearing what the eunuch was reading, followed by a series of questions:

> *So Philip ran to him, and heard him reading the prophet Isaiah, and said, "Do you understand what you are reading?" And he said, "How can I, unless someone guides me?" And he asked Philip to come up and sit with him. The place in the Scripture which he read was this: "He was led as a sheep to the slaughter; and as a lamb before its shearer is silent, so He opened not His mouth. In His humiliation His justice was taken away, and who will declare His generation? For His life is taken from the earth." So the eunuch answered Philip and said, "I ask you, of whom does the prophet say this, of himself or of some other man?" Then Philip opened his mouth, and beginning at this Scripture, preached Jesus to him. Now as they went down the road, they came to some water. And the eunuch said, "See, here is water. What hinders me from being baptized?" (Acts 8:30-36).*

So, Philip asked the first question:

- "Do you understand what you are reading?"

With this great question, Philip entered into a spiritual dialogue with this stranger. The amazing things is that the eunuch requested that Philip help him interpret Scripture:

- "How can I, unless someone guides me?"

Philip recognized the passage as Isaiah 53, and knew immediately that it was speaking of Jesus. The eunuch did not have that insight. So, the eunuch asked another question:

- "I ask you, of whom does the prophet say this, of himself or of some other man?"

Here was Philip's opening. God had prepared the eunuch's heart to question the text of Scripture. He did not understand it.

"Then Philip opened his mouth, and beginning at this Scripture, he evangelized Jesus to him" (Acts 8:35, translation mine)

Here we find three important verbs:

- Philip opened [ἀνοίγω] his mouth

- Philip began [ἄρχομαι] from that Scripture

- Philip evangelized [εὐαγγελίζω] him about Jesus.

Personal evangelism in three verbs. These three verbs elucidate four points:

1. Opening one's mouth; communicated by words out of his mouth

2. Beginning the conversation from where the person is at spiritually—which was an issue of Bible interpretation

3. Addressing the person's spiritual point of need—Philip made it a point to start the conversation by answering his question

4. Evangelizing to him about Jesus—that is, the life of Jesus, His death, and resurrection.

Each word is important here! Philip opened (ἀνοίγω) his mouth. Later we find God opening a heart (Acts 16:14)—using the same verb. Philip opened his mouth (ὁ στόμα). Later we find Peter testifying that God used his mouth to share the gospel (Acts 15:7). Philip began from that Scripture (Isaiah 53:7-8). If you are having a gospel conversation and someone brings up a Bible passage—any Bible passage—take that as a sign from God, ask God to help you find it, look it up, and talk about it—and its context. In the context of almost any verse there is a way to get into the gospel.

Isaiah 53 is a very powerful passage to get into the gospel, which was in this case used by Philip. He evangelized (εὐαγγελίζω) the eunuch concerning Jesus (ὁ Ἰησοῦς). He worked his way to the gospel of Jesus through this passage. Then Philip must have called upon him to repent and be baptized—was this not the pattern of preaching used by Peter in Acts 2:38? The eunuch therefore requested baptism.

So far, the three patterns of preaching we have seen have been impromptu evangelism methods. This fourth example involves another kind of impromptu evangelism.

Impromptu Apologetics (Acts 26)

In Acts 26 Paul had already been incarcerated for quite some time. He had survived a plot to kill him while he was being transferred as a prisoner from one place to another (Acts 23). He was sent to Governor Felix, who would request to see Paul often, hoping to receive a bribe from him (Acts 24:26). Because Paul did not give him a bribe, he remained in prison until Portius Festus became governor. Festus—wanting to do the Jews a favor—planned to send Paul back to Jerusalem. Paul, remembering that the Lord had told him, "you must bear witness at Rome" (Acts 23:11), appealed to Caesar. Festus replied to Paul, "You have appealed to Caesar? To Caesar you shall go!" (Acts 25:12).

However, in a strange twist, to please the curiosity of Agrippa and the antagonism of the Jews, Festus coordinated a special event, where Paul would be the jester before a group of gathered guests. Paul would be forced to state his case before hundreds of people, Governor Festus and King Agrippa included. Interestingly, this occasion allowed Luke to pen perhaps the most forceful gospel presentation in the Book of Acts, including a personal invitation of salvation to King Agrippa.

Luke laid out the setting of this event for his readers:

So the next day, when Agrippa and Bernice had come with great pomp, and had entered the auditorium with the commanders and the prominent men of the city, at Festus' command Paul was brought in (Acts 25:23).

In that first century auditorium, King Agrippa and his wife, were brought in. Other men also brought their wives. It was going to be a spectacle! Later Paul wrote, "For we have been made a spectacle to the world" (1 Corinthians 4:9). Surely, this is a fulfillment of Jesus' prophecy, "You will be brought before governors and kings for My sake, as a testimony to them and to the Gentiles" (Matthew 10:18).

Consider then the choice verbs penned to illustrate the essence of this preaching opportunity:

Then Agrippa said to Paul, "You are permitted to speak for yourself." So Paul stretched out his hand and answered for himself: "I think myself happy, King Agrippa, because today I shall answer for myself before you concerning all the things of which I am accused by the Jews" (Acts 26:1-2).

- Then Agrippa said [φημί] to Paul,
  - "You are permitted [ἐπιτρέπω] to speak [λέγω] for yourself."
- So Paul stretched out [ἐκτείνω] his hand
- And answered [ἀπολογέομαι] for himself:
- "I think [ἡγέομαι] myself happy
- "Because I shall answer [ἀπολογέομαι] for myself
- "Concerning the things of which I am accused [ἐγκαλέω] of the Jews."

Paul, given the opportunity to speak for himself before this great crowd, began by raising his hand. This action in a large group is reminiscent of Paul's sermon in Acts 13. Notice the interesting verb Luke used to describe how Paul responded. He answered (ἀπολογέομαι, from which comes the English word apologetics) for himself. Consider then, that this verb is used once in Luke's introductory narrative, at the beginning of Paul's discourse, and when Festus interrupted Paul:

And as he was saying these things in his defense [ἀπολογέομαι], Festus said with a loud voice, "Paul, you are out of your mind; your great learning is driving you out of your mind" (Acts 26:24 ESV).

Notice that Luke echoed Paul and said that Paul was "giving an answer" (ἀπολογέομαι). Three times in Acts 26 the verb ἀπολογέομαι is associated with this speech of Paul. Paul spoke this verb twice in Acts 26:1-2 at the beginning of his speech. Luke summarized Paul's speech using the verb once in Acts 26:24. This usage represents the highest concentration of this verb found only ten times in the entire New Testament—seven of which come off the pen of Luke.

What "much learning" Festus was referencing above is uncertain. The learned Luke did not appear to include any references by Paul to secular philosophy in Acts 26, nor did he use Stoic or Epicurean terminology. Rather, it seems that Paul's Holy Spirit-given tenacity, forcefulness in presenting the gospel, and clarity in addressing King Agrippa before such a great crowd shocked Festus and his plan to make Paul into a spectacle.

Luke thrice used a verb that carries with it significant historical-methodological importance. The term "apologetics" is derived as a transliteration from this same Greek verb, ἀπολογέομαι, meaning "to speak in one's own defense." If one considered the means in which Paul spoke to "defend himself," one would have difficulty finding any type of theistic argument in Acts 26. His address did not consist of what would be considered "Classical Apologetics." There was no "meeting in the middle" between various systems of thought. Paul did not build any "bridges" to secular reasoning. He did not address any other religious systems with unprejudiced dialogue. He did not cite the "Five Proofs of the Existence of God." Rather, Paul directly and respectfully shared of his hope in the gospel of Jesus Christ.

This same verb is also found in Acts 24:10 at the beginning of Paul's imprisonment:

> Then Paul, after the governor had nodded to him to speak, answered: "Inasmuch as I know that you have been for many years a judge of this nation, I do the more cheerfully answer [ἀπολογέομαι] for myself" (Acts 24:10).

In Acts 24 Paul addressed the reason for his unlawful imprisonment. But in similar fashion to Acts 26, Paul also included aspects of the gospel in his initial appeal to Felix.

In Luke 12, in one of his sending passages, Jesus used the same verb when describing the very situation in which Paul found himself. He promised that the Holy Spirit would provide a proper answer:

> "Now when they bring you to the synagogues and magistrates and authorities, do not worry about how or what you should answer [ἀπολογέομαι], or what you should say [λέγω]. For the Holy Spirit will teach you in that very hour what you ought to say" (Luke 12:11-12).

Would the Holy Spirit, who infuses Scripture with His breath, actually teach arguments from the secular world to prop up divine revelation? The Bible clearly states, "The LORD knows the thoughts of man, that they *are* futile" (Psalm 94:11). Rather, as in these examples of the use of the verb ἀπολογέομαι in the New Testament, the Holy Spirit assists followers of Christ to give an answer related to the gospel of Christ. They were not seeking to use secular arguments to defend or prove the validity of the Bible, gospel, or the resurrection of Christ. They were rather expounding the gospel and its place in their actions.

In Acts 26, Paul had less than a day to prepare himself to be placed in front of a large crowd and give an answer as to what the gospel is and how he went about proclaiming the gospel. And he did just that. Paul in Acts 26 gave the example of Biblical Apologetics for all who were to imitate him—all in response to a last-minute invitation.

Special Event Evangelism (Acts 28)

Whereas the assembly in Acts 26 could be considered a somewhat hostile crowd—wherein Paul was given very little preparatory time—the crowd in Acts 28 was an inquisitive group of Jews from Rome. This second invitation was at the prompting of Paul, and it is highly likely that Paul had Scripture scrolls available to him for discussion and consideration. Whereas Acts 26 was an evening affair, the Acts 28 meeting was an all-day affair. In this brief segment, Luke summarized concepts that are essential to all invitational evangelism, such as special meetings at church or home, or multi-church evangelistic crusades:

And it came to pass after three days that Paul called the leaders of the Jews together. So when they had come together, he said to them: "Men and brethren, though I have done nothing against our people or the customs of our fathers, yet I was delivered as a prisoner from Jerusalem into the hands of the Romans, who, when they had examined me, wanted to let me go, because there was no cause for putting me to death. But when the Jews spoke against it, I was compelled to appeal to Caesar, not that I had anything of which to accuse my nation. For this reason therefore I have called for you, to see you and speak with you, because for the hope of Israel I am bound with this chain."

Then they said to him, "We neither received letters from Judea concerning you, nor have any of the brethren who came reported or spoken any evil of you. But we desire to hear from you what you think; for concerning this sect, we know that it is spoken against everywhere."

So when they had appointed him a day, many came to him at his lodging, to whom he explained and solemnly testified of the kingdom of God, persuading them concerning Jesus from both the Law of Moses and the Prophets, from morning till evening. And some were persuaded by the things which were spoken, and some disbelieved.

So when they did not agree among themselves, they departed after Paul had said one word: "The Holy Spirit spoke rightly through Isaiah the prophet to our fathers, saying, 'Go to this people and say: "Hearing you will hear, and shall not understand; and seeing you will see, and not perceive; for the hearts of this people have grown dull. Their ears are hard of hearing, and their eyes they have closed, lest they should see with their eyes and hear with their ears, lest they should understand with their hearts and turn, so that I should heal them."' Therefore let it be known to you that the salvation of God has been sent to the Gentiles, and they will hear it!" And when he had said these words, the Jews departed and had a great dispute among themselves (Acts 28:17-29).

Paul had a pre-crusade event with the Jewish leaders to introduce himself. Notice that he did this three days after arriving in Rome. He did not allow moss to collect under his feet. He took the initiative and called together a meeting of the leaders.

Here were Paul's pre-event activities:

- After three days that Paul called [συγκαλέω] the leaders of the Jews together

- So when they had come together [συνέρχομαι], he said [λέγω] to them

- Then they said [λέγω] to him:

  o We neither received [δέχομαι] letters from Judea concerning you, nor have any of the brethren who came reported [ἀπαγγέλλω] or spoken [λαλέω] any evil of you

  o But we desire [ἀξιόω] to hear [ἀκούω] from you what you think; for concerning this sect, we know that it is spoken against [ἀντιλέγω] everywhere (Acts 28:17-22).

The heart of Paul's event evangelism is found in verse 23-24:

- So when they had appointed [τάσσω] him a day

- Many came [ἥκω] to him at *his* lodging

- To whom he explained [ἐκτίθημι] and solemnly testified [διαμαρτύρομαι] of the kingdom of God

- Persuading [πείθω] them concerning Jesus from both the Law of Moses and the Prophets, from morning till evening

- And some were persuaded [πείθω] by the things which were spoken

- And some disbelieved [ἀπιστέω] (Acts 28:23-24).

Notice that while Paul had the same goal in mind as was described of his synagogue evangelism in Acts 17:2-4, the only overlapping verb is the verb "to persuade" (πείθω). Even the negative response is a different verb, being "disbelieve" (ἀπιστέω) in Acts 28:24 and "disobey" (ἀπειθέω) in Acts 17:5.

It is in this volatile setting of opposing sides that Luke chose to allocate more space in the Book of Acts to explain the aftermath of the meeting—and to make a link with one of the most quoted Old Testament portions in the New:

- So when they did not agree [ἀσύμφωνος + εἰμί] among themselves

- They departed [ἀπολύω] after Paul had said [λέγω] one word: "The Holy Spirit spoke rightly through Isaiah the prophet to our fathers, saying, 'Go to this people and say: "Hearing you will hear, and shall not understand; and seeing you will see, and not perceive; for the hearts of this people have grown dull. Their ears are hard of hearing, and their eyes they have closed, lest they should see with *their* eyes and hear with *their* ears, lest they should understand with *their* hearts and turn, so that I should heal them."' Therefore let it be known to you that the salvation of God has been sent to the Gentiles, and they will hear it!" (quoting Isaiah 6:9-10)

- And when he had said [λέγω] these words

- The Jews departed [ἀπέρχομαι] and had a great dispute [ἔχω + συζήτησις] among themselves (Acts 28:25-29).

Luke explained the aftermath of the special event at the home where Paul was under house arrest in Rome. All the makings for planning a good special event are found in this example, from contacting leaders and hearing of their interest, to agreeing on a date, time, and location, to hosting the event, and the follow-up. It is indeed amazing to comprehend the clarity and power of God's intentions as revealed in the Book of Acts.

Christ in His Great Commission said, "Go and preach." And in the Book of Acts we find the followers of Christ obeying the command to "Go and preach." The pages of the Book of Acts provide a roadmap of descriptive and prescriptive guidelines for Christ's blood-bought Church to obey His Great Commission.

The New Testament does not leave us in the dark as to how the Great Commission of Jesus was fulfilled in the Book of Acts. God included sufficient examples in Acts to provide patterns for obedience of Christ's Great Commission. Ours is to consider these examples and to submit to what God is communicating through them.

THOMAS P. JOHNSTON

CHAPTER SIX

THEY EVANGELIZED
—εὐαγγελίζω—

There are approximately 165 Greek verbs used to explain evangelizing in the Bible. The two main verbs used in the New Testament for preaching the gospel are κηρύσσω (to preach) and εὐαγγελίζω (to evangelize). Εὐαγγελίζω (to evangelize) is found 55 times in the New Testament (depending on the Greek text) and κηρύσσω (to preach) is found 61 times. One big difference between these verbs is the fact that the verb κηρύσσω (to preach) is found in Mark's Great Commission as a command to all followers of Christ. It is also found in two other commands of Christ, Matthew 10:7, 27, and in Paul's command to Timothy in 2 Timothy 4:2. The verb εὐαγγελίζω (to evangelize), however, is never used as a command or in the imperative mood. Rather, εὐαγγελίζω is used as a participle 21 times. In English a participle is delineated by adding "-ing" at the end of a verb stem. Hence for evangelize, the participle is "evangelizing." One of these 21 uses is in Acts 14:7:

And there they kept evangelizing [εὐαγγελίζω] (Acts 14:7 HCSB).

A participle use of the verb lends itself to narrative—the telling of an event or occurrence. Hence, εὐαγγελίζω was used predominantly in participle off the pen of Luke in Luke and Acts (12 times) and seven times off the pen of Paul, and twice in 1 Peter.

The verb εὐαγγελίζω was used in narrative sections to describe the preaching activity of Jesus (Luke 8:1; 20:1) and of the disciples (Luke 9:6) in Luke. In Acts it was used to describe the missionary activity of the Apostles (Acts 5:42), the scattered disciples (Acts 8:4), Philip in Samaria (Acts 8:12), God (Acts 10:36), some men (Acts 11:20), Paul and his team (Acts 14:7, 15, 21), and Paul and Barnabas in Antioch (Acts 15:35).

The verb κηρύσσω (to preach) was also used in participle form 19 times. In the Gospels it was used three times to describe the preaching of John the Baptist (Matthew 3:1; Mark 1:4; Luke 3:3). It was used six times of Jesus (Matthew 4:23; 9:35; Mark 1:14, 39; Luke 4:44; 8:1). And it was used of the obedience of the former demoniac from Gerasenes (Luke 8:39). In Acts of the Apostles it was used for Moses being proclaimed around the Roman Empire (Acts 15:21) and of Paul's ministry (Acts 20:25; 28:31). It is interesting to note that the verb εὐαγγελίζω (to evangelize) was never used in a command or imperative. Therefore, this chapter will focus on the methodology of evangelizing as exemplified in some of the New Testament verbs used to describe this activity.

Differences Between Preaching and Evangelizing

There are quite a number of interesting differences between the concepts of "preaching" and "evangelizing":

- Preaching often refers to prepared remarks; evangelizing usually involves extemporaneous speech

- Preaching is typically indoors, within the walls of a church, while evangelizing is often done outside in the open air

- Preaching is usually done by ordained men, in some cases authorized by the state-church; however, all Christians should evangelize

- Preaching is often limited to men; evangelizing is commanded of both men and women

- The audience for preaching is mainly Christian with some non-Christian people; whereas the target audience for evangelizing is only non-Christians.

The lucid reader may find other differentiations between the two verbs. These examples illustrate the potential impact in the English language of translating every use of "evangelize" in the New Testament as "preach." It is virtually impossible to gauge the impact on the English culture worldwide from 600+ years of translating "evangelize" as "preach."

Evangelize That They May Hear

Hebrews 4:2 used the verb *evangelize* (εὐαγγελίζω), along with two other verbs, that of *blending* (συγκεράννυμι) and that of *hearing* (ἀκούω), as well as the noun *faith* (ὁ πίστις):

> For indeed the gospel was preached to us as well as to them; but the word which they heard did not profit them, not being mixed with faith in those who heard it (Hebrews 4:2).

Consider that absent from this verse is the message of the gospel. Rather the emphasis was on the listener—and that which was or was not in his heart, "faith." In the Second Council of Orange of 529 A.D., to accommodate infant baptism, the hearer was rendered passive or neutral upon the reception of "salvation." All the power of salvation was vested, not in evangelizing, nor in the "gospel of Christ" (Romans 1:16), but rather in the Christological nature of the water being poured on the head—that is, in the Holy Spirit acting in, with, and by "the water of baptism" to convert the totally passive recipient of the Sacrament. The inactive recipient of infant baptism had no need to hear the gospel, neither to repent of his or her sin, nor to give verbal assent to the propositions of the gospel. Simultaneously the necessity for evangelizing was swept away very early in the history of the Western Church.

Nowhere in the Bible do we find the recipient of the gospel message numb to its proposals. The gospel always demands a response. And therefore, in the New Testament, the hearers of the gospel always respond one way or another. Jesus cried out, "He who has ears to hear, let him hear!" (Matthew 13:9). To illicit a response from the hearer, the hearer needs to hear. And to hear the gospel propositions, there must be a method of hearing. Hearing necessitates evangelizing. Followers of Christ are not left to dredge culture or inventory their preferences to determine how to communicate the gospel. In the New Testament God has explained how His gospel ought to be communicated.

Luther's Reformation Find

Galatians 1:8-9 served the Protestant Reformers as the hermeneutical basis for the Protestant Reformation. In 1517, when

Martin Luther initiated what became the Protestant Reformation, he read Galatians in both Latin and Greek texts. It was not until 1522 that he translated the New Testament into German. In both the Latin and the Greek the word "evangelize" is used three times in two verses. The following is a modernized version of the 1382 First Edition Wycliffe translation of Galatians 1:8-9:

> But though we, or an angel of heaven, evangelize to you, besides that that we have evangelized to you, cursed be he. As I before said, and now again I say, if one shall evangelize out-taken that that you have taken, cursed be he (Galatians 1:8-9 modernized Wycliffe First Edition, 1382).

The reader will note that the verb "evangelize" was used in Wycliffe's First Edition rather than "preach the gospel," as is currently in vogue. Translating "evangelize" (εὐαγγελίζω) as "evangelize" clarifies in this passage that the predominant issue is the method of evangelizing, not the message. Consider, for example, the following translation of the 1605 French Geneva:

> Thus, if even we ourselves, or an angel from heaven evangelize you other than how we evangelized you, may he be accursed. As we have already said, now I will say it again, if someone evangelizes you other than what you have received, may he be accursed (Galatians 1:8-9, translation mine).

In verse 8 the focus appears to be the method of evangelizing. In verse 9 Paul brings in the message received through evangelizing. Translating the verb "evangelize" (εὐαγγελίζω) into the phrase "preaching the gospel" subtly shifts the focus of Paul's argument from method and message to pure message. This small but significant interpretive difference changes the application of the entire epistle of Paul to the Galatians. Meanwhile, the driving force behind the Protestant Reformation is diffused.

Martin Luther's preliminary problem with Rome's Catholicism was the sale of indulgences for the forgiveness of sins. Johannes Tetzel came to Wittenberg to sell Papal Indulgences. As Luther wrestled with this practice, his eyes fell on Galatians 1. Here the Apostle Paul gave immutable authority to his previous method of evangelism. Where was this immutable example to be found? Luther found it in the pages of the Book of Acts. In Acts Luther could not find the selling of Indulgences. Tetzel's approach to preaching the gospel was therefore an "other" method. The verses that established the prescriptive importance of the preaching methods in the Book of Acts were Galatians 1:8-9. In these verses, the Apostle Paul canonized his method of evangelizing as the divine example for all of church history. If anyone, including an angel or Paul himself, were to deviate from his methodology as found in the Book of Acts (the only inspired and extant witness of Paul's early methodology), he was to be accursed—excommunicated.

So, by this logic Martin Luther examined the method of Johannes Tetzel—then he examined the Book of Acts. Luther could not find Tetzel's methodology in Acts. Therefore, Tetzel and his method were to be rejected. Hence, it was Luther's theology of evangelism that led to the Protestant Reformation. Further, this same logic can easily be applied to contemporary methodologies for evangelism. First, consider the contemporary methodology. Next, study the Book of Acts. If the method does not parallel a method in the Book of Acts, it should be questioned.

Now why did God use the verb "evangelize" among the many other verbs used for proclaiming the gospel?

A Brief Introduction to Evangelizing

The Greek verb for *evangelize* (εὐαγγελίζω) is found 54, 55, or 56 times in the Greek New Testament, depending upon which text one is using. For our purposes, I will use the Greek Orthodox New Testament in which the verb is found 55 times, with an additional 22 times in the Greek Old Testament. Here are some usage summaries that may prove helpful:

- Luke and Acts combined use the verb 25 times: Luke, 10 times; Acts, 15 times;

- Paul used the verb 25 times;

- Other books used it 5 times: Matthew, once; 1 Peter, twice; Revelation, twice.

The fact that the verb was used 22 times in the Greek Old Testament provides helpful context for its use. For example, every use of "evangelize" in the Old Testament came from a translation

THOMAS P. JOHNSTON

of the Hebrew verb *bashar*. Hebrew lexicons generally translate *bashar* as "bring good news." Thus, for good or ill, that translation has been transferred into the New Testament. The implication is that "evangelizing" means to "bring," "carry," or "travel with" something. Missing from this lexical transference is the idea of "speaking" a message.

Consider two ways of translating Isaiah 52:7, where the Greek verb for "evangelize" is found twice:

> How beautiful upon the mountains are the feet of him who brings good news, who publishes peace, who brings good news of happiness, who publishes salvation, who says to Zion, "Your God reigns" (Isaiah 52:7 ESV).

> How beautiful upon the mountains are the feet of him who evangelizes, who publishes peace, who evangelizes good, who publishes salvation, who says to Zion, "Your God reigns!" (Isaiah 52:7, translation mine).

Consider that this verse was so powerful to encourage evangelizing for the Apostle Paul that he quoted it in Romans 10:15. "Brings good news" mutes the meaning of this important verb. Using the verb "evangelize" trumpets its power.

Perhaps the most important part of this chapter is to look in the pages of the Bible to deduce the meaning of the verb "evangelize" as opposed to the many other proclamational verbs in the New Testament. The six uses of "evangelize" in 1 Corinthians provide a perfect petri dish to clarify a definition of "evangelize" in the New Testament.

Defining Evangelizing

The New Testament book of 1 Corinthians lends itself to developing a definition of what Paul meant when he used the verb "evangelize" (εὐαγγελίζω). It has a total of six uses of this verb. The two uses in 1 Corinthians 15:1-2 prove very helpful for definitional purposes.

The first 8 verses of 1 Corinthians 15 distinguish themselves in being the clearest New Testament definition of the gospel. The Book of Romans gives us the "Roman Road" for salvation. Luke's Great Commission (Luke 24:46-47) provides a concise synopsis of the gospel from the mouth of Jesus. In 1 Corinthians 15 Paul discussed the reception of the gospel, then the gospel, and then focused the rest of the chapter on the resurrection from the dead.

It is precisely in the first two verses that Paul melted his propagation of the gospel with the Corinthian reception of the gospel. In these verses, he twice used the verb evangelize:

> Moreover, brethren, I declare to you the gospel by which I evangelized [εὐαγγελίζω] you, which also you received and in which you stand, by which also you are saved, if you retain it by what manner I evangelized [εὐαγγελίζω] you—unless you believed in vain (1 Corinthians 15:1-2, translation mine).

Paul was the evangelist that God used to bring the gospel and to bring salvation to the Corinthian believers to whom Paul was writing. Hence, the verb evangelize, as used in this context, refers specifically to preaching the gospel to non-believers. Further it also refers to the method and message of their first salvific hearing of the gospel—that first hearing by which they were saved. Therefore, Paul's use of "evangelizing" presupposed a specific audience, that of unsaved persons.

People continue to be "evangelized" until they are saved. Once a person is saved, the communication of the gospel they receive is no longer called "evangelizing." Biblical terminology for post-conversion reception of the gospel for edification changes to "preaching" or "teaching."

The verb "preaching" in English is much more generic in its usage. For example, English translations of the Bible translate dozens of Greek verbs as preach and proclaim, rendering differentiation difficult. Likely the most important reason that English has unified all these verbs together is the "Sacrament of Ordination" by which only certain "approved and appointed" persons are authorized to "preach" publicly. Consider, for example, the translation of the common verb "speak" [λαλέω] in Acts 8:25 in KJV, NKJ, and HCSB versions:

> And they, when they had testified and preached [λαλέω] the word of the Lord, returned to Jerusalem, and preached the gospel [εὐαγγελίζω] in many villages of the Samaritans (Acts 8:25 KJV).

> So when they had testified and preached [λαλέω] the word of the

> Lord, they returned to Jerusalem, preaching the gospel
> [εὐαγγελίζω] in many villages of the Samaritans (Acts 8:25 NKJ).

> Then, after they had testified and spoken [λαλέω] the message of
> the Lord, they traveled back to Jerusalem, evangelizing
> [εὐαγγελίζω] many villages of the Samaritans (Acts 8:25 HCSB).

The translators of the King James Version, from their high church Anglican context, could not help themselves. They were drawn to use the technical term "preach" when its subject was the Apostles Peter and John, rather than the common word "speak." Then when it came to the verb "evangelize," they repeated the use of the verb "preach"—to translate a very different Greek verb.

Just like the muffling of the verb "speak" in Acts 8:25, so "evangelize" was muffled in all its 55 uses. All other proclamational terms were generalized under the comfortable umbrella of "preaching." This author is very grateful that the Holman Christian Standard Bible for 9 years has included six uses of the verb *evangelize* (1999-2008), and seven in their 2009-2016 edition:

> Then, after they had testified and spoken the message of the
> Lord, they traveled back to Jerusalem, evangelizing many villages
> of the Samaritans (Acts 8:25 HCSB).

> Philip appeared in Azotus, and he was traveling and evangelizing
> all the towns until he came to Caesarea (Acts 8:40 HCSB).

> And there they kept evangelizing (Acts 14:7 HCSB).

> After they had evangelized that town and made many disciples,
> they returned to Lystra, to Iconium, and to Antioch
> (Acts 14:21 HCSB).

> After he had seen the vision, we immediately made efforts to set
> out for Macedonia, concluding that God had called us to
> evangelize them (Acts 16:10 HCSB).

> My aim is to evangelize where Christ has not been named, so that
> I will not build on someone else's foundation
> (Romans 15:20 HCSB).

> For Christ did not send me to baptize, but to evangelize—not with
> clever words, so that the cross of Christ will not be emptied of its
> effect (1 Corinthians 1:17 HCSB).

Using "preach" to translate the 55 New Testament uses of the verb "evangelize" makes it difficult to distinguish in Bible translations when and where lay people are permitted to preach and when they are not. Likewise, in the King James Version, the seventeenth century Anglican state-church anti-evangelism and anti-lay preaching was superimposed on the translation of εὐαγγελίζω ("evangelizing"). This redefinition resulted in harnessing Bible readers so that they would not read and heed the calls of Christ for all His followers to "evangelize."

According to 1 Corinthians 15:1-2, "evangelizing" (εὐαγγελίζω) is the verbal proclamation of the gospel to unsaved persons, culminating in some of them coming to believe in that gospel.

First Corinthians 1:17 adds other dimensions in understanding the verb "evangelize":

> *For Christ did not send me to baptize, but to evangelize [εὐαγγελίζω]—not with clever words, so that the cross of Christ will not be emptied of its effect* (1 Corinthians 1:17 HCSB).

In this important context, Paul combined purpose language (reason for being sent) with "evangelizing." In this he followed the example of Jesus:

> *But He said to them, "I must evangelize [εὐαγγελίζω] the rule of God to the other cities also, because for this purpose I have been sent"* (Luke 4:43, translation mine).

Here, Jesus also confirmed that a reason He was sent by God was to "evangelize." He was not to stay long in one place. His calling from God was to be on the move—sharing the gospel in the harvest fields as He went.

Several points on the use of "evangelize" in 1 Corinthians 1:17. First, Paul placed evangelizing as a priority above baptism. In other words, evangelizing took primacy over the ritual of baptism for Paul. If baptism is considered the outward confession of a new believer's commitment to Christ, then one may construe from this statement that for Paul, evangelizing lost people was a priority over leading people to submit to Christ. In other words, evangelism was a priority over discipleship. (There will be more about this delicate balance in later chapters.)

Second, the power of the gospel can be annulled by the proclaimer. Effectiveness in evangelizing was not defined by using clever words or catchy analogies. Paul was to preach the cross of Christ in power and simplicity. If the focus of the proclamation of the gospel moves from the cross of Christ to the fancy words of the proclaimer, the amazing power of the gospel can actually be nullified.

Paul also used the verb evangelize three times in 1 Corinthians 9. In 1 Corinthians 9:16, Paul called a woe upon himself, should he ever cease from evangelizing:

> For if I evangelize [εὐαγγελίζω], I have nothing to boast of, for necessity is laid upon me; yes, woe is me if I evangelize [εὐαγγελίζω] not! (1 Corinthians 9:16, translation mine).

Like a crescendo, in 1 Corinthians 9:16, Paul called a woe upon himself if he did not evangelize. This woe echoes down through the ages to every church leader and every child of God. Paul was willing to call a curse upon himself if he ceased evangelizing. "God, take me out if I stop evangelizing!" The next verse continued with this theme by offering two alternatives related to evangelizing— willingness and unwillingness. One would receive a reward. The other was considered a duty. Then in verse 18, Paul brought another warning, concerning financial abuse in gospel ministry:

> What is my reward then? That when I evangelize [εὐαγγελίζω], I may present the gospel of Christ without charge, that I may not abuse my authority in the gospel (1 Corinthians 9:18, translation mine).

Paul was warned by the Holy Spirit that there existed the abuse of the gospel for financial gain. Again, loaded into the definition of "evangelize" in 1 Corinthians, the Holy Spirit has provided some powerful warnings for its proper use and function.

While a thorough study of the 55 uses of the verb evangelize (εὐαγγελίζω) in the New Testament may prove to be both useful and challenging, may this overview of the six uses in 1 Corinthians prove sufficient to whet the reader's appetite as to the potential benefits of related study.

Proclamational Verbs in the Great Commission Passages

Building from the concept of "evangelizing," Jesus Himself used other specific verbs when He sent out His disciples before His crucifixion, and when He charged His people through the ages after His resurrection. In the Book of Acts the Apostle Paul also received several specific commissions (e.g. Acts 9:15; 18:9-10; 22:18, 21). And there are also commissionings sprinkled throughout the Epistles (e.g. Ephesians 6:19-20; Colossians 1:28-29; 2 Timothy 1:8; 2:2; 1 Peter 2:9-10).

This section will only highlight the five Great Commissions of Jesus to His disciples after His resurrection. Each of these commissions casts a distinctive hue on the totality of Christ's mandate to His followers. And in each of these commissions Jesus used particular verbs to move His disciples into action.

John

In John, Jesus commissioned His disciples to follow His example. He told them, "As the Father has sent Me, I also send you" (John 20:21). The sending (ἀποστέλλω) of Jesus was to be mimicked by the sent (πέμπω) disciples. In fact, these disciples were not sent out in a general sense, but rather sent out with a specific mission—such as gathering in the harvest!

Luke and Acts

Luke focused on the message of the gospel in Jesus' commissioning. Here, we find in a nutshell the main points of the gospel as later we find proclaimed throughout the Book of Acts. In Luke 24:46-47 Jesus explained the centrality of His death and resurrection. Then in the next verse He highlighted that "repentance and remission of sins" was the vital response based on His death and resurrection. In fact, "repentance and remission of sins" was to be preached (κηρύσσω) to all nations. He continued, "You are witnesses of these things" (Luke 24:48). Yet, while saying in Luke, "to all nations beginning in Jerusalem," in Acts 1:8 Jesus developed the expansion of the witness of that gospel: Jerusalem, Judea, Samaria, and the remotest parts of the earth. Also in Acts, while Jesus did not repeat the verb *preach* (κηρύσσω), He repeated

His injunction that the disciples were to be testifiers (ὁ μάρτυς), "And you shall be witnesses to Me."

Mark

Mark 16:15 also used the same main verb as in Luke 24:47. Jesus commanded His disciples to "preach" (κηρύσσω) the gospel. Jesus highlighted the need to proclaim the gospel to everyone everywhere. He then continued, as recorded by Mark in the next verse, by addressing two opposite responses to this gospel proclamation: belief and unbelief.

Matthew

In Matthew 28:19, Jesus used the verb μαθητεύω, which was translated "teach" in the King James Version (KJV), and "make disciples" by John Darby in his 1884 English translation of the New Testament. Most translations followed Darby's precedent after 1884. Just like Mark focused on some that believe and others that do not believe, in Matthew Jesus commissioned His disciples to "win disciples" from out of all nations. Rather than focusing on those who did not believe, Jesus focused only on "them" who were to become disciples of Jesus through the testimony of the apostles. These few, designated as "them," were to be baptized: "baptizing them." For this reason, it may be that instead of "teach" as in the KJV or "make disciples" (as in the Darby), a better translation may be "win disciples."

It is clear from the use of "them" that only "won disciples" were to be baptized. Thus, the proclamation and witness was not to go unheeded or to be without aim. Rather, the testifying of the followers of Jesus was to focus specifically to "win" them as disciples. That was to be their focus as they built Christ's Church.

All five of these Great Commissions conform to and complement one another amazingly as portrayed in the chart below. The main verbs for proclamation used by Jesus in these commissionings are twice κηρύσσω, "to preach," twice to be "a witness" (ὁ μάρτυς), and once to "win disciples" (μαθητεύω). Jesus used amazingly powerful verbs to communicate his marching orders to His Church!

What Is Commanded in the Great Commission?
A Linear View of the Five Great Commission Passages

Call	Geographic Extent			Method			Message		Nurture	Example	Power	Fulfillment
Sent; go	"All the world … to all creation"	"To all nations, beginning from Jerusalem"	(1) Jerusalem, (2) Judea, (3) Samaria, (4) uttermost parts of the earth	Preach; proclaim; testify	With the result of winning disciples		The Gospel: "the Christ should suffer and rise again from the dead the third day"	The Message: "repentance for the forgiveness of sins … in His name"	(1) baptizing (2) teaching to obey	Christ	Holy Spirit	Prophetically stated
John 20:21; Matt 28:19; Mark 16:15	Mark 16:15	Luke 24:47	Acts 1:8	Mark 16:15; Luke 24:47-48; Acts 1:8	Matt 28:19		Mark 16:15; Luke 24:46	Luke 24:47	Matt 28:19-20	John 20:21	Acts 24:49	Luke 24:47; Acts 1:8

See also "A Linear View of the Five Great Commission Passages" (Johnston, *Charts for a Theology of Evangelism* [Nashville: Broadman, 2007], 14-15).

Other Verbs for Evangelizing

So far we have seen the verb "evangelize" (εὐαγγελίζω) and the verb "preach" (κηρύσσω) and the verb "to be" with the noun "a witness" (ὁ μάρτυς). As the reader may guess, these are not the only verbs used for evangelizing in the New Testament, not even to mention verbs used in the Old Testament prophecies about evangelism. Whereas Jesus used the verb "to be" for "to be My witnesses" in Luke and Acts, in other places we actually find the verb "bear witness" in relation to evangelism:

> But the following night the Lord stood by him and said, "Be of good cheer, Paul; for as you have testified [διαμαρτύρομαι] for Me in Jerusalem, so you must also bear witness [μαρτυρέω] at Rome" (Acts 23:11).

In this, another of God's commissionings of Paul, God used two cognates of the verb "to bear witness." As you "have testified" (διαμαρτύρομαι) of Me in Jerusalem, so you must also "bear witness" (μαρτυρέω) at Rome. Both of these verbs are related to being a witness (ὁ μάρτυς). But Jesus did not use these verbal forms as recorded in Luke and Acts. As I mentioned at the beginning of this chapter there are at least 165 different Greek verbs[1] used in the New Testament and in the Old Testament Septuagint that explain what Christ meant when He sent out His disciples to evangelize. He did not leave Himself without a witness!

---

[1]Charts of these verbs are available at:
http://www.evangelismunlimited.com/charts.php.

CHAPTER SEVEN

FELLOW WORKERS
—συνεργέω—

Amazing as is the energized power of God's word and the work of the Holy Spirit through His word, God has also chosen to expand the breadth of His work in the world to include human instruments! The Great Commission of Jesus made that clear. Jesus called His followers to "Go!" and "Preach!" And His disciples did just that, they "Went!" and they "Preached!" The underlying assumption behind Jesus sending out His disciples is that He wants to work with and through His people—and as can be expected, we are called His "Fellow workers," even His ambassadors.

Πρεσβεύω —"Ambassadoring"

One word which highlights the nature of this unique interrelationship of God working through man is the verb πρεσβεύω, meaning to "act as an ambassador":

> Now then, we are ambassadors for Christ, as though God were pleading through us: we implore you on Christ's behalf, be reconciled to God (2 Corinthians 5:20).

The word "ambassador" does not originate from a Greek noun, as one may expect. Rather "ambassador" comes from the Greek verb πρεσβεύω. The actual form of the verb is πρεσβεύομεν: the present active indicative first-person plural of πρεσβεύω. The present active implies that Paul and Timothy were acting as ambassadors at the time of writing. The plural form is consistent with the fact that Paul included Timothy as a co-author of that book. But even more importantly, the first-person plural implies that Paul was including his audience as part of the ambassadorial work. Paul affirmed this same idea in 1 Corinthians 11:1 when he wrote, "Imitate me, just as I also *imitate* Christ." But what is the activity of being an ambassador, or "ambassadoring"?

Paul explained the activity of ambassadoring in 2 Corinthians 5:18-6:2. Ambassadoring is the ministry of reconciling others to Christ. It is the second stage of God's reconciling the world to Himself through Christ. Stage One: Jesus dying a substitutionary death for mankind. Stage Two: Saved persons telling others of the reconciliation available in Christ. This ministry of reconciliation in 2 Corinthians 5:18-19 finds its expression in "ambassadoring" for Christ. When we ambassador for Christ it is as though God is pleading through us—God literally uses the sounds created by our vocal cords and by the air coming out of our mouths. He speaks His message by the words shaped off our tongues and through lips. And what does God say? He says, "We implore you on behalf of Christ, 'Be reconciled to God.'" The words of God that He will put on our lips, are conjoined as a call to commitment!

Charted out, this process is communicated as follows (2 Corinthians 5:20):

Evangelist	Christ	God
Now then, we are ambassadors	For Christ,	As though God...
...were pleading through us:		
We urge you	On Christ's behalf	
"Be reconciled...		...to God!"

The power of this verse is clear. Man speaks for God on behalf of Christ!

But Paul's teaching did not end there. He then penned one of the clearest New Testament verse on the substitutionary atonement.

For He made Him who knew no sin to be sin for us, that we might become the righteousness of God in Him (2 Corinthians 5:21).

Charted out as above, this verse may look as follows:

Evangelist	Christ	God
		He made…
	Him who knew no sin to be sin	
For us		
That we might become		The righteousness of God
	In Him	

The absolutely clear teaching of this verse, especially in this context of God cooperating with mankind, is that man has NO part in his own salvation. Salvation is all from God. The reason that salvation is all from God is that it is all of Christ, *Solus Christus*. Even more amazing in this verse is this: God's salvation clothes saved man with the righteousness of God! Imputed righteousness—an alien righteousness, one that is not generated nor issues from man or his efforts, but from God alone. This unearned and undeserved righteousness is given as a free gift to all those who would receive it!

After clearly clarifying that salvation is all of God in Christ, Paul then returned to more fully describe the concept of ambassadorship:

> *We then,* as *workers together* with Him *also plead with* you *not to receive the grace of God in vain* (2 Corinthians 6:1).

In this verse Paul used a synonymous verb to elaborate the idea of ambassadoring, that is the verb συνεργέω, meaning "to work together with." This third verse can be laid out as follows:

Evangelist	Christ	God
We then, as workers together…	*…With Him*	
Also plead with you "Receive not in vain…		…The grace of God."

Paul expanded on ambassadorship by issuing a second exhortation. After "Be reconciled with God," the second urging is "Don't receive the grace of God in vain." The "in vain" is the same words that Paul used in 1 Corinthians 15:2, "unless you believed in vain." Were the Corinthian church members to change Paul's delivered gospel, they would be turning their faith into vain belief. Thus, if we are to be acting as ambassadors of God in Christ, one or the other of these exhortations is sure to be on our lips. Exhortation #1 is directed to the unsaved, "Be reconciled." Exhortation #2 is directed to Christians, "Don't receive this gospel in vain."

Following these two ambassadorial exhortations comes 2 Corinthians 6:2—one of the most amazing verses in the New Testament, wherein Paul exemplifies how a proper gospel invitation is to be organized and given.

Συνεργέω —"Working Together"

Even as God ambassadors through man, implying a top-down relationship, God also co-labors with man, implying a side-by-side relationship. In the above passage, we noted that Paul used the verb συνεργέω, meaning "to work together," in 2 Corinthians 6:1. It is used of man "working together" with God in spiritual work—surely an intimidating prospect. In the New Testament the verb συνεργέω is often linked to its cognate noun ὁ συνεργός, meaning "fellow worker." Consider the amazing thought that man is asked not only to represent God in ambassadoring, but even to "co-labor" with Him!

For we are God's fellow workers [ὁ συνεργός]. You are God's field, God's building (1 Corinthians 3:9 ESV).

Does the sovereign and omnipotent God really need the help of fallible humans to accomplish His work? He really doesn't need human help at all, does He? After all, God was certainly able to create the world by speaking a few words without any human help. He devised the Ten Commandments without human involvement. So why does He need us for anything? The answer is, He doesn't! Rather, God chooses to work together with His people. One way that He has chosen to operate in this world is by using the human agency of His people. This theme of God cooperating with His people in divine activity is central in the writings of the Apostle Paul.

Paul not only used the συνεργέω word group to describe divine-human cooperation, he also used these words to describe human-human cooperation. Paul used the term "my fellow worker(s)" six times, and implied "my fellow workers" in Colossians 4:11. He used "our fellow worker" three times and used the word three other times related to men—for a total of 13 New Testament uses. However, in the two uses cited above, συνεργέω in 2 Corinthians 6:1 and ὁ συνεργός in 1 Corinthians 3:9, both are related to man cooperating with God in divine activity.

These examples of cooperative work between God and man found in Paul—using the verb συνεργέω—is preceded by a use of this verb the Gospel of Mark. Following Christ's resurrection and His Great Commission to the disciples, Mark summarized the ongoing proclamation of the gospel in the last verse of his Gospel:

> And they went out and preached everywhere, the Lord working with [συνεργέω] them and confirming the word through the accompanying signs. Amen (Mark 16:20).

Here in Mark, the Lord was the subject of the verb συνεργέω, indicating that He was working in, with, and by the followers of Jesus—as they went out preaching the gospel everywhere, in obedience to Christ's Great Commission. A chart of this verse may look as such:

Evangelists	The Lord
And they went out [ἐξέρχομαι]	
And preached [κηρύσσω] everywhere	The Lord working with [συνεργέω] them
	And confirming [βεβαιόω] the word
	Through the accompanying [ἐπακολουθέω] signs. Amen.

The disciples went forth and they preached. As they did so, Christ fulfilled His promise to be with them unto the ends of the earth

(Matthew 28:20). His cooperative work included first a confirmation of the word and second signs that followed the preaching (the literal meaning of ἐπακολουθέω). These signs were given "after" the preaching as a confirmation, and not "before" the preaching as a type of preparatory grace to add relevance, credibility, or power to the gospel.

Paul wrote, "we are God's fellow workers." He added, "*as* workers together *with Him.*" God has chosen to use His people in His work in the world. Therefore, Paul and Barnabas, when they returned from their first missionary journey explained what God had done through them:

> And when they arrived and gathered the church together, they declared all that God had done [ποιέω] with them, and how he had opened [ἀνοίγω] a door of faith to the Gentiles (Acts 14:27 ESV).

Consider the power of these words. The subject of the verb ποιέω ("to do") is God. What "God had done"—with, through, or by them. And how God "had opened [ἀνοίγω] the door of faith to the Gentiles." Again, as Paul and Barnabas described their evangelism ministry, it was not them ministering, but God ministering through them. God opened the door of faith—it was not Paul and Barnabas who opened that "door of faith." Consider that this symbiotic relationship was an echo of God's original call of Barnabas and Paul in Acts 13:2: "Set apart for me Barnabas and Saul for the work [τὸ ἔργον] to which I have called them" (ESV).

Christ's followers cannot be lazy during harvest and expect God to bring in the harvest without them—especially when Christ Himself has clearly sent them out into the fields! Nor should they be so deluded to think that they are responsible to effectuate the spiritual results of their evangelism—results that only God can work. God works in combination with His people. It is a partnership decreed by Christ in the Great Commission. This cooperative work includes the use of the same verbs to describe the actions of God and of man in the evangelism process.

This cooperation work between God and man is exemplified in the famous Mars Hill Sermon of Paul. Paul addressed the gathered philosophers:

Therefore having overlooked the times of ignorance, God is now declaring to men that all everywhere should repent (Acts 17:30 NASB).

Who was speaking? Was it God or Paul? It was not God speaking, but rather Paul. And yet Paul told these philosophers, "God is now declaring." Consider the interrelationship being communicated. It was surely puzzling to these philosophers.

Paul followed a similar pattern in Antioch of Pisidia. There he quoted a Messianic prophecy to explain why he was planning to preach to the Gentiles:

Then Paul and Barnabas grew bold and said, "It was necessary that the word of God should be spoken to you first; but since you reject it, and judge yourselves unworthy of everlasting life, behold, we turn to the Gentiles. For so the Lord has commanded us:

'I have set you as a light to the Gentiles, that you should be for salvation to the ends of the earth.'"

Now when the Gentiles heard this, they were glad and glorified the word of the Lord. And as many as had been appointed to eternal life believed (Acts 13:46-48).

Paul used the Messianic prophecy in Isaiah 49:6 to justify his own preaching to the Gentiles. Because the coming Messiah, Jesus, was prophesied to preach to the Gentiles, so Paul could do likewise. Therefore, if Jesus was sent to the Gentiles, so was Paul—and so are all Christ's followers by virtue of Christ's Great Commission. Later, Paul added this command: "Imitate me, just as I also *imitate* Christ" (1 Corinthians 11:1).

God's cooperative partnership in evangelism is not optional. It is obligatory. We can accomplish nothing outside of God's working in, with, and through us. However, while God is involved in evangelism in a general sense, He is also involved in the details of the gospel ministry.

Διανοίγω—Man Opening and God Opening

One of several Greek verbs used both of God and man in evangelism is διανοίγω, meaning "to open." We find the verb tied to Paul's methodology of sharing the gospel in Acts 17:3. In

109

Acts 17:2, Luke used the verb "to be accustomed to" (ἔθω) to described Paul's ministry in the Book of Acts. Luke provided his readers with a baseline for Paul's standard ministry practice:

> Then Paul, as his custom was [ἔθω], went in to them, and for three Sabbaths reasoned with them from the Scriptures, explaining [διανοίγω] and demonstrating [παρατίθημι] that the Christ had to suffer and rise again from the dead, and saying, "This Jesus whom I preach to you is the Christ" (Acts 17:2-3).

Luke's only other use of the word "custom" was of Jesus going to the synagogue on the Sabbath day and reading the Scriptures (Luke 4:16). In the case of Paul's custom, it was also to enter the synagogue—much like Jesus. However, Paul did more than just read. He "reasoned," "explaining," "demonstrating," and "preaching." Four verbs in a linear sequence!

The second verb listed here is the verb "explaining." It comes from the Greek verb διανοίγω, "to open." Here is the idea: Paul was "opening" the Scriptures and "establishing" (παρατίθημι) the truth claims of the death and resurrection of Jesus to the Jews in the synagogue. This was done in the context of "reasoning" or "disputing" (Deuteronomy 25:1) and with the assistance of παρατίθημι, meaning "demonstrating" or "setting forth." Once Paul had done his job, then God entered the picture and began to elicit a response in the hearts of those who were listening.

In Acts 17, Luke summarized the response of the hearers as follows:

> And some of them were persuaded [πείθω]; and a great multitude of the devout Greeks, and not a few of the leading women, joined Paul and Silas (Acts 17:4).

Luke used the verb "persuade" (πείθω) in the passive "were persuaded" to describe the response of some of the Thessalonians. It is important to note that not all were persuaded.

Luke explained the theology behind this persuasion when in another place, he narrated the conversion of Lydia from Thyatira. In this passage, he again used the verb "to open" (διανοίγω). The question to keep in mind is, who is doing the opening?

> And on the Sabbath day we went out of the city to the riverside,

where prayer was customarily made; and we sat down and spoke to the women who met there. Now a certain woman named Lydia heard us. She was a seller of purple from the city of Thyatira, who worshiped God. The Lord opened [διανοίγω] her heart to heed the things spoken by Paul (Acts 16:13-14).

Notice that it was not Paul who opened (διανοίγω) Lydia's heart. It was the Lord. "The Lord opened her heart to heed the things spoken by Paul." The Lord used the very words that proceeded through the lips of Paul to open Lydia's heart to the gospel. Who then drew Lydia to Christ? Was it the words of Paul alone? No. Was it the power of God working in, with, and by the words of Paul? Yes. It was Paul and God co-laboring to bring Lydia to Christ. Paul was ambassadoring. He called on Lydia to be reconciled to God. God then gave her a hearing of faith, and she responded by the power and work of God. Thus, Luke could write: "The Lord opened her heart"!

The Greek New Testament includes 78 uses of the verb ἀνοίγω, meaning "to open." But it uses the verb διανοίγω only 8 times, meaning "to open completely." The following chart considers the eight New Testament uses of this last verb:

New Testament Uses of "Open Completely" – Διανοίγω

Christ opens the ears and mouth of a mute man	A firstborn child opens the womb	Paul opens the Scriptures in a synagogue	Christ reveals who He is	Christ explains the Scriptures	Christ opens the disciples' minds to understand the Scriptures	God opens Lydia's heart to receive Paul's evangelizing
Mark 7:34, 35	Luke 2:23	Acts 17:2-3	Luke 24:31	Luke 24:32	Luke 24:45	Acts 16:14

Surely, this verb displays God's inter-working with man.

Ἀκούω or Ἀθετέω —"Listens" or "Rejects"

Close on the heels of man opening and God opening follows the reception of the gospel proclaimer. Luke makes it clear by including both reception and rejection in the same passage:

> *"The one who listens [ἀκούω] to you listens [ἀκούω] to Me, and the one who rejects [ἀθετέω] you rejects [ἀθετέω] Me, and he who rejects [ἀθετέω] Me rejects [ἀθετέω] the one who sent Me"* (Luke 10:16 NASB).

Verses like this may make naturalistic man squeamish. Yes, from the mouth of Jesus, if a person listens to or hears the gospel from the mouth of a follower of Christ, he is truly and actually listening to and/or hearing from Christ Himself! This same idea is found throughout the Old Testament from Moses to Ezekiel. Perhaps the fourfold use of the verb "to reject" (ἀθετέω) is even more sobering. If the words of the evangelist are rejected, it is not merely a rejection of Jesus, but it represents a rejection of God Himself!

Both in acceptance and in rejection, there is a symbiotic communion between the evangelist, Christ, and God.

Several other texts parallel this idea within the Gospels. One context is found in the Sermon on the Mount and the Sermon on the Plain:

> *"Blessed are you when others revile you and persecute you and utter all kinds of evil against you falsely on my account. Rejoice and be glad, for your reward is great in heaven, for so they persecuted the prophets who were before you"* (Matthew 5:11-12 ESV).

> *"Blessed are you when people hate you and when they exclude you and revile you and spurn your name as evil, on account of the Son of Man! Rejoice in that day, and leap for joy, for behold, your reward is great in heaven; for so their fathers did to the prophets. … Woe to you, when all people speak well of you, for so their fathers did to the false prophets"* (Luke 6:22-23, 26 ESV).

Notice the "on Mmy account" in Matthew 5:11 and "on account of the Son of Man" in Luke 6:22. In both these cases the persecution which Christ honors refers to the clear and direct persecution that comes when one verbally aligns one's life with Christ.

A third context is within the Sending Sermons of Jesus in Luke 10, as above and as in Matthew 10. A fourth powerful context describing this same symbiotic union with Christ in the reception of the gospel is found in the Upper Room Discourse:

> *"Truly, truly, I say to you, whoever receives [λαμβάνω] the one I*

send receives [λαμβάνω] me, and whoever receives [λαμβάνω] me receives [λαμβάνω] the one who sent me" (John 13:20 ESV).

Therefore, in John 13 Jesus repeated the same Greek verb four times, highlighting the symbiotic interrelationship between the disciple who He sends out in evangelism, Jesus Himself, and God who sent Jesus:

> *"Remember the word that I said to you, 'A servant is not greater than his master.' If they persecuted Me, they will also persecute you. If they kept My word, they will keep yours also. But all these things they will do to you for My name's sake, because they do not know Him who sent Me. If I had not come and spoken to them, they would have no sin, but now they have no excuse for their sin. He who hates Me hates My Father also"* (John 15:20-23).

This last Scripture includes a section corresponding to Luke 10:16 noted above. "If they persecuted Me, they will also persecute you. If they kept My word, they will keep yours also" (John 15:20). Both the negative and positive reception were again reaffirmed by Jesus.

The idealistic or triumphalistic young Christian may expect everyone to accept Jesus Christ as easily as he received Jesus. However, through initiative evangelism the new evangelist quickly learns that not all people are open to hearing the gospel. Paul also had a touch of this idealistic attitude, of which God had to warn him, as noted in Acts 22:18-21. Paul wanted to stay and evangelize in Jerusalem. He was sure that his classmates would be open to the gospel just as he himself was. They knew his former life. They were his pals. God told him.

> *"Make haste and get out of Jerusalem quickly, for they will not receive [παραδέχομαι] your testimony concerning Me"* (Acts 22:18).

Paul's idealistic response to God was to rely on his prior relationship and life with them.

> *"So I said, 'Lord, they know that in every synagogue I imprisoned and beat those who believe on You. And when the blood of Your martyr Stephen was shed, I also was standing by consenting to his death, and guarding the clothes of those who were killing him'"* (Acts 22:19-20).

113

God never responded to Paul's objection, but rather He repeated His command, "Depart, for I will send you far from here to the Gentiles" (Acts 22:21).

As God's sovereign will would have it, even as Paul told his story in Acts 22, this Jerusalem audience of his peers confirmed God's prior warning—though it was made 20 years earlier. They immediately called for the death penalty:

> And they listened to him until this word, and then they raised their voices and said, "Away with such a fellow from the earth, for he is not fit to live!" (Acts 22:22).

Truly, as we proclaim "Enter by the narrow gate!" we quickly find out, "Wide is the gate and broad the way that leads to destruction, and there are many who go in by it" (Matthew 7:13). We also learn: "Narrow is the gate and difficult the way that leads to life, and there are few who find it" (Matthew 7:14).

This promised and exemplified antagonism is totally different in a state-church model. In this model, the state-church approved proclaimer goes forth with the vested authority of the government, its army, and its police. There is no room for "He who rejects you." Likewise, the state-church presumes to have Christ's authority by authorizing those who can preach. They decide that all should listen to them. There is no particular group defined by, "He who listens to you." Further, the state-church determines who is worthy to be listened to through monopolizing the oil of ordination. None of these passages account for the circumstance of the state-church model. In some cases, the state-church interrelationship was so extreme that those who rejected the state-church were consigned to Inquisition and Martyrdom. Hence, part of properly applying the "Union with Christ" verses cited above, is to understand them to apply to unity under the "Christ-sanctioned" state-church.

John explained God's action in the world in very simple terms:

> He came to His own, and His own did not receive [παραλαμβάνω] Him. But as many as received [λαμβάνω] Him, to them He gave the right to become children of God, to those who believe in His name: who were born, not of blood, nor of the will of the flesh, nor of the will of man, but of God (John 1:11-13).

The same verb for "receive" found four times in John 13:20 is also found here in John 1:12, and with a prepositional prefix in John 1:11. In John 1:13, God made it very clear that when it comes to His working in the world, He is not under any man's obligation. He is not obligated to follow the will of any man, nor the will of any flesh and blood. Who was meant by "He who listens to you listens to Me" (Luke 10:16) is completely in God's hands. He has not released this authority to man in any way. As His word goes forth "He has mercy on whom He wills, and whom He wills He hardens" (Romans 9:18).

God has explained Himself clearly enough in the Bible. God only guides certain persons. In Psalm 25 they are designated as "those who fear Him":

> Who is the man who fears the LORD? Him will he instruct in the way that he should choose [αἱρετίζω] (Psalm 25:12 ESV).

To unpack this verse: there is a particular subset of humanity designated by their fear of the Lord. God will instruct those He determines "fear Him." He will show them the way that they should choose (Hebrew *bachar*; Greek αἱρετίζω). God will help those who fear Him "to choose." They will have freedom of conscience. The Greek verb "to choose" (αἱρετίζω) relates to the noun for "choice" (ἡ αἵρεσις), which being transliterated into English is the word "heresy." In a state-church system, having one's own freedom to choose is "heresy." Luther found against this, using a verse in 1 Corinthians to show that choices are necessary:

> There must, indeed, be factions [ἡ αἵρεσις] among you, so that those who are approved may be recognized among you (1 Corinthians 11:19 HCSB).

Again, the basic meaning of the noun ἡ αἵρεσις is "choice or option" (Friberg). Therefore, the word is used substantively to refer to a "sect, faction, party, or division." However, its basic meaning is merely "a choice." God chooses to work through those who fear Him. And He instructs those who fear Him—and only those who fear Him—to know the way that they should choose. The only way for God to exercise His sovereign will is for man to be allowed to exercise his free will.

Building from God's instruction is submission to Christ's

instructions. If a person—in submission to Christ's instructions—is sharing the gospel. Then the listener has the choice to either accept or reject that gospel. In the case of the proclaimer, he is acting as an ambassador of Christ. He is speaking on Christ's behalf. Rejecting the listener is in fact rejecting Christ. And rejecting Christ is rejecting His Father who sent Him.

> With the pure You prove Yourself pure, but with the crooked You prove Yourself shrewd (Psalm 18:26 HCSB).

God's supernatural inter-working within and among humanity is a humbling thing. Some are considered "pure" and some are considered "crooked." Similarly, as we submit to the words of Christ we will face acceptance and rejection. God will cover us with a special union with Himself and Christ as we herald His gospel!

Yes, ambassadoring for Christ is a high and holy calling. Co-laboring with God is daunting and intimidating. And yet this is just what God has called us to do. God wants to use you and me. In our weakness, He is made strong. And in it all, He alone is worthy of all the glory.

CHAPTER EIGHT

REPENT
—μετανοέω—

Repent! Quite a gnarly term! Basically, it implies that God has it right and mankind has it wrong. God's ways are always higher than man's ways and His thoughts are always higher than man's thoughts. Man's thoughts are always wrong; God's thoughts are always right. The only time man can come close to getting it right is when his thoughts approach God's thoughts.

Even for the saved and born-again believer in Jesus Christ his thoughts are always wrong. The key is understanding the "his" in "his thoughts." Even with the Holy Spirit pouring through his psyche, man's fallen nature has a profound corrupting influence. Redeemed man need always approach God humbly, in prayer, asking Him for His help and His guidance, because man's thoughts are always wrong. The Christian must always approach the word of God humbly, seeking guidance and counsel from God, for his thoughts can easily deceive him. The truly born-again Christian must maintain a constant posture of humility and submission toward God and toward His word.

As for non-Christians, there are two choices. One choice is that they have not heard the Good News of Jesus. They are living in ignorance and sin. They are bound for an eternity in hell. The other choice is that they have heard and rejected submission to Jesus. They have refused to repent. They do not acknowledge that they are wrong—filled with wrong thoughts and on the wrong road. Sure, their conscience convicts them; but because of pride they will not submit to the first verb of the gospel—Repent! They refuse to admit that all their ways, all their thoughts, and all their doings are wrong.

There is a way that seems right to a man, but its end is the way of death (Proverbs 14:12; 16:25 ESV).

> *Every way of a man is right in his own eyes, but the LORD weighs the heart* (Proverbs 21:2 ESV).

As for the lost, they stumble over the first command of the gospel, they refuse to repent.

Are the above paragraphs overstatement? Not at all. Perhaps the major problem with easy-believism and shallow Christianity comes down to the omission of one verb—Repent! God decried the false prophets in the days of Jeremiah, because they refused to preach repentance:

> *Thus says the LORD of hosts: "Do not listen to the words of the prophets who prophesy to you, filling you with vain hopes. They speak visions of their own minds, not from the mouth of the LORD. They say continually to those who despise the word of the LORD, 'It shall be well with you'; and to everyone who stubbornly follows his own heart, they say, 'No disaster shall come upon you'"* (Jeremiah 23:16-17 ESV).

> *"I did not send the prophets, yet they ran; I did not speak to them, yet they prophesied. But if they had stood in my council, then they would have proclaimed my words to my people, and they would have turned them from their evil way, and from the evil of their deeds"* (Jeremiah 23:21-22 ESV).

Omitting or ignoring the preaching of repentance is no small matter. It commanded the stern rebuke of God. Consider also, for example, God's warning against the unrepentant hearer of the word of God in Deuteronomy 29:

> *"Beware lest there be among you a man or woman or clan or tribe whose heart is turning away today from the LORD our God to go and serve the gods of those nations. Beware lest there be among you a root bearing poisonous and bitter fruit, one who, when he hears the words of this sworn covenant, blesses himself in his heart, saying, 'I shall be safe, though I walk in the stubbornness of my heart.' This will lead to the sweeping away of moist and dry alike. The LORD will not be willing to forgive him, but rather the anger of the LORD and his jealousy will smoke against that man, and the curses written in this book will settle upon him, and the LORD will blot out his name from under heaven* (Deuteronomy 29:18-20 ESV).

There is a dire need for the constant preaching of repentance for man to remain humble before the Lord and tender to all His counsels.

In all the contemporary debate about whether or not to use an "Invitation System" or whether or not a "Sinner's Prayer" is valid, the true weight of the issue is the danger of omitting repentance from the gospel message. Jesus always called His followers to turn from their sins, their selfish pride, and their fallen thought systems and to follow after Him. Perhaps turning from self is the most important part of the call of Jesus, "Follow Me!" While those who responded to Jesus had to "follow" Jesus, in order to "follow" after Him they had to begin by unfollowing everything else. They had to unfollow their old manner of life with its thoughts and words and deeds. In other words, they had to turn 180 degrees to follow after Christ.

Ἐπιστρέφω —"Turn!"

Is not a "180-degree turn" the root meaning behind the Greek verb μετανοέω ("to repent")? Μετὰ (meta) as a prefix in this verb implies "against," "after," "behind." The noun νοός (noos) means "mind." Hence when combined the concept is, "change your mind." The idea behind the verb *repent* is to turn away from sin, selfishness, and pride and turn to Christ.

Another verb used in the New Testament for turning is the Greek verb ἐπιστρέφω ("to turn back"). Similarly, the call to repent is the call for persons to change their minds about themselves and what they are doing and thinking, and rather to turn around and to follow after Christ.

Consider, for example, the powerful preaching of Ezekiel to the circumcised Jews of his day:

> Say to them, As I live, declares the Lord GOD, I have no pleasure in the death of the wicked, but that the wicked turn [ἀποστρέφω] from his way and live; turn back [ἀποστροφή], turn back [ἀποστρέφω] from your evil ways, for why will you die, O house of Israel? (Ezekiel 33:11 ESV).

Three times in Hebrew, God through Ezekiel used the Hebrew verb *shub* (meaning "to turn"). It is translated as such in our English.

However, the translators of the Greek Septuagint translated the first use of *shub* with the Greek verb ἀποστρέφω (meaning "to turn around"). The second and third uses they translated with a noun and a verb, ἀποστροφή-ἀποστρέφω—turning-turn. The implication is, "Turn around, yes, turn around!" The Jews in the days of Ezekiel had the same problem "that is common to man"—a fleshly nature that "kicks against the goads." This nature must be subdued. There is only one way to subdue human pride. It is the way of repentance.

Repentance is not complete at conversion. It merely begins at the foot of the cross. The entire Christian life is one of constant repentance. Solomon called it "living in the fear of God." Paul called it "taking off the old" and "putting on the new"! Jesus called it "denying oneself":

> *"If anyone desires to come after Me, let him deny himself, and take up his cross daily, and follow Me"* (Luke 9:23).

Jesus spoke of man denying that he knows the right way of doing things. The "daily" need not only relate to taking up the cross. Self-denial is also a daily struggle. The entire Christian life is one of dying to self-will and self-sufficiency, followed by humble submission to God and to His words.

As the Christian grows in humble reliance on God, he grows to put into practice another admonition of Solomon, to trust in the Lord:

> *Trust in the LORD with all your heart, and do not lean on your own understanding. In all your ways acknowledge him, and he will make straight your paths* (Proverbs 3:5-6 ESV).

Every time he opens and reads about the wicked, the fool, or the naïve in the Bible, the follower of Christ dare not point his finger and look at other people—unless he has not first pointed the three or four remaining fingers directly at himself. Only Christ is worthy. Only Christ is holy. Only Christ is righteous and just. Humanity exists as fallen wretches helplessly caught in the clutches of sin. If it was not for the initiating grace of God in salvation and His sustaining grace in sanctification, mankind would be hopelessly lost in sin.

Yes, the word "repent" packs a powerful punch. It calls on people to change their minds. Change their minds about their sin, their sinful nature, and their sinful thought processes. A parallel idea is communicated through the verb ἐπιστρέφω, "to turn." Jesus used this verb when He translated and quoted the prophet Isaiah:

> "'For this people's heart has grown dull, and with their ears they can barely hear, and their eyes they have closed, lest they should see with their eyes and hear with their ears and understand with their heart and turn [ἐπιστρέφω], and I would heal them'" (Matthew 13:15 ESV).

True repentance calls on all humanity to "turn!" Turn from their wicked ways. Turn from their sins! Turn from their miserable and miserly thoughts. All the thoughts of men combined are nothing and less than nothing. All the thoughts and doings of men are meaningless.

> All the nations are as nothing before him, they are accounted by him as less than nothing and emptiness (Isaiah 40:17 ESV).

And yet to know that He loves the world—Amazing!

The power of the command to repent was harnessed by Jesus and included in the summary statement of His early gospel preaching. Then this same verb was used to relate the intended impact and response to the gospel message in Luke's Great Commission.

The Spiritual Battle Around Repent

Because the word *repent* has a distinctly religious meaning, it allows philosophers to equivocate with its meaning. Yet, according to the Bible, repent implies that mankind was headed in the exact opposite direction of the demands of God. Yet God through His Good News informed humanity of its sinful state, hopeless and helpless, locked in to receive the full wrath of God. Mankind was found guilty and doomed to spend eternity in hell. He had no hope in himself.

> But God, who is rich in mercy, because of His great love with which He loved us, even when we were [spiritually] dead in our trespasses, made us alive together with Christ (by grace you have

been saved) (Ephesians 2:4-5).

The idea of salvation was God's. The work was God's. Man's salvation was fully and completely wrought for him, even while he was still living in a state of spiritual rebellion. For this reason, man can get no glory from his salvation or in thinking that he can save himself. He could not and cannot initiate his own salvation, nor could he or can he even remain in saving faith. Man is hopeless and helpless under the hand of a totally loving and completely sovereign God.

He must begin by repenting—turning from what he is, has, and does, and turn around, completely change his mind, 180 degrees, and turn to what Jesus would have him be, have, and do. Not even one iota of human action or thinking can enter into this mix. Human thinking is of no account to God. Socrates, Plato, Aristotle are nothing to God. Spinoza, Hume, and Kierkegaard are meaningless to Him.

> *Stop regarding man, whose breath* of life *is in his nostrils; for why should he be esteemed?* (Isaiah 2:22 NASB).

That word "repent" cannot remain idle in Scripture. It packs too powerful a punch. History has not been good to this term. It has treated *repent* with disrespect. Allocating a uniquely philosophical or religious connotation to the term *repent* allowed it to be adapted and become nuanced in its meaning. In the fourth century, Jerome—or one of his contemporaries—advanced a slight grammatical adaptation to the verb *repent*. They changed it to "do penance." It was revised from being a "change of mind" to becoming an "act of penance"—some action or good deed that a person was to perform. This grammatical shift affected the first command of Christian preaching from calling on a change of heart to calling potential converts to perform an action.

The three steps in this shift were: (1) turn around; (2) repent; and (3) do penance. The New Testament uses the verb μετανοέω ("to repent") 34 times. Therefore, in order to seal the change, new Bible translations had to be updated to read, "do penance." Meanwhile older Latin Bibles were declared invalid. It was convenient that the Latin Vulgate was a translation of the Greek. Most Western Church parishioners did not know Greek. Further, it was convenient that the church had a relationship with the state. Use of the new translation of Jerome could be enforced by the power of the state.

For example, here are two examples of the 69 uses of "penance" in the 1899 Douai-Rheims Bible:

> And in those days cometh John the Baptist preaching in the desert of Judea. And saying: Do penance: for the kingdom of heaven is at hand (Matthew 3:1-2 DRA).

> In those days John the Baptist came preaching in the wilderness of Judea, "Repent, for the kingdom of heaven is at hand" (Matthew 3:1-2 ESV).

> From that time Jesus began to preach, and to say: Do penance, for the kingdom of heaven is at hand (Matthew 4:17 DRA).

> From that time Jesus began to preach, saying, "Repent, for the kingdom of heaven is at hand" (Matthew 4:17 ESV).

Jerome did not chose to retain the lexical meaning of repent (μετανοέω) as a change (μετὰ) of mind (νοός). He rather reassigned its focus to the *result* of changing one's mind, renewed action. For Jerome, the renewed action required by true repentance was for a person to "do penance." Thus, he paraphrased the Greek verb μετανοέω as "do penance." There is only one problem with this substitution of words: it changed the meaning of the words of Christ and the others who used it. Christ never said, "Do acts of penance." Christ said, "Repent." He said, "Change your mind." Turn from idols and idolatry and turn to me. Similarly, Paul spoke of the wonderful conversion of the Thessalonians as a "turning to" and a "turning from":

> For they themselves report concerning us the kind of reception we had among you, and how you turned to God from idols to serve the living and true God, and to wait for his Son from heaven, whom he raised from the dead, Jesus who delivers us from the wrath to come (1 Thessalonians 1:9-10 ESV).

In this case, the Thessalonian believers "turned" to God and simultaneously turned away from their idols and idolatry. If there was an act involved, it was the act of removing the idols from their homes.

Repent > Pentance
≠

In the case of "do penance," acts of penance became an idol or a crutch upon which people placed their faith, without focusing on a "change of heart." Their trust shifted to their actions (fulfilling prescribed acts of penance) and no longer rested uniquely on the finished work of Christ on the cross, who said, "It is finished!" (John 19:30). Even as Jerome's translation grew to be the preferred Latin text of Scripture, so the light of the gospel message dimmed in Western state-churches. Salvation by the Sacraments soon replaced salvation by the Scriptures alone, by faith alone, by grace alone, by Christ alone, and to the glory of God alone. Pope Damasus' commissioning of Jerome's Latin translation in A.D. 382 marks a milestone in the advancement of Sacramental thought within the state-church structure of the Western Church.

What can be learned from the spiritual warfare over the translation of this one word—"repent"? First, it is important to note that "Every word of God is tested" (Proverbs 30:5 NASB). This one word packs a powerful punch. Second, the following admonitions must be taken seriously, even as it relates to Bible translation:

- *Awake, sleeper* (Ephesians 5:14).

- *Be on the alert* (Matthew 24:42, 43; 25:13; Mark 13:35, 37; Acts 20:31; 1 Corinthians 16:13; Ephesians 6:18; 1 Peter 5:8).

- *Beware* (Matthew 7:15; 10:17; 16:6, 11; Mark 8:15; 12:38; Luke 12:1, 15; 20:46; Philippians 3:2).

- *Take heed that no one deceives you* (Matthew 24:4; cf. Colossians 2:8).

- *Take heed* (Mark 13:23, 33; Acts 13:40; 1 Corinthians 10:12; Colossians 4:17).

- *Watch out* (Matthew 16:6; Mark 8:15; Luke 11:35).

- *Watch yourselves* (2 John 8).

These are just samples of many similar admonitions in the New Testament.

Third, the reader may consider that translation work is important, as is discernment in the use of a good Bible translation. Reading from a good Bible translation is not a secondary matter.

Rather original language texts and their proper translation are foundational to *every other* doctrinal and practical discipline!

Fourth, practice follows translation. <u>Deviancy in translation eventuates deviancy in doctrine and practice</u>. Submission to a good Bible translation favors right practice. Fifth, understanding the linguistic battle lines of spiritual warfare is vital—knowing what words were fought over can be transferred to the present, wherein those same words represent the same spiritual battles.

Repent in the New Testament

As far as "repent," there are six chronological time periods in the preaching of repentance in the New Testament. First, it was used as the primary verb to describe John the Baptist's message. Second, *repent* appeared in summaries of the preaching of Jesus. Third, the command to *repent* was preached by the disciples after Jesus sent them out. Fourth, "repentance" became the central focus of preaching in the Great Commission in Luke. Fifth, *repent* played a role in the preaching of the Book of Acts. And sixth, Jesus called on five of the seven churches in Revelation 2-3 to *repent.* It appears only proper to consider that all biblical preaching should draw hearers to "repent!"

Repentance in John the Baptist's Preaching

First, the command to "repent" was the only verb listed in the summary of John the Baptist's preaching in Matthew 3:

> In those days John the Baptist came preaching in the wilderness of Judea, and saying, "Repent, for the kingdom of heaven is at hand!" (Matthew 3:1-2).

Further, Mark 1:4 and Luke 3:3 summarized the preaching of John the Baptist as preaching a "baptism of repentance." Therefore, the preaching of John the Baptist in these two books consisted of two nouns, "baptism" and "repentance." It must be stated up front that the Gospel of John nowhere uses the verb "repent" nor the noun "repentance." John focused his narrative on John the Baptist preparing the way for and differentiating himself from the coming Messiah. This does not imply that John the Apostle was against "repentance"—an argument from silence. Rather it implies that

John the Apostle used other synonymous concepts to describe God's requirement that man should repent.

John the Baptist's preaching of repentance in Matthew, Mark, and Luke illicit several key questions:

- How did John the Baptist's preaching of repentance prepare the way for Jesus?

- Did the preaching of repentance end when John the Baptist's ministry was fulfilled?

- Does preaching repentance continue to prepare the way for Jesus today?

Seeking to answer these questions is the narrow purpose of this section and a broader purpose of this chapter.

Repentance in Jesus' Preaching

Second, Jesus used the verb *repent* quite a number of times in His preaching. Consider the nine uses of μετανοέω (to repent) in Luke:

"Woe to you, Chorazin! Woe to you, Bethsaida! For if the mighty works which were done in you had been done in Tyre and Sidon, they would have repented long ago, sitting in sackcloth and ashes" (Luke 10:13).

"The men of Nineveh will rise up in the judgment with this generation and condemn it, for they repented at the preaching of Jonah; and indeed a greater than Jonah is here" (Luke 11:32).

And Jesus answered and said to them, "Do you suppose that these Galileans were worse sinners than all other Galileans, because they suffered such things? I tell you, no; but unless you repent you will all likewise perish. Or those eighteen on whom the tower in Siloam fell and killed them, do you think that they were worse sinners than all other men who dwelt in Jerusalem? I tell you, no; but unless you repent you will all likewise perish" (Luke 13:2-5).

"I say to you that likewise there will be more joy in heaven over one sinner who repents than over ninety-nine just persons who need no repentance" (Luke 15:7).

"Likewise, I say to you, there is joy in the presence of the angels

of God over one sinner who repents" (Luke 15:10).

"Abraham said to him, 'They have Moses and the prophets; let them hear them.' And he said, 'No, father Abraham; but if one goes to them from the dead, they will repent.' But he said to him, 'If they do not hear Moses and the prophets, neither will they be persuaded though one rise from the dead'" (Luke 16:29-31).

"Take heed to yourselves. If your brother sins against you, rebuke him; and if he repents, forgive him. And if he sins against you seven times in a day, and seven times in a day returns to you, saying, 'I repent,' you shall forgive him" (Luke 17:3-4).

Consider, then, that Jesus was not hesitant to use the verb *repent*. Our example from the Lamb of God, the Son of Love, is to preach that persons should repent. This concept was central in His preaching. In one instance, Jesus affirmed, "I have not come to call *the* righteous, but sinners, to repentance [ἡ μετάνοια]" (Luke 5:32). This same emphasis was echoed in Christ's Great Commission in Luke, as is noted below.

Repentance in Preaching of the Disciples

Third, Jesus sent out His disciples to call out to their hearers to repent:

So they went out and preached that people *should repent. And they cast out many demons, and anointed with oil many who were sick, and healed* them (Mark 6:12-13).

Consider that two verbs in combination to describe their preaching was "preach" (κηρύσσω) and people should "repent" (μετανοέω). The parallel passage in Luke is as follows:

And they departed and went through the villages, preaching the gospel [εὐαγγελίζω] and healing everywhere (Luke 9:6 ESV).

Where Mark had "went out" Luke had "departed and went through." Where Mark had "preached that people should repent" Luke had "evangelized" (εὐαγγελίζω). And where Mark had casting out demons, anointing the sick with oil, and healing, Luke had "healing everywhere." The different verbs used to explain the same events are quite interesting. Needless to say, for the purposes of this section, repentance was a part of the disciples' preaching during the ministry time of Jesus on earth.

Repentance in the Great Commission in Luke

The fourth point regards the use of "repent" in Luke's Great Commission. Luke's commissioning provides a robust view of the five Great Commissions as to the mission and purpose of Christ for His disciples on earth. This mission and purpose, following the guidelines of Luke's commissioning, were carried forth by Luke when he wrote the Acts of the Apostles. Christ's commissioning in Luke marked the last recorded words of Jesus in Luke's account of the life of Jesus:

> Then He said to them, "These are the words which I spoke to you while I was still with you, that all things must be fulfilled which were written in the Law of Moses and the Prophets and the Psalms concerning Me." And He opened their understanding, that they might comprehend the Scriptures. Then He said to them, "Thus it is written, and thus it was necessary for the Christ to suffer and to rise from the dead the third day, and that repentance and remission of sins should be preached in His name to all nations, beginning at Jerusalem. And you are witnesses of these things. Behold, I send the Promise of My Father upon you; but tarry in the city of Jerusalem until you are endued with power from on high" (Luke 24:44-49).

The word *repentance* in this text is not the verb "repent" but rather the noun *repentance* (ἡ μετάνοια). As such, *repentance* is the fulcrum of what is to be preached to all nations. The requisite response of *repentance* provides the only contingency or necessity for a person to receive "remission of sins." *Repentance* finds its place in Christ's Great Commission in Luke in these ways:

1. The suffering and resurrection of Christ encapsulated the core content of the message—what is preached:

    a. Jesus remains the central focus of the message—His person, His worth, His virtue, His glory.

    b. Man and his response of repentance are subordinate to the suffering and resurrection of Christ being preached "in His name."

2. Repentance in His name:

a. Drives the momentum of the message—the purpose for which the core content is preached.

b. Discloses the desired result of the message—the end driving the message's focus.

c. Reveals the requisite response to the message—how the hearer ought to respond to the preached content.

d. Expresses the Holy Spirit's invitation to the receptive soul—He will drive the sinner to repent.

3. Remission of sins in His name explains the result of reception of the message—how the hearer ought to respond to the preached content.

When I taught evangelism at a Registered Baptist Church school in Russia, I learned that the Russian Baptists calculated decisions for Christ by the number of "those who repented"—perhaps equivalent to public confession of sins (Acts 19:18). That method of figuring conversions rang true in light of Luke's Great Commission. Easy-believism has crept into gospel preaching—preaching the gospel and omitting the need to repent. May there be a resurgence of obedience to preaching repentance for the remission of sins.

Repentance and Confession in John's Gospel

A parenthetical note may be necessary in considering the Gospel of John. John's Gospel does not use the verb "repent" (μετανοέω) or the noun "repentance." However, by looking at Matthew 3, a valid link can be made between the verbs "repent" (μετανοέω) and "confess" (ἐξομολογέω) as a response to genuine repentance:

> In those days John the Baptist came preaching in the wilderness of Judea, "Repent [μετανοέω], for the kingdom of heaven is at hand." ... Then Jerusalem and all Judea and all the region about the Jordan were going out to him, and they were baptized by him in the river Jordan, confessing [ἐξομολογέω] their sins (Matthew 3:1-2, 5-6 ESV).

Therefore, one can include the four uses of "confess" in John to represent a parallel thought to the result of true repentance, along with John's development of the idea of believing (πιστεύω).

Repentance in Apostolic Preaching

Fifth, *repent* did have a role in the preaching of the Book of Acts. Out of the five times that the verb *repent* (μετανοέω) is used, three times it comes from the lips of Peter. All three are imperatives (commands):

> And Peter said to them, "Repent and be baptized every one of you in the name of Jesus Christ for the forgiveness of your sins, and you will receive the gift of the Holy Spirit" (Acts 2:38 ESV).

> "Repent therefore and be converted, that your sins may be blotted out, so that times of refreshing may come from the presence of the Lord" (Acts 3:19).

> "Repent therefore of this your wickedness, and pray God if perhaps the thought of your heart may be forgiven you" (Acts 8:22).

Note the two changes Peter's Pentecost Sermon. First, the dual commands of Christ "repent" (μετανοέω) and "believe" (πιστεύω) found in Mark 1:15, became at Pentecost "repent" (μετανοέω) and "be baptized" (βαπτίζω) in the name of Jesus Christ. Second, being baptized in the name of Jesus also became the outward sign of inwardly believing in Jesus. Then in Acts 3, Peter paired the verb *repent* with its parallel "turn" or "convert" (ἐπιστρέφω). In Acts 8, in his personal exhortation to Simon the Sorcerer, Peter coupled "repent" with "pray." Hence, here is the progression:

- Repent and believe, Mark 1
- Repent and be baptized, Acts 2
- Repent and turn, Acts 3
- Repent and pray, Acts 8.

The concept of *repent* also made its way into missionary work among the Gentiles. In the early church of Antioch, "a large number who believed turned to the Lord" (Acts 11:21 NASB)— inverting the order of repent and believe. Paul evangelized the

Gentile crowd to "turn" (ἐπιστρέφω) in Acts 14:15, later using the verb "repent" (μετανοέω) in his sermon to the Gentiles in Athens (Acts 17:30). Paul shared that he preached that men should repent (μετανοέω) before King Agrippa, Festus, and all the prominent men and women of the city in Acts 26:20. Not long after he spoke these words, Paul was interrupted by Governor Festus, the organizer of the event.

Repentance in Revelation

Sixth, in Revelation, the verb *repent* finds itself eight times on the lips of Jesus as He gave warning to five of the seven churches:

> "'Remember therefore from where you have fallen, and repent and do the deeds you did at first; or else I am coming to you, and will remove your lampstand out of its place—unless you repent'" (Revelation 2:5 NASB).

> "'Repent therefore; or else I am coming to you quickly, and I will make war against them with the sword of My mouth'" (Revelation 2:16 NASB).

> "'And I gave her time to repent; and she does not want to repent of her immorality. Behold, I will cast her upon a bed of sickness, and those who commit adultery with her into great tribulation, unless they repent of her deeds. And I will kill her children with pestilence; and all the churches will know that I am He who searches the minds and hearts; and I will give to each one of you according to your deeds'" (Revelation 2:21-23 NASB).

> "'Remember therefore what you have received and heard; and keep it, and repent. If therefore you will not wake up, I will come like a thief, and you will not know at what hour I will come upon you'" (Revelation 3:3 NASB)

> "'Those whom I love, I reprove and discipline; be zealous therefore, and repent'" (Revelation 3:19 NASB).

It seems logical to consider that Christ's message has not changed to churches today. Repent is an important part of the Great Commission of Jesus in Luke, and repent is a strong focus of Christ's challenge to the churches in Revelation. Through these six chronological time periods, from John the Baptist to the Book of Revelation, the need for preaching repentance remains constant.

Repent and Believe

Closely tied to repenting in the preaching of Jesus was the twin verb "to believe." Repenting provides the divinely commanded response to one's own rebellious state. Believing indicates the volitional placing of trust in a place outside of oneself, that is, in Jesus Christ. While the verb "believe" will be considered in detail in the next chapter, some words about the inter-connectedness of these two terms will be considered here.

Mark summarized the early preaching of Jesus as follows:

> Now after John was put in prison, Jesus came to Galilee, preaching the gospel of the kingdom of God, and saying, "The time is fulfilled, and the kingdom of God is at hand. Repent [μετανοέω], and believe [πιστεύω] in the gospel" (Mark 1:14-15).

In this context, then, the present plural command "to repent" (μετανοέω) is tied by a conjunction to the present plural command "to believe" (πιστεύω). The order of these verbs is helpful. One cannot repent without the prior work of the Holy Spirit breaking the hardened self-willed heart of man. It is only when broken from our sin that we can consider that we need to change our ways. The Bible does not recommend a small change of some habits. Jesus commanded a 180-degree turn in which we release complete control of our lives and place control into the hands of Christ.

Once a person is ready to relinquish control of his entire life caught in the clutches of sin, then Jesus tells him to "believe the Good News." The surrender does not remain in a vacuum. Control is concretely placed in the Person and work of Jesus, "in His name." The repentant gives his life to Christ, who died on the cross for his sins and rose again from the grave for him. The repentant takes "self" off the throne of his life—through repentance—and places Christ on the throne of his life through believing in Him. Repentance makes a person open to believing, because they see their need for salvation.

Repentance and Remission of Sin

Gospel proclamation in Luke's Great Commission includes two dual concepts. The first dual relates to the death and resurrection of Jesus. The second dual extends the availability of repentance and remission of sins in His name:

> Then He said to them, "Thus it is written, and thus it was necessary for the Christ to suffer and to rise from the dead the third day, and that repentance and remission of sins should be preached in His name to all nations, beginning at Jerusalem" (Luke 24:46-47).

This remission of or cleansing from sin is available "in His name." It is this phrase which links the two verses together. Because of the death and resurrection of Jesus, remission of sins is available. However, there is a prerequisite to remission of sins. It is repentance. Here Luke used the noun "repentance" (ἡ μετάνοια) rather than the verb "to repent" (μετανοέω). The noun focuses on the concept, the verb on the action. Jesus here, off the pen of Luke, sent out His disciples to preach that persons needed to repent.

When Jesus said, "believe the good news" He was forecasting the Good News that He would die on the cross and be raised from the dead, which is the gospel. In Luke 24, the passage where we find Luke's Great Commission, Jesus is interpreting His death and resurrection for His disciples. They did not understand and some were even skeptical about the resurrection. Jesus had to explain why He had to die and why He rose again. Jesus merged His explanation of this truth with His commissioning of His followers through all ages, places, and times.

The gospel as described in Luke 24:46-47 provides a thematic grid or prism (1) from the mouth of Jesus; and (2) off the pen of Luke—by which all the preaching in the Book of Acts can be interpreted.

A proper understanding of any text or portion of the Bible is greatly assisted by understanding the broad themes of the author. Hence, the Pharisees sought to understand the Central Interpretive Motif of Jesus when they asked Him, "Which is the great commandment in the Law?" (Matthew 22:36; Mark 12:28). Jesus answered first a love for God and second a love for one's neighbor. In so doing, Jesus "showed His hand" as to how He approaches the great themes of Scripture—that is, giving the priority to God, while not ignoring the horizontal duties commanded by God.

Likewise, it is important to understand how to properly interpret the Book of Acts, and in particular the sermons in the Book of Acts. That said, Luke's synopsis of the gospel, from the mouth of Jesus in Luke 24 is an important thematic statement to properly understand not only the climax of Luke's Gospel—the death and resurrection of Jesus—but also to interpret and apply the preaching of that gospel in the Book of Acts. Hence, a proper interpretation of all the evangelistic sermons in Acts should seek to see how the speaker approached:

1. The suffering of Christ on the cross

2. His resurrection

3. The call to repentance

4. Remission of sins.

All of these elements were important to Jesus as He interpreted His death and resurrection to His disciples and simultaneously, as He sent out His disciples to evangelize the world. And it is no surprise that the call to repentance is the hinge between the message and the response to that message.

> So they went out and preached that people should repent (Mark 6:12).

Case Studies on Repentance

If repentance is a part of the Great Commission given by Jesus in His post-Resurrection Preaching, then it follows that repentance should be exemplified in the Bible. For Jesus, the people of Nineveh were raised up as an example of genuine repentance in Matthew and Luke. An examination of Acts also shows how repentance was effectuated in the apostolic church. Here follow some examples of repentance or the lack of it.

Repentance in the Book of Jonah

Jesus used the repentance of the persons in Nineveh in a rebuke to His hearers in Matthew 12 and Luke 11:

> "The men of Nineveh will rise up in the judgment with this generation and condemn it, because they repented at the

preaching of Jonah; and indeed a greater than Jonah is here" (Matthew 12:41; cf. Luke 11:32).

In these virtually identical verses, the Holy Spirit recommends to the reader to consider the example of repentance in the Book of Jonah. The repentance of Nineveh was typified by wearing sackcloth and fasting, accompanied by prayer and turning from evil (Jonah 3:5-8). Another time Jesus used the example of Nineveh's repentance by their wearing of sackcloth and ashes:

> *"Woe to you, Chorazin! Woe to you, Bethsaida! For if the mighty works which were done in you had been done in Tyre and Sidon, they would have repented long ago in sackcloth and ashes"* (Matthew 11:21; cf. Luke 10:13).

Here Jesus associated true repentance with a change of clothing and a sign of contrition. These were two of the signs of repentance exemplified in Nineveh after the preaching of Jonah. They are outward signs of an inward broken heart, a humble heart, a repentant heart. Among many verses on this topic, Psalm 34 speaks of the broken heart:

> *The LORD is near to the brokenhearted and saves the crushed in spirit* (Psalm 34:18 ESV).

Saul (Paul) in Acts 9

Saul's conversion is perhaps the most striking for several reasons. First, Saul was an aggressive persecutor of the church, his conversion was an act of God's providence. It provides a precedent for God saving antagonistic persons throughout the history of the churches. Second, Saul became the Apostle Paul, the main character in the second half of the Book of Acts. Third, Saul became the Apostle Paul who authored 13 or 14 letters in the New Testament. In his letters, Paul sometimes referred to his salvation and spiritual development. His spiritual experiences became the collective spiritual experiences of the entire church through his writings. And fourth, the spiritual growth of Saul to Paul is one of the few overt examples of spiritual growth in the Book of Acts. For these reasons, the conversion of Paul is one of the central accounts in the New Testament. But, what of repentance in Paul?

1. How did Paul receive the proclamation of "repentance and remission of sins"?

2. How did Paul respond to the proclamation of "repentance and remission of sins"?

A pre-conversion experience of Saul that cannot be overlooked is his participation in the martyrdom of Stephen. Stephen clearly preached the need for repentance, citing numerous Old Testament Scriptures. In his conclusion, Stephen called his hearers "stiff-necked and uncircumcised of heart and ears" (Acts 7:51). His hearers were shocked and stunned at his mighty words. Yet, it was not until he mentioned Jesus that they charged at him:

> *When they heard these things they were cut to the heart, and they gnashed at him with their teeth. But he, being full of the Holy Spirit, gazed into heaven and saw the glory of God, and Jesus standing at the right hand of God, and said, "Look! I see the heavens opened and the Son of Man standing at the right hand of God!" Then they cried out with a loud voice, stopped their ears, and ran at him with one accord; and they cast him out of the city and stoned him. And the witnesses laid down their clothes at the feet of a young man named Saul. And they stoned Stephen as he was calling on God and saying, "Lord Jesus, receive my spirit." Then he knelt down and cried out with a loud voice, "Lord, do not charge them with this sin." And when he had said this, he fell asleep (Acts 7:54-60).*

Was Saul first in the audience to charge him and begin carrying him off? Could Saul have been leader of the "Synagogue of the Freedmen" from Cilicia and Asia who argued with Stephen and set him up for arrest in Acts 6:9-15? Clearly Saul heard the message of repentance from the mouth of Stephen.

Stephen had seen the heavens open and beheld the Son of Man standing at the right hand of God. Later, on a road to Damascus, Saul himself was struck by a light from heaven, and heard a voice saying, "I am Jesus, whom you are persecuting" (Acts 9:5).

Saul's repentance was communicated in several ways. First, he fell to the ground in submission in Acts 9:4. Second, he trembled at the words of Jesus in Acts 9:6. Third, he obeyed what Jesus told him to do in Acts 9:6. Fourth, he fasted while he waited on the Lord in Acts 9:9, unlike his predecessor King Saul in 1 Samuel 28:20-25. Fifth, he was praying (Acts 9:11). Sixth, God gifted him with scales of physical blindness, which reminded him of his own spiritual blindness (Acts 9:18). Seventh, he, a Pharisee of Pharisees, received baptism from Ananias (Acts 9:18). Therefore, while Ananias did not preach the death and resurrection of Jesus, Saul had heard that from Stephen and in other discussions with Christians. While it did not state that Paul "repented," he showed repentance by submitting to and obeying the commands of Christ. While it does not specifically say that Paul "believed" in the name of Jesus, by Acts 9:20 he was preaching that Christ was the Son of God in the synagogues of Damascus.

Cornelius in Acts 10

Just as considering the repentance of Saul necessitated some digging into the text of Scripture, the same is true for Cornelius. Cornelius was described by four characteristics, showing a heart that was tender to God's word (Acts 10:2):

1. He was a pious, religious, or devout man

2. He feared God with all his household

3. He gave alms generously to the people

4. He prayed to the Lord always.

Perhaps these four characteristics show that the word of God had done its plowing on the heart of Cornelius. Cornelius appears to resemble the contrite heart whom the Lord does not despise according to Psalm 51:17. His repentant heart was exemplified by his being obedient to the promptings of the Lord through the dream that the Lord gave him.

Peter, in his sermon at the home of Cornelius, listed two prerequisites for those welcome to or favorable to God: (1) fearing Him; and (2) working righteousness (Acts 10:35). These qualities do not save a man, but rather reveal a heart upon which the Holy Spirit is working. Consider, however, that although Jesus "loved" the Rich Young Ruler for his obedience of the Ten Commandments, this Young Ruler went away sad and unsaved (Mark 10:21-22). It is "repentance ... in the name of Jesus" that saves.

The Philippian Jailer in Acts 16

The Philippian Jailer cried out to Paul and Silas, "Sirs, what must I do to be saved?" (Acts 16:30). Merely by asking this question, the jailer showed a repentant disposition of heart. His question paralleled the brokenness of heart exemplified by the crowd at Pentecost, "Brothers, what shall we do?" (Acts 2:37 ESV). Peter in that case stated, "Repent" and show your repentance by being baptized, and display your faith in Jesus by being baptized "in the name of Jesus Christ" (Acts 2:38). Likewise, in his question, the Philippian Jailer showed a repentant heart, open to the gospel. Therefore, Paul and Silas focused on the second verb in the gospel, "Believe on the Lord Jesus Christ and you will be saved" (Acts 16:31).

The Philosophers Who Followed in Acts 17

In Acts 17 we find Paul's sermon to the Epicurean and Stoic philosophers in Athens. Paul's message was heckled when he began to speak of Jesus and the resurrection. Therefore it was an unfinished sermon. And yet it did elicit a response. Some openly mocked Paul. Others were casually interested. And "some men joined him and believed" (Acts 17:34).

Consider that the verb "joining" is paired with "believe," much as "repent" is paired with "believe" in gospel proclamation. The act of joining or cleaving (κολλάω) to Paul and his preaching was synonymous in this instance with an attitude of repentance from dead works and thoughts.

The Revival in Acts 19

Acts 19 tells of a true citywide revival in Ephesus. The repentance in this revival was exemplified in two ways: one verbally and the other practically. Verbally "many of those who believed came confessing and telling their deeds" (Acts 19:18). The beginning of true repentance is the acknowledgement of sin. Here we have an example of the public acknowledgement of sin—which often accompanies true revival. From a practical point-of-view, the cost of the books destroyed as a sign of "leaving the old life behind" was worth about 50,000 pieces of silver (Acts 19:19). Or, if one piece of silver is equivalent to one day's wage (depending on the job and economy) 50,000 times $50 equals 2.5 million dollars of books burned. Burning the old life and leaving it behind is necessary for true repentance to take place. Likewise, water baptism signifies death to the old life and coming alive to a new life in Christ (Romans 6:4). The ongoing nature of this process was explained by Paul as putting off the old and putting on the new (Ephesians 4:22-24; Colossians 3:8-10).

Simon the Sorcerer in Acts 8

An interesting case study in the topic of repentance relates to the truthfulness of the salvation of Simon the Sorcerer. In Acts 8:13, Luke wrote that "Simon himself also believed; and when he was baptized he continued with Philip." In Simon, the Holy Spirit gives us an example of false repentance. The dubious nature of Simon's repentance is a reminder of the need for repentance before and accompanying faith.

Consider that the Apostles were sent to check on the revival in Samaria in the verse after Simon's supposed conversion took place (Acts 8:13-14). Consider also that Simon was amazed by the miracles and signs of Philip, perhaps rather than being amazed at the message of salvation. Although Simon had been called "the great power of God" (Acts 8:10), it was Philip who had great powers from God. Consider also that Simon wanted to pay money to receive the power to give the Holy Spirit. All these features lend suspicion as to his salvation.

Yet something else that leads to the conclusion that Simon's conversion, and thus his repentance, was disingenuous:

> And when Simon saw that through the laying on of the apostles' hands the Holy Spirit was given, he offered them money, saying, "Give me this power also, that anyone on whom I lay hands may receive the Holy Spirit." But Peter said to him, "Your money perish with you, because you thought that the gift of God could be purchased with money! You have neither part nor portion in this matter, for your heart is not right in the sight of God. Repent therefore of this your wickedness, and pray God if perhaps the thought of your heart may be forgiven you. For I see that you are poisoned by bitterness and bound by iniquity." Then Simon

answered and said, "Pray to the Lord for me, that none of the things which you have spoken may come upon me" (Acts 8:18-24).

Peter took three warnings from the Book of Deuteronomy, showing that he classified Simon's request for spiritual power among the highest indications of his being a rogue Christian:

- *No part of portion*—comes from Deuteronomy 18:1, wherein the Levites have no inheritance in the land of Israel (cited in Acts 8:21).

- *A man or a woman who has been wicked in the sight of the LORD your God*—is found in Deuteronomy 17:2 (also cited in Acts 8:21).

- *Poisoned by bitterness and bound by iniquity* (cited in Acts 8:23)—comes from Deuteronomy 29:18, describing a person who is "following the dictates of his own heart"; Deuteronomy cited four consequences of such a response:

  o *The LORD will not be willing to forgive him*

  o *But rather the anger of the LORD and his jealousy will smoke against that man*

  o *And the curses written in this book will settle upon him*

  o *And the LORD will blot out his name from under heaven* (Deuteronomy 29:20 ESV).

Peter commanded Simon to "repent and pray." Yet, even after these stern rebukes from the Book of Deuteronomy, Simon retorted, "[You] pray for me" (Acts 8:24). He did not request prayer for a change of his heart (repentance), but rather prayer that he might avoid the consequences of his sinful request. It is clear from his response that:

1. His heart was not tender to the warnings of the word of God

2. Nor did he understand the importance and severity of Peter's warning

3. Nor was he willing to humbly obey what Peter requested of him.

Consider the ineffectiveness of water baptism to produce life-change in the case of Simon the Sorcerer, apparently having been baptized without a repentant heart.

The example of Simon recalls the false repentance exemplified by Cain, Esau, and King Saul. All three were worried about facing the consequences of their sin. Not one was concerned about their own heart condition nor their severed relationship with God:

> *Lest there* be *any fornicator or profane person like Esau, who for one morsel of food sold his birthright. For you know that afterward, when he wanted to inherit the blessing, he was rejected, for he found no place for repentance, though he sought it diligently with tears* (Hebrews 12:16-17).

Just as believing in Jesus is important, so also is the first command of the gospel—the command "to repent." Moving on to the second command without obedience of the first engenders a self-seeking faith that is counter-productive to a spirit of genuine repentance.

THOMAS P. JOHNSTON

CHAPTER NINE

BELIEVE
—πιστεύω—

The second verb in the dual gospel command of Jesus is the verb "to believe" (πιστεύω). Obedience to the verb "believe" is triggered by repentance. Repenting (μετανοέω) gives the context for "believing"—it is the why and what of believing. Without knowing what is the purpose of believing and its place in responding to repentance, believing can be shallow or misplaced. There are times in Scripture that repenting is used alone to describe what is necessary for salvation. There are times in Scripture that believing is used all by itself to describe salvation. Therefore, there must be some overlap in usage of these concepts. For example, the Gospel of John never uses the verb "repent" or the noun "repentance." Does this imply that John's Gospel contradicts Luke's Great Commission, which states that "repentance and remission of sins should be preached in His name to all nations, beginning in Jerusalem"? (Luke 24:47). Not at all. The same Holy Spirit that inspired Luke as an author in writing the biography of Jesus also inspired John who wrote the Gospel of John. The difference lies in focus and emphasis. Each has its legitimate emphasis and focus!

Believing in the New Testament is an active verb. It is something that wells up from within the heart of man and is applied to a person, place, or thing. As can be expected in any word in the Bible, there are many gems and nuggets of truth hidden away in the New Testament usage of this term. There are a number of perplexing issues that are also revealed by a thorough study of the verb "to believe" (πιστεύω).

The verb *believe* (πιστεύω) is found 248 times in the New Testament. It is used at least 96 times specifically in contexts of people putting their faith and trust in Jesus: in Jesus, in the name of

Jesus, in the words of Jesus, or in the miracles of Jesus. It is used in the context of absolute assurance of salvation. But then it is also used of equivocal half-hearted belief. It is used of belief in God, belief in prayer, belief in the prophets, and as a description of followers of Christ, as believers. It is an amazing word. In this chapter, I will seek to do justice to this verb. But I must confess from the outset that it is a rich and deep verb. These next few pages will only serve as an overview of this important active verb.

Not Believing and Believing

To introduce the subject of believing, the New Testament, and especially the author John juxtaposes true belief with unbelief. Whereas John uses the verb πιστεύω (to believe) 100 times in his Gospel, 27 times that he uses this verb it is in a negative context. For example, in the famous conversation with the ruler Nicodemus in John 3, the first two uses of the verb πιστεύω are in a negative context:

> "If I have told you earthly things and you do not believe, how will you believe if I tell you heavenly things?" (John 3:12).

Here Jesus reprimanded Nicodemus for not understanding the concept of a spiritual "new birth." He was responding to the question of Nicodemus, "How can these things be?" from verse 9. So, due to Nicodemus' misunderstanding of the spiritual analogy of the new birth, it was clear to Jesus that Nicodemus lacked faith in three ways:

- Faith in Jesus

- Faith in what Jesus said

- A hearing of faith provides (1) spiritual insight into Christ's teaching; and (2) a proper context for understanding.

Jesus then used the term πιστεύω (to believe) in a positive context in verses 15 and 16, only to return to the negative in verse 18. Let's look at verses 14-16:

> "And as Moses lifted up the serpent in the wilderness, even so must the Son of Man be lifted up, that whoever believes [πιστεύω] in Him should not perish but have eternal life. For God

so loved the world that He gave His only begotten Son, that whoever believes [πιστεύω] in Him should not perish but have everlasting life" (John 3:14-16).

Here in these verses, Jesus laid out the positive side of believing. That is, if someone specifically believes in Jesus, he will have eternal life. In this case John twice used the simple verb ἔχω in the Greek, meaning "to have" or "to hold." There is no need to complicate what is quite simply taught by Jesus off the pen of the Apostle John. Everyone who "believes" in Jesus has or holds eternal life.

But then in verse 18, Jesus clarified His point:

"He who believes [πιστεύω] in Him is not condemned; but he who does not believe [μή πιστεύω] is condemned already, because he has not believed [μή πιστεύω] in the name of the only begotten Son of God" (John 3:18).

After three positive uses of the verb πιστεύω (to believe) Jesus then returned to the negative usage two further times. In these seven uses of the verb believe, we have a 2-3-2 pattern. Two negative, three positive, and two more negative.

As a very important side-note here: The sign of a false prophet or false teacher is the teaching of the positive side of the equation without teaching the negative side—even when they are both located in the same text side-by-side. The prophet Jeremiah addressed the danger of this "Positive-Only Thinking" in Chapter 23 of his book:

"But in the prophets of Jerusalem I have seen a horrible thing: they commit adultery and walk in lies; they strengthen the hands of evildoers, so that no one turns from his evil; all of them have become like Sodom to me, and its inhabitants like Gomorrah." ... Thus says the LORD of hosts: "Do not listen to the words of the prophets who prophesy to you, filling you with vain hopes. They speak visions of their own minds, not from the mouth of the LORD. They say continually to those who despise the word of the LORD, 'It shall be well with you'; and to everyone who stubbornly follows his own heart, they say, 'No disaster shall come upon you'" (Jeremiah 23:14, 16-17 ESV).

Likewise, Jesus when He taught about the love of God for the world, "that whoever believes in Him should not perish but have everlasting life," also taught the negative side. What of those who do not believe? In verse 18 Jesus reiterated that those who "do not" actively believe in the name of the only begotten Son of God are "condemned already."

So, we have in these words of Jesus two sides of a spectrum. One side is believing and the other not believing. On the believing side, Jesus gave clear assurance of salvation. At least 28 occurrences of the verb πιστεύω (to believe) are accompanied by very strong statements assuring those who believe that Christ has fully and completely redeemed them from their sins. He has paid it all. Our sins are atoned for full and free.

On the other hand, Jesus gave clear testimony of the perdition for those who do not believe. Just as in John 3:18, there are a host of verses coming off the pen of every New Testament author that those who do not repent and believe are doomed to an eternal hell. Just like the positive side of the equation, this negative side is incontrovertible to anyone who believes in the inspiration of the Bible.

So, this chapter will be organized as follows: First, it will begin with statements of assurance of salvation using the verb "believe." Then, this chapter will consider eight case studies related to biblical belief. Finally, it will address two aspects of believing in relation to evangelism. Jesus clearly communicated assurance of salvation in contexts He used the verb πιστεύω (to believe).

Statements of Assurance

Because one of the chief roles of Satan is to slander the people of God before the throne of God (see Job Chapter 1), it seemed propitious to begin this chapter by providing solace to the weary soul. Satan is called "the accuser of the saints":

> *And the great dragon was thrown down, the serpent of old who is called the devil and Satan, who deceives the whole world; he was thrown down to the earth, and his angels were thrown down with him. And I heard a loud voice in heaven, saying, "Now the salvation, and the power, and the kingdom of our God and the*

> *authority of His Christ have come, for the accuser of our brethren has been thrown down, who accuses them before our God day and night"* (Revelation 12:9-10 NASB).

This wicked foe is a slanderer. He slanders mankind in their minds. He slanders through other people. He is a liar and the father of lies. He has never told the truth. He cannot and never will tell the truth—although he may come very close to it. Satan is always deceiving others. And the only weapon in the Christian's armor is the Sword of the Spirit—which is the word of God—to arm Christ's followers to ward off the fiery darts of Satan that seek to steal, kill, and destroy.

One way Satan destroys people is to tell them that there is no hope. Not so. In Christ and Christ alone there is great hope. Jesus died and He rose again from the dead. That truth provides hope and assurance.

Further, Psalm 51:17 explains that the Lord does not despise the contrite heart. Therefore, all true believers in Jesus come to Him with a contrite heart. Not merely a contrite heart on the day of their salvation, but a continuously contrite heart. A heart that diligently seeks the Lord. A heart that presses forward into knowing and serving the Lord. This same humble and broken heart, this same repentant heart, exposes the Christian to be susceptible to the wiles of the Devil. He may think that he is spiritually lost and without hope. On the other hand, Satan might tempt the Christian to think that all is fine, and he has no need for Jesus! Whatever the temptation of Satan, it is the words of the word of God that provide protection from his attacks.

The Apostle Paul based his assurance of salvation on the Person of Jesus Christ:

> *For this reason I also suffer these things; nevertheless I am not ashamed, for I know whom I have believed [πιστεύω] and am persuaded that He is able to keep what I have committed to Him until that Day* (2 Timothy 1:12).

Through the intense persecution that Paul suffered, he received one spiritual adrenalin rush after another, helping him handle the persecution that came his way. He absorbed this infusion of spiritual power by the agency of the written word of God. Consider, for example, Paul's advice to Timothy, his son in the faith:

You, however, continue in the things you have learned and become convinced of, knowing from whom you have learned them; and that from childhood you have known the sacred writings which are able to give you the wisdom that leads to salvation through faith which is in Christ Jesus (2 Timothy 3:14-15 NASB).

Notice the phrases "and become convinced [assured] of" and "from whom you have learned them." The assurance Paul recommended to Timothy did not come via the thoughts of men, but this assurance came through the God-breathed Holy Scriptures.

The Apostle John shared his spiritual purpose in writing. No hidden agenda with John. His specific thought when he wrote the Gospel of John was to give his believing readers assurance of salvation!

Now Jesus did many other signs in the presence of the disciples, which are not written in this book; but these are written so that you may believe [πιστεύω] that Jesus is the Christ, the Son of God, and that by believing [πιστεύω] you may have life in his name (John 20:30-31 ESV).

God wrote the sixty-six books of His love letter, using the pens of forty authors, so that those who read His words would believe in Jesus Christ. Then, by believing in Jesus, they would have life in His name! While that is God's purpose generally, it is especially God's purpose in the Gospel of John—the Gospel of Belief. God wants those who believe in Jesus to have assurance of salvation. And this assurance is directly linked to who Jesus was and what He did, particularly as related to His death and resurrection. The very clear basis upon which any assurance of salvation rests is the finished nature of salvation in the death and resurrection of Jesus, "It is finished!" (John 19:30).

God's work of saving souls did not merely end with Abraham. Rather Abraham became an example for all who believe on God's words. Consider therefore that Abraham believed the "word of the LORD":

And behold, the word of the LORD came to him [Abraham] ... And

> he believed the LORD, and he counted it to him as righteousness
> (Genesis 15:4, 6 ESV).

Abraham's belief in the "word of the LORD" triggered the imputation of his sins:

> Now it was not written for his sake alone that it was imputed to him, but also for us. It shall be imputed to us who believe [πιστεύω] in Him who raised up Jesus our Lord from the dead, who was delivered up because of our offenses, and was raised because of our justification (Romans 4:23-25).

While assurance is communicated to humanity by the imputed (from the outside) righteousness of Christ placed within man's soul, there is nevertheless a particularity. This mysterious but very real transaction is only performed on those who believe. The condemnation of Jesus related to unbelievers remains active:

> "He who believes [πιστεύω] in the Son has everlasting life; and he who does not believe [μή πιστεύω] the Son shall not see life, but the wrath of God abides on him" (John 3:36).

The Apostle Paul and Silas responded with a propositional truth claim to the Philippian Jailer in answer to his plea, "What must I do to be saved?":

> So they said, "Believe [πιστεύω] on the Lord Jesus Christ, and you will be saved, you and your household" (Acts 16:31).

They replied to the Philippian Jailer with an imperative, "Believe...." The result of believing? "You will be saved, you and your household." The key for his salvation was placing his complete trust in Jesus.

Two verses from John's pen are striking in relation to assurance. These verses have clearly communicated God's saving purposes in evangelism situations:

> "Truly, truly, I say to you, whoever hears [ἀκούω] my word and believes [πιστεύω] him who sent me has eternal life. He does not come into judgment, but has passed from death to life" (John 5:24 ESV).

In this verse, assurance comes from two places: a proper hearing, "whoever hears [ἀκούω] my word," and a response of believing, "and believes [πιστεύω] him who sent me." If both of these concepts are well ordered, then the hearer is affirmed to have "everlasting life." As to the slight riddle, "believes him who sent me," this phrase is found on several occasions by Jesus. It simply means believing that God sent Jesus. Rather than Muhammed being "the prophet" of Allah, true faith believes that God, the Creator of heaven and earth, sent His one and only Son Jesus, to live a sinless life, and to die a substitutionary death for the sins of the world. He was raised on the third day, and He lives today interceding for His people!

Another key verse on assurance is in the First Epistle of John:

> These things have I written unto you that believe [πιστεύω] on the name of the Son of God; that ye may know that ye have eternal life, and that ye may believe [πιστεύω] on the name of the Son of God (1 John 5:13 KJV).

Here the word of God is the agent of salvation, as noted in an earlier chapter, "I have written … that ye may believe." In this verse, John cited Jesus who said the same thing as recorded in the Gospel of John:

> "Most assuredly, I say to you, he who believes [πιστεύω] in Me has everlasting life" (John 6:47).

So, the Apostle John wrote the book of First John to give those "who believe in the name of the Son of God" assurance—assurance of eternal life! In a way, John was repeating what he had already written in John 20:31, "these are written that you may believe."

So, believing in Jesus is the goal of the Scriptures, but what kind of believing does God desire as portrayed in His word?

Eight Case Studies

Assurance of salvation necessitates genuine believing in Jesus Christ. It is interesting to note that three New Testament authors in four New Testament books use the verb "believe" (πιστεύω) to describe those who did not have a full and genuine faith. In the introduction of this chapter I described the two ends of the spectrum of believing, belief and unbelief. There are, however, several biblical examples of something other than a full-hearted faith. In each of these cases the verb πιστεύω (to believe) is used, and yet there is a flaw as to these people's faith.

Demons in James 2

The search for false faith begins with the faith of demons. James, the half-brother of Jesus, brought up the faith of demons in an *ad extremum* argument to prove that "Faith Alone," being devoid of proper corresponding (succeeding) works was proven to be void. James wrote:

> You believe that there is one God. You do well. Even the demons believe—and tremble! (James 2:19).

So, James was saying that true faith always results in life-change or "works." In Hebrews 11:6, true faith was described as believing (1) that God exists; and (2) that He is a rewarder of those who diligently seek Him. From this definition then, while demons believe Point 1, they must fall short on Point 2. They are not working for a reward from God. Further, as to the argument of James, true faith, being preceded by a repentant heart, will continue to lead to the diligent seeking of God. Part of pursuing God includes obeying those admonitions taught in His word. Hence, true faith is an obedient faith.

Simon the Sorcerer in Acts 8

In Acts 8 we are simultaneously introduced to Philip the Evangelist and his antithetic Simon the Sorcerer. Their similarities and differences make an interesting study. However, by the time Simon crossed paths with Philip, we read that he believed, was baptized, and continued with Philip. Was his faith genuine? While his example was noted previously from the point-of-view of repentance, it also applies as regards to his faith.

> Then Simon himself also believed [πιστεύω]; and when he was baptized he continued with Philip, and was amazed, seeing the miracles and signs which were done (Acts 8:13).

At first glance all seems well with Simon—until he saw that the Holy Spirit was given by the laying on of hands. It was his seeming inability to give out the Holy Spirit that birthed in him an evil ploy.

151

He offered the Apostles Peter and John money so that he would also receive that same power that they had. The irony was that he had that power if he was in Christ under Christ's authority.

Luke recorded Simon's sinister request for this gift:

> "Give me this power also, that anyone on whom I lay hands may receive the Holy Spirit" (Acts 8:19).

Peter's rebuke was harsh and to the point:

> But Peter said to him, "Your money perish with you, because you thought that the gift of God could be purchased with money! You have neither part nor portion in this matter, for your heart is not right in the sight of God. Repent therefore of this your wickedness, and pray God if perhaps the thought of your heart may be forgiven you. For I see that you are poisoned by bitterness and bound by iniquity" (Acts 8:20-23).

Peter, citing Deuteronomy 18 affirmed that Simon had "neither part nor portion" in this matter. Further, Peter commanded him to repent, which he did not do. Rather, he asked Peter to pray for him. In the classic pattern of false repentance of Cain, Esau, and King Saul, all Simon cared about was the punishment for his sin, not the sin itself.

So, in Simon the Sorcerer, we have someone who believed without a repentant heart, and we find a person who believed only for his own personal gain. Personal gain may have also guided Judas Iscariot to betray Jesus. Clearly Simon represents a dangerous follower of Jesus who believed and was baptized. True saving faith necessitates the foundation of repentance. And true saving faith is a sacrificial faith, not a self-seeking faith.

The Faith of the Shallow Soil

The second soil in Jesus' Parable of the Sower is sometimes called "the shallow soil." This soil's commitment is described in Matthew as hearing the word and "immediately receiving it with joy" (Matthew 13:20). Likewise, in Mark, "when they hear the word, immediately receive it with gladness" (Mark 4:16). However, in Luke the verb "believe" (πιστεύω) is used rather than the word "receive" (λαμβάνω):

"But the ones on the rock are those who, when they hear, receive the word with joy; and these have no root, who believe [πιστεύω] for a while and in time of temptation fall away" (Luke 8:13).

These persons, who receive the word on the shallow soil of their hearts, appear to believe, as long as it benefits them. Once persecution comes because of the word, they stumble, as emphasized in Mark's Gospel:

"Afterward, when tribulation or persecution arises for the word's sake, immediately they stumble" (Mark 4:17).

On the other hand, true saving faith perseveres through trials. It is sacrificial faith:

"And you will be hated by all for My name's sake. But he who endures to the end shall be saved" (Mark 13:13).

The Jews who Believed in John 8

In several New Testament contexts, we find people named "Jews who believed." In some contexts this designation seems to be an innocuous description of their religious background. This appears to be the case in John 11:45 and 12:11. However, there are two passages where the context displays a lukewarm faith among the "Jews who believed [πιστεύω] in Him." This first is found in John 8:31, "Then Jesus said to those Jews who believed in Him." What follows is a progressively more hostile interaction where the Jews become combative. They falsely affirm, "We are Abraham's offspring, and have never been in bondage to anyone" (John 8:33). They accuse Jesus by stating, "We were not born of fornication" (John 8:41). They go on to say to Jesus, "Do we not say rightly that You are a Samaritan and have a demon?" (John 8:48). And "Now we know you have a demon" (John 8:52). Finally, "They took up stones to throw at Him; but Jesus hid Himself" (John 8:59).

Surely there was something deficient in the belief of these antagonistic Jews in John 8. Surely, they were not submissive to the teachings of Christ. Perhaps they were like other fair-weather believers who followed Jesus as long as He was healing people and feeding them (John 10:31-33). The moment He started teaching, they became combative!

The Jews who Believed in Acts 21

Another quandary relates to the words of those at the church in Jerusalem, the "many myriads of Jews who have believed [πιστεύω]." Here is the verse in which they are described:

> And when they heard *it*, they glorified the Lord. And they said to him, "You see, brother, how many myriads [ἡ μυριάς = ten thousand] of Jews there are who have believed, and they are all zealous for the law" (Acts 21:20).

Several contextual points about these Jews. First, neither these myriads of Jews nor the Apostles were hospitable to Paul and his team, but rather a Cyprian named Mnason (Acts 21:16). Second, they had a misplaced zeal, they were "zealous for the law," rather than zealous for the gospel, zealous for Jesus, or zealous for lost souls. These myriads appear to be from the same group who opposed Paul in his Book of Galatians. Third, they encouraged him to use his own money to pay for a Jewish head-shave ritual for himself and for four others, a political ploy to assuage rumors circulating against Paul. Fourth, when Paul was being beaten after "all the city was disturbed," no one stood up for Paul, neither from among the Apostles who had encouraged him to get a head-shave, nor from among the "myriads of Jews who have believed" who had a misplaced zeal.

Their zeal was "for the law." Paul's zeal was for the cross of Christ. Paul wrote the Corinthian church, "I determined not to know anything among you except Jesus Christ and Him crucified" (1 Corinthians 2:2). In Ephesians, Paul recommended for armor on the feet, "a readiness [or zeal] for the gospel of peace" (Ephesians 6:15). It appears that these Jews were zealous for the Law much like those who created problems for Paul in Acts 15:1, 5.

The Pharisees Who Believed in Acts 15

In Acts 15:5 we have a group of men who are from the "sect of the Pharisees who believed." These men opposed Paul, who himself had been a Pharisee. Here is the verse in which they are described using the verb "believe" (πιστεύω):

> *But some of the sect of the Pharisees who believed [πιστεύω]*

rose up, saying, "It is necessary to circumcise them, and to command them to keep the law of Moses" (Acts 15:5).

Apparently, these from the Pharisees added to what was said previously by "certain ones who had come down from Judea." This former group merely advocated for circumcision to be added to believing for assurance of salvation:

> And certain men came down from Judea and taught the brethren, "Unless you are circumcised according to the custom of Moses, you cannot be saved" (Acts 15:1).

Thanks to the tenacity of Paul, these men did not prevail, and many of the Reformation *Solas* can be traced back to Peter's discourse in Acts 15:7-11.

All to say, that the teachings of Acts 15 were helpful not only in the first century, but also for the sixteenth century Protestant Reformation, and even to the present day. Some have belief in Christ, but they have added certain encrustations of religious ritual to faith in Jesus. It is a very dangerous problem. A mixed faith is a deficient faith. No one in heaven, or on earth, or under the earth is worthy other than Jesus (Revelation 5:3). Only the Lamb is worthy. Jesus did it all. And Jesus and Jesus alone saves!

Those Who Believed in John 2

Jesus told His disciples to be "Wise as serpents and gentle as doves" (Matthew 10:16). Likewise Jesus modelled this wisdom in John 2, then early in John the crowds were becoming endeared to Him. We read in John 2:23, "Many believed [πιστεύω] in His name when they saw the signs which He did." Jesus however, did not reciprocate "belief" in them.

The Apostle John wrote:

> But Jesus did not commit [πιστεύω] Himself to them, because He knew all men, and had no need that anyone should testify of man, for He knew what was in man (John 2:24-25).

The verb for "commit" in John 2:24 is a translation of the Greek πιστεύω (to believe). Because of context, the translators did not use the word "believing" for Jesus. They rather said that Jesus did not commit or entrust Himself to them. We appear to have a play on the word "believe." John was counter-positioning Jesus and the crowds. The crowds had a shallow amazed "belief" in Jesus. Jesus, however, knowing all things, was not infatuated with it nor did He reciprocate a commitment to them. Perhaps their faith was some type of "fair-weather" faith as noted above.

The Believing Rulers in John 12

Perhaps the most interesting case in this study of half-hearted faith commitments is communicated by John in Chapter 12. John spoke of the rulers who "believed" in Jesus, but were hesitant to confess Him publicly, lest they be kicked out of the synagogue.

> Nevertheless even among the rulers many believed [πιστεύω] in Him, but because of the Pharisees they did not confess Him, lest they should be put out of the synagogue; for they loved the praise of men more than the praise of God (John 12:42-43).

These rulers clearly "believed [πιστεύω] in Him." Yet their faith was only half-hearted. They desired to avoid potential persecution for believing in Jesus. John added that these men "love the praise of men more than the praise of God." One wonders if they were really saved or not. Would these words of Jesus have applied to them?

> "Everyone therefore who shall confess Me before men, I will also confess him before My Father who is in heaven. But whoever shall deny Me before men, I will also deny him before My Father who is in heaven" (Matthew 10:32-33 NASB).

Paul in Galatians 1:10 wrote of his commitment to pleasing God and not men:

> For am I now seeking the favor of men, or of God? Or am I striving to please men? If I were still trying to please men, I would not be a bond-servant of Christ (Galatians 1:10 NASB).

As for the rulers mentioned in John 12, it would seem that Nicodemus was one of these men. He was a ruler of the Jews, and fearing to be seen by men, came to Jesus by night (John 3:1-2). Joseph of Arimathea was also one of these rulers. Yet something happened during and after the death of Jesus on the cross that caused them to take a stand for Him by requesting and burying His body:

After this, Joseph of Arimathea, being a disciple of Jesus, but secretly, for fear of the Jews, asked Pilate that he might take away the body of Jesus; and Pilate gave him permission. So he came and took the body of Jesus. And Nicodemus, who at first came to Jesus by night, also came, bringing a mixture of myrrh and aloes, about a hundred pounds. Then they took the body of Jesus, and bound it in strips of linen with the spices, as the custom of the Jews is to bury. Now in the place where He was crucified there was a garden, and in the garden a new tomb in which no one had yet been laid. So there they laid Jesus, because of the Jews' Preparation Day, for the tomb was nearby (John 19:38-42).

So both Joseph of Arimathea and Nicodemus confessed Jesus before men, loving the praise of God more than the praise of men, turning from their former embarrassment toward their Savior.

This last type of half-hearted faith may still be more common in today's churches. It represents a level of believing without a corresponding verbal confession of allegiance. These believers may go to church, but they otherwise hide their faith from their family, friends, and associates. And yet, there is something freeing and cathartic that comes with a verbal witness. The pleasure of Christ rests upon those who freely profess His name. Whereas He is ashamed of those who are ashamed of Him.

"For whoever is ashamed of Me and My words in this adulterous and sinful generation, of him the Son of Man also will be ashamed when He comes in the glory of His Father with the holy angels" (Mark 8:38).

Having considered eight biblical examples of those who "believed" and lived with a shallow faith, calling persons "to believe" is an important part of evangelism. In this next section we will consider the place of calling persons to believe as part of sharing the gospel.

The Role of Believing in Evangelism

The verb *believe* (πιστεύω) was used 100 times in the Gospel of John. The Holy Spirit as the ultimate author of the Bible, worked through John as the human instrument inspiring His Gospel. In so doing, we have off the pen of this author a rich use of this important verb. Certain of these uses relate directly to the means by which the gospel is communicated and received.

This next portion will address the end of the gospel conversation, wherein a person is admonished to respond to the gospel. These examples display what is commended and conveyed by the Holy Spirit to communicate true salvation.

Believing as an Invitation to the Gospel

There are approximately 14 times that the verb πιστεύω (to believe) is used in a verbal call to commitment, depending on how a call to commitment is defined. Five of these calls to commitment are in the form of a question:

1. *And when He had come into the house, the blind men came to Him. And Jesus said to them, "Do you believe [πιστεύω] that I am able to do this?" They said to Him, "Yes, Lord"* (Matthew 9:28).

2. *Jesus heard that they had cast him out; and when He had found him, He said to him, "Do you believe [πιστεύω] in the Son of God?"* (John 9:35).

3. *"And whoever lives and believes [πιστεύω] in Me shall never die. Do you believe this?"* (John 11:26).

4. *Jesus answered them, "Do you now believe [πιστεύω]?"* (John 16:31).

5. *"King Agrippa, do you believe [πιστεύω] the prophets? I know that you believe"* (Acts 26:27 ESV).

Six other calls to commitment are not in question form:

1. *As soon as Jesus heard the word that was spoken, He said to the ruler of the synagogue, "Do not be afraid; only believe [πιστεύω]"* (Mark 5:36).

2. *Jesus said to him, "If you can believe, all things* are *possible to him who believes [πιστεύω]"* (Mark 9:23).

3. *Jesus answered them, "This is the work of God, that you believe [πιστεύω] in him whom he has sent"* (John 6:29 ESV).

4. *"While you have the light, believe [πιστεύω] in the light, that you may become sons of light." These things Jesus spoke, and departed, and was hidden from them* (John 12:36).

5. *Then Jesus cried out and said, "He who believes [πιστεύω] in Me, believes [πιστεύω] not in Me but in Him who sent Me"* (John 12:44).

6. *Then Philip said, "If you believe [πιστεύω] with all your heart, you may." And he answered and said, "I believe [πιστεύω] that Jesus Christ is the Son of God"* (Acts 8:37).

Here are sample New Testament calls to commitment using the verb πιστεύω (to believe). There are also other calls to commitment in the New Testament, for example: "Come to Me" (Matthew 11:28) and "Follow Me" (Mark 1:17). These calls to commitment are descriptive. They also have a prescriptive element in that they can properly be used as models for calling people to believe in or follow after Christ.

The Object of Believing

Or consider this progression in John, with a special look at the object of faith. Here are some examples from John of the verb *believe* with an object:

- *And His disciples believed [πιστεύω] in Him* (John 2:11).

- *And they believed [πιστεύω] the Scripture* (John 2:22).

- *Many believed [πιστεύω] in His name* (John 2:23).

- *And many more believed [πιστεύω] because of His own word* (John 4:41).

- *And many of the people believed [πιστεύω] in Him* (John 7:31).

- *As He spoke these words, many believed [πιστεύω] in Him* (John 8:30).

- *And many believed [πιστεύω] in Him there* (John 10:42).

- *Then many of the Jews … believed [πιστεύω] in Him* (John 11:45).

- *Many of the Jews went away and believed [πιστεύω] in Jesus* (John 12:11).

- *Nevertheless even among the rulers many believed [πιστεύω] in Him* (John 12:42).

Believing "in Him"—that is, in Jesus—is found six times. Believing "in Scripture" is found one time, as is "His own word." Believing "in His name" and "in Jesus" are also found one time each. So, clearly, the object of faith or belief in the Gospel of John is Jesus Christ and His words.

In the Book of Acts, the response of belief is found in 31 passages—to describe a saving response to the gospel. In 16 of these Scriptures we read specific objects of "belief" (πιστεύω):

- "Believed" (without object) as a designation (Acts 2:44; 4:32; 8:13; 11:21; 13:48; 14:1; 15:5; 16:34; 17:12, 34; 18:27; 19:2; 18; 21:20, 25)

- "Believing" after hearing the word (Acts 4:4)

- "Believing" the teaching of the Lord (Acts 13:12)

- "Believing" the word of the gospel (Acts 15:7)

- "Believing all things which are written in the Law and in the Prophets" (Acts 24:14)

- "Believing" the prophets (Acts 26:27)

- "Believing" in the Lord (Acts 5:14; 9:42; 14:23; 18:8)

- "Believing" in the Lord Jesus Christ (Acts 11:17; 16:31)

- "Believing" in this Man (Acts 13:38-39)

- "Believing" in Him (Acts 10:43; 19:4)

- "Believe on You" (Acts 22:19)

- "Believed Philip" (Acts 8:12).

All these designations co-relate to one another. The recipient of the gospel ought not to pick and choose between objects of faith. Believing one implies believing all the others. No other object of belief should be added to these lists—if they are not specifically found in Scripture. The Bible provides all the necessary objects of belief throughout its pages.

Whether it is in calling for commitment or examining a response of belief in those who hear the gospel, the verb "believe" (πιστεύω) is a legitimate and acceptable verb that can and should be used as we tell others about Jesus.

Believing as a Response to the Gospel

In the last example of the use of *believe* in a call to commitment, we found the Ethiopian Eunuch responding also using the verb "believe" (πιστεύω). "I believe," said the eunuch, "that Jesus Christ is the Son of God" (Acts 8:37). This conversation provides an example of instantaneous initiative evangelism, where Philip learned that God was at work in the Ethiopian Eunuch's heart when he heard him reading the Scriptures. The Scriptures had prepared the eunuch's heart to hear and respond to the gospel. Upon meeting Philip, after a conversation of an appropriate length, the eunuch requested baptism. It was at this point that Philip asked him if he believed "with all his heart." The eunuch responded as noted above. His commitment to Christ was conveyed verbally through a confession from his lips.

The following are other New Testament conversations that resulted in the hearer responding to the gospel using the verb believe (πιστεύω):

- *Immediately the father of the child cried out and said with tears, "Lord, I believe [πιστεύω]; help my unbelief!"* (Mark 9:24).

- *Then they said to the woman, "Now we believe [πιστεύω], not because of what you said, for we ourselves have heard Him and we know that this is indeed the Christ, the Savior of the world"* (John 4:42).

- *"Also we have come to believe [πιστεύω] and know that You are the Christ, the Son of the living God"* (John 6:69).

- *Then he said, "Lord, I believe [πιστεύω]!" And he worshiped Him* (John 9:38).

- *She said to Him, "Yes, Lord, I believe [πιστεύω] that You are the Christ, the Son of God, who is to come into the world"* (John 11:27).

- *"Now we are sure that You know all things, and have no need that anyone should question You. By this we believe [πιστεύω] that You came forth from God"* (John 16:30).

According to these verses, the verb "believe" is sufficient to describe a positive response to the gospel.

Believe (πιστεύω) is a powerful verb. By its use the authors of the Bible communicated the absolute assurance of an eternal salvation that is offered in the gospel. Also, by use of this same verb, God warns those who would seek to adhere to a shallow or self-seeking belief. "Believing in Jesus Christ" describes the essence of the gospel call and the attitude that God desires in those who would come to Him for salvation.

CHAPTER TEN

A HEARING OF FAITH
—ἀκούω—

By the time he arrived at Chapter 4 in Hebrews, the Apostle Paul made an interesting point. Appropriating the people of Israel as his example, he combined two very important concepts. First, he used the verb "evangelize" (εὐαγγελίζω). Then to that he added the verb "hearing" (ἀκούω), the noun "hearing" (ἡ ἀκοῆς), and the noun "with faith" (ὁ πίστις):

> For indeed we were evangelized [εὐαγγελίζω], just as they; but the word of their hearing [ἡ ἀκοῆς] did not profit them, not being mixed with faith [ὁ πίστις] in those who heard [ἀκούω] (Hebrews 4:2, translation mine).

The order can be considered as follows:

They were evangelized

Their hearing was unprofitable

Their hearing was not mixed with faith in those who heard.

The subject of the last phrase is "the hearing" of the middle phrase. Hence, there is something important about "the hearing."

While evangelizing and believing (faith) are individually very important concepts, this chapter explores components that link these two together, the principle of *hearing*. *Hearing* is closely linked to the concept of evangelizing. In fact, the absolute necessity of *hearing* the gospel is the focal point of Evangelicalism. People need to "hear" prior to their responding to the gospel. So also, there is the proper type of *hearing*. This *hearing* stands independently of the efforts, effectiveness, and persuasiveness of the proclaimer. There is a spiritual quality in the *hearing* that transcends mere natural *hearing*. Hebrews 4 combined and explained the order and importance of each of these components: evangelizing, hearing, and faith.

Six deductions may be derived from the "Us-Them" comparison-contrast of the author of Hebrews:

1. Evangelized (εὐαγγελίζω)—the same method of communication was made to two groups, "We" and "They":

   a. In other words, the evangelist evangelized wielding the same introduction, content, conclusion, and call to commitment.

   b. The human side of the communication was identical.

2. The word (ὁ λόγος)—the identical message was communicated to both groups:

   a. There was no variance in the verbal, cognitive, or emotive elements of the message.

   b. They both heard identical words with similar analogies and emphases.

3. Of their hearing (ἡ ἀκοῆς)—both groups did in fact have an adequate hearing of the message—"in those who heard":

   a. It was not a partial or incomplete hearing for either group.

4. Hearing (ἀκούω)—the author described two separate means of hearing (or ingesting the message)—unprofitable and profitable:

   a. There were two (and only two) ways listed of absorbing the properly and fully communicated message into their minds and souls.

5. Profit (ὠφελέω)—two opposite results sprung up from how the message was heard—unprofitable and profitable:

   a. The passage later explained that the product of the unprofitable hearing was not entering the promised rest.

   b. The outcome of a profitable hearing was entering that rest.

6. Blending (συγκεράννυμι)—the author clearly defined the distinction involved:

   a. The need for a proper mixing of both hearing (ἀκούω) and faith (ἡ πίστις).

Here is a restatement of this important verse:

> *For indeed we were evangelized, just as they; but the word of their hearing did not profit them, not being mixed with faith in those who heard* (Hebrews 4:2, translation mine).

The Apostle Paul addressed a parallel principle in Romans, reversing the order of "hearing" and "faith."

> *So then faith comes by hearing, and hearing by the word of God* (Romans 10:17).

From the standpoint of Romans, Paul explained that *hearing* must precede faith. He explained that faith emanates from or flows from *hearing*. Thus, faith (or believing) finds its origin in a prerequisite *hearing*. God has so constructed His divine plan of salvation that He uses the *hearing* of the word of God as the trigger for faith to be quickened in the heart of man.

These verses highlight two different aspects related to the origination of faith. In Romans 10, Paul underlined that faith detonates in the human soul through the literal hearing of the words of God. In Hebrews 4, Paul emphasized that a profitable hearing occurs only when faith already exists within the person— blending the hearing with the faith that is already there. So then, there seems to be two sides of the same coin. As far as the principle of believing the message of salvation, faith and hearing are simultaneous ideas. Faith and a hearing of faith are both dependent upon hearing.

In Hebrews 4, Paul focused on the co-mingling of faith and hearing that takes place during the hearing. This mixture blends into a profitable result within the hearer. In the context of Romans 10, Paul addressed the absolute necessity of a person to hear in order to respond with faith. The issue at stake lies between a carnal hearing and a spiritual hearing. In a carnal hearing, the ear is deaf to spiritual truth. In a spiritual hearing, the ear is awake to spiritual truth.

As to the reality that all men do not believe equally upon hearing the gospel, Paul quoted Isaiah 53:1 in Romans 10:16 (one verse prior to the verse cited above):

> But they have not all obeyed the gospel. For Isaiah says, "LORD, who has believed our report?" (Romans 10:16).

Reminiscent of God explaining to Isaiah, "Keep on hearing, but do not understand" (Isaiah 6:9), Isaiah in Chapter 53 used a universal interrogative, "who?" Paul interpreted Isaiah's question, providing him an answer:

> Isaiah: Who has believed our report?

> Paul: Not all have obeyed the gospel.

In classic understatement Paul responded, "not all," to Isaiah's query. "Not all" who hear the gospel will obey it. The differentiation between the "wide road" and "narrow road" as explained by Jesus becomes apparent in evangelism.

Even the verb "obey" in the phrase "they have not all obeyed the gospel" is a contraction from the verb "to hear" (ἀκούω). In the case of "obey" in Romans 10:16, the verb ὑπακούω literally means "harken, listen to, yield to, surrender to, obey." It combines the preposition for "under" (ὑπὸ) with our theme verb for this chapter (ἀκούω). The resulting combination (ὑπὸ + ἀκούω) corresponds to "coming under the authority of what is heard." So, not everyone who hears the gospel will respond positively to it by obeying its mandates to repent and believe.

Nevertheless, the New Testament confirms the importance of a proper "hearing" to lead to a positive response to the gospel. The theme verb for this chapter, ἀκούω ("hearing") and its cognates, are used 466 times in the New Testament—a nice-sized pool of uses from which to make firm conclusions as to the meaning of the verb. This chapter will unpack the concept of "hearing" in the Bible, showing its necessity in the work of the gospel.

The Need to Hear

Paul brought out the need "to hear" the gospel in his classic sequence of rhetorical questions in Romans 10:14-15:

> How then will they call on him in whom they have not believed? And how are they to believe in him of whom they have never heard [ἀκούω]? And how are they to hear [ἀκούω] without someone preaching? And how are they to preach unless they are sent? As it is written, "How beautiful are the feet of those who preach the good news [εὐαγγελίζω]!" (Romans 10:14-15 ESV).

Here Paul used an inverted chronology of the evangelizing process by starting with the beginning of salvation, "calling on Christ," and working his way back to the preacher being sent out. In this reverse chronology, we find these points being made by Paul:

- Sending out precedes preaching

- Preaching results in hearing

- Hearing results in the heart believing

- Believing leads to the voice calling out.

It must be noted that the word "preacher" in verse 14 comes from the verb "to preach" (κηρύσσω) in a participle form, clearly translated in the ESV, "And how are they to hear without someone preaching?" The difference lies in the meaning of the text. Verse 14 does not focus on the person preaching, the preacher, but rather the verb or the act of preaching.

However, for the purposes of this chapter, it is important to note the pivotal importance of the verb in the middle of this sequence—hearing (ἀκούω). After a person is sent out to preach, and after the preaching is done, then there is a certain kind of "hearing" that must take place for the word to be planted, received, and bear fruit in a person's soul. In this sequence by Paul, the proper response is flagged by the word "believe." Believing is then followed by a verbal calling out to the Lord for salvation. The Scripture that initiated Paul's series of rhetorical questions was from Joel 2:32, "Whoever calls on the name of the LORD shall be saved."

The main ministry of those who are called to obey the Great Commission is to cause people to hear the gospel that they may have the opportunity to "call upon the name of the Lord to be saved." It all begins with the necessity of hearing to believe and obey the gospel. A pivotal tenet of evangelism is the necessity of verbally "hearing" the gospel.

Hearing in John

The idea of hearing and believing is found sprinkled throughout the four Gospels. In the Book of John, a classic verse on hearing and believing is found in John 5:24:

> "Truly, truly, I say to you, whoever hears [ἀκούω] my word and believes him who sent me has eternal life. He does not come into judgment, but has passed from death to life" (John 5:24 ESV).

In this verse, Jesus combined the circumstance of a person hearing His word and simultaneously believing. Once these two conditions had been met, then he was to receive "eternal life." Building from John 1:11-13, the condition of receiving and believing could not be met by the will of the flesh, nor by the will of man, but only by God Himself. Therefore, in the supernatural interaction described in John 5:24, while an evangelist is necessary for someone to hear the gospel, only God can give a "hearing with believing," and only God can give "eternal life." Of necessity, for God to act, the only condition to be met is the necessary "hearing" of the word of God!

And yet John 5:24 does not stand alone as far as hearing. In John 1, the disciples of John the Baptist hear Jesus and they immediately follow Him (John 1:37, 40). In John 4:42, we have the astonishing statement of the people of Sychar:

> Then they said to the woman, "Now we believe, not because of what you said, for we ourselves have heard [ἀκούω] Him and we know that this is indeed the Christ, the Savior of the world" (John 4:42).

This verse also combines hearing (ἀκούω) and believing, along with a testimony of Jesus as the Christ. In verse 39 the townspeople believed "because of the word of the woman." Then in verse 42 they believed because of His words. Later Jesus drew a line in the sand. The line of salvation depended upon a proper hearing of His words, both positively, as well as negatively:

> *"It is written in the prophets, 'And they shall all be taught by God.' Therefore everyone who has heard [ἀκούω] and learned from the Father comes to Me"* (John 6:45).

> *"He who is of God hears [ἀκούω] God's words; therefore you do not hear [οὐ + ἀκούω], because you are not of God"* (John 8:47).

There is much more in John about a proper hearing. For example, consider Jesus' teaching on being the good shepherd in John 10:

- *The sheep hear his voice* (v. 3)

- *And the sheep follow him, for they know his voice* (v. 4)

- *All who ever came before Me are thieves and robbers, but the sheep did not hear them* (v. 8).

Likewise, just prior to His death, Jesus said to Pilate, "Everyone who is of the truth hears [ἀκούω] My voice" (John 18:37).

Several Case Studies in John

John's Gospel is filled with interesting examples of understanding and misunderstanding. The following are several case studies to whet the reader's appetite. These case studies portray the centrality of a proper hearing, as well as diversity in hearing.

Nicodemus in John 3

When Jesus mentioned the unalterable necessity of being born again to enter the kingdom of God, Nicodemus answered with two somewhat sarcastic questions:

> *Nicodemus said to him, "How can a man be born when he is old? Can he enter a second time into his mother's womb and be born?"* (John 3:4 ESV).

Through these questions and one found in verse 9, "How can these things be?" Nicodemus showed that he had a carnal hearing. Yet if we continue to read the Gospel of John, we find Nicodemus joining Joseph of Arimathea in removing the body of Jesus from the cross

(John 19:38-42). His original carnal hearing was transformed into a spiritual hearing.

The Woman at the Well in John 4

The Samaritan woman that Jesus met at the well of Sychar asked Him several questions which displayed that she did not have spiritual comprehension at first:

> *The woman said to him, "Sir, you have nothing to draw water with, and the well is deep. Where do you get that living water?"* (John 4:11 ESV).

In the course of the conversation, this woman who at first did not have a spiritual understanding of "living water" was granted a spiritual understanding. Many in her city believed in Jesus because of the word that she surmised, "Can this be the Christ?" (John 4:29 ESV).

The Crowds in John 6

The crowds in John 6 wanted to use force to make Jesus their king. Jesus, wise to their superficial delight from receiving a free meal from Him, departed from them. They displayed their lack of a "hearing of faith" in their response to Jesus:

> *Then they said to him, "What must we do, to be doing the works of God?" Jesus answered them, "This is the work of God, that you believe in him whom he has sent." So they said to him, "Then what sign do you do, that we may see and believe you? What work do you perform? Our fathers ate the manna in the wilderness; as it is written, 'He gave them bread from heaven to eat'"* (John 6:28-31 ESV).

In this very sad interchange, Jesus urged the crowd to "believe in Him." They, however, having hardened and blinded hearts, only wanted more food as a sign—even after He had just fed them—5,000 people—the day before. The ongoing blindness of this crowd was proven at the end of Chapter 6, when all of them departed from Jesus, save the twelve apostles. Peter spoke for the twelve when Jesus asked them, "Do you also want to go away?"

> *But Simon Peter answered Him, "Lord, to whom shall we go? You have the words of eternal life. Also we have come to believe and*

know that You are the Christ, the Son of the living God"
(John 6:68-69).

Peter and the other disciples had a "hearing of faith." Although Jesus qualified His statement with regard to Judas saying, "one of you is a devil" (John 6:70). Even among the twelve there was diversity in hearing. On another sad note, none of those who experienced the miracle of Jesus received a hearing of faith through the miracle. One hundred percent—5,000 out of 5,000—of those who fed their stomachs with the bread and fish turned from Jesus. None of them responded in faith by Jesus' obvious miracle. Likewise today, even miracles cannot open the heart and bring the greater miracle of a hearing of faith.

It is the words of Christ that are powerful unto salvation. It is these same words that are powerful unto rejection and persecution. These case studies from John show the complexity of a hearing of faith. In the case of Nicodemus and the Woman at the Well, both started with a carnal hearing, but were granted a spiritual hearing during or after their conversations with Jesus. On the other hand, the crowd in John 6, although they had seen miracles of Jesus were not granted a hearing of faith. Just as "hearing" [ἀκούω] is important in the Book of John, so it is also important in the other Gospels.

Hearing in the Other Gospels

The principle of hearing is taught and exemplified in the other Gospels as well. Jesus taught the absolute necessity of hearing to believe. He also affirmed that there were variations in hearing. In His Parable of the Sower, Jesus considered four distinct ways of hearing. We begin by looking at the need to hear in Matthew, Mark, and Luke.

Four Opportunities to Hear

In the Parable of the Sower, there is one condition that is met by all four soils. Prior to displaying their distinctive features, all four of the soils had the same opportunity to "hear":

"All who hear [ἀκούω] the word of [God's] kingdom..."
(Matthew 13:19, translation mine).

171

"Is he who hears [ἀκούω] the word and..." (Matthew 13:20, 22, 23).

All four soils heard, and all four soils heard the same message—that is, the word.

This same Parable with a similar emphasis is also recorded in Mark 4 and Luke 8. In these and other places Jesus further accentuated the theme of "hearing" in a declaration repeated eight times:

"He who has ears to hear [ἀκούω] let him hear [ἀκούω]" (Matthew 11:15; 13:9, 43; Mark 4:9, 23; 7:16; Luke 8:8; 14:35, translation mine).

For emphasis, Jesus employed a double use of the verb "to hear" (ἀκούω): "to hear" + "hear!" Therefore, "He who has ears to hear let him hear" (Ὁ ἔχων ὦτα ἀκούειν ἀκουέτω). In Mark, then, Jesus added a warning to this declaration:

Then He said to them, "Take heed what you hear [ἀκούω]. With the same measure you use, it will be measured to you; and to you who hear [ἀκούω], more will be given" (Mark 4:24).

In this context, the treasure gifted by God consists not of material things, but of verbal things. This statement runs parallel with the teaching in the Psalms and Proverbs that the word of God values far more than silver or gold. Mark ends his Chapter 4 with the winds and the waves "harkening" unto Jesus' words:

And they feared exceedingly, and said to one another, "Who can this be, that even the wind and the sea obey [ὑπακούω] Him!" (Mark 4:41).

The word "obey" is literally "to listen with attention" or "to submit," hence to obey.

Considering the Prominence of a Carnal Hearing

In the Parable of the Sower, Jesus built on His theme of "having ears to hear." He differentiated the miracle of hearing with understanding with that of hearing without understanding. In an interlude spoken only to His disciples (Matthew 13:10-17; cf. Mark 4; Luke 8), Jesus explained a two-tier hearing: a hearing with understanding and a hearing without understanding. The point of Jesus was this: not everyone had or has a hearing with understanding. To affirm this point Jesus cited Isaiah 6:9-10:

> And he [the Lord] said, "Go, and say to this people: 'Keep on hearing, but do not understand; keep on seeing, but do not perceive.' Make the heart of this people dull, and their ears heavy, and blind their eyes; lest they see with their eyes, and hear with their ears, and understand with their hearts, and turn and be healed" (Isaiah 6:9-10 ESV).

God sent out His prophet Isaiah to His own people—that is, to the circumcised people of Israel—preparing Isaiah that they would hear His message but not comprehend it. They would see but would not perceive. Lest they see with their eyes, hear with their ears, understand with their hearts, and repent to be saved. God did not give Isaiah the positive side of hearing, only the negative—the positive must be deduced as the opposite of the negative. The circumcised people of Israel would not be receptive to God's message through Isaiah. Jesus applied this Old Covenant commissioning of the prophet Isaiah to the New Covenant evangelist spreading the word of the gospel. The general population would be like the circumcised people of Israel in the time of Isaiah. They would hear but not understand (cf. Matthew 7:13-14).

Isaiah responded, "How long? O Lord" (Isaiah 6:11). Jesus answered this question in the Parable of the Sower. As the gospel of the rule (kingdom) of God over individual hearts was to going forth, only a small percentage would respond positively with a hearing of faith, repentance, and belief in Jesus Christ as Lord and Savior. God answered Isaiah's question, the one Man—Jesus—was the coming Root of Jesse (Isaiah 11:1, 10). This Jesus would be the Savior of His remnant, His tenth, His terebinth, His portion, His holy seed (Isaiah 6:13).

The general population will always remain without understanding. Likewise, God gifts only a predetermined percentage from every tribe, tongue, and nation with a hearing of faith. This mysterious design of God has caused consternation among the people of God for centuries. Furthermore, Satan has used this principle to further his schemes of "dividing brothers" (Proverbs 6:19). Yet, even with this discord, God's purposes are being perfectly accomplished—nothing happens outside His sovereign will! And the Parable of the Sower teaches how God sovereignly designates four kinds of hearing among the peoples of the world.

Types of Hearing

There are four receptions of the gospel foretold in the Parable of the Sower. First, there is the wide road with no understanding. Jesus said that the Wicked One snatches the seed out of the heart before it is sown (Matthew 13:19). Is this not the spiritual battle displayed when the word of the gospel goes forth? Evangelism attracts the birds of the air to come. Satan himself lurks about to snatch the seed from a person's heart before it can take root. Is this not the carnal or natural hearing?

The last reception Jesus mentioned is the "good soil." This soil represents a person who hears the word, understands it, and bears fruit. Here we find a picture of the profitable or spiritual hearing as described in Galatians 3:2 and 5 (considered below). Theirs was the "hearing of faith." This hearing represents the good soil.

There is another type of hearing taught in the Parable of the Sower, someone who hears and then turns back. The shallow soil, we are told in Matthew, "hears the word and immediately receives it with joy" (Matthew 13:20 ESV). This representative group of people produce no root. **The location of their deficiency is within themselves.** They have the same opportunities as the other soils: same message and same messenger. Yet, tribulation and persecution drive them to denounce the same word that originally brought them joy.

The weed-infested soil is the third soil. This group of people receives the word, but never bears fruit. They have beautiful stalks and leaves, but they bring no fruit to maturity. Theirs is also a deficiency in hearing with faith.

What can be learned from these soils? There are a variety of responses to the hearing of the gospel. It is not the evangelist's fault if seed does not fall on good soil. Not everyone is good soil.

The wise evangelist will test the soil to discern its receptivity (soils 2-4) or its unreceptivity (soil 1). If it is receptive, he should share the gospel and bring them to as immediate a response as possible. It will take time for the qualities of soils 2-4 to differentiate.

Strong opposition comes to the Christian who holds to the absolute necessity for hearing prior to believing. Although it is clearly taught by Jesus in Matthew, Mark, Luke, and John, other forms of sharing the gospel and responding to it have been formulated. These comments may prepare the evangelist for pushback against the doctrine of "Hearing Alone."

Pushback to Hearing Alone

There exists significant pushback against the doctrine of "Hearing Alone" on three levels:

1. On the absolute need to hear the gospel to respond

2. On the prominence of a carnal hearing

3. On the reality of a differentiated or segmented hearing.

These points have been addressed above. The issue of "hearing" is under attack in other ways. As sometimes happens, pragmatics can trump doctrine. New methodologies are developed which are considered "effective." Being "wise as a serpent" (Matthew 10:16) encourages the Christian to examine everything:

> But test everything; hold fast what is good (1 Thessalonians 5:21 ESV).

Once something is found to be "good," then we can firmly cling to it. Four methodologies have diminished the absolute necessity of "hearing" and responding to what is heard to be saved.

Evangelism by Exemplary Lifestyle Alone

Contemporary culture asks the question: Is there not some other way for a person to be saved other than hearing and believing? The answer to this rhetorical question, to which many contemporaries may desire an affirmative answer, is, "No!" There is no other way. Paul's propositional statement has no wiggle room, "Faith *comes* by hearing, and hearing by the word of God" (Romans 10:17).

While seeking to live an exemplary life is quite laudable, it cannot communicate man's total depravity and the righteousness of Christ alone for salvation. Jesus Himself, who lived a perfect and sinless life, was poorly received in His hometown. Mark 6 recounts that after hearing (ἀκούω) Jesus, those in Nazareth were astonished, offended, and unbelieving (Mark 6:2, 3, 6). If Jesus' perfect lifestyle did not open the hearts of those who knew Him best, surely we cannot be "greater than our Master"? (John 15:20).

In fact, even the miracles of Jesus did not tenderize people's hearts to His message. Consider this interesting interchange in John:

> *"I and the Father are one." The Jews picked up stones again to stone him. Jesus answered them, "I have shown you many good works from the Father; for which of them are you going to stone me?" The Jews answered him, "It is not for a good work that we are going to stone you but for blasphemy, because you, being a man, make yourself God"* (John 10:30-33 ESV).

So, here in John 10, their opposition to the words of Jesus was so strong that they were ready to kill Him, even after He raised Lazarus from the dead. It was not the miracles of Jesus that opened their hearts, rather His words and teachings resulted in the Jews hating Him!

Salvation Merely by Good Works

A number of scenarios may be presented to prove that it is not necessary to limit ourselves to the Pauline "hearing and believing." Posited conceptions include:

- Those who have responded to the Light through general revelation planted in their hearts by God

- Those who have dreams about God, Christ, or a messenger of Christ coming to them

- Those who have responded to crumbs of "truth" about God from within their false religions

- Those who have never heard the gospel.

Those never having the opportunity to hear the gospel cannot be condemned to an eternal hell, can they? The answer to this question cast the Apostle Paul on a lifelong journey of evangelism. It is laudable and necessary to desire that as many people as possible be saved. But the answer to this dilemma lies not in changing one's doctrinal convictions, but in changing one's practice to conform to the biblical pattern. When the biblical boundaries of hearing and believing are lost, total depravity and total inability are likewise jettisoned—and with them every other major doctrine of biblical Christianity.

State Religion

A third reason for significant pushback comes with the notion that a human governmental system should preside over the conscience of man. To optimize such an arrangement, a number of doctrines must be tweaked. Foremost among these is forecasting a general or universal salvation. Jesus' teachings about the many and the few became an overstatement by the Master:

> *"Enter by the narrow gate; for wide* is *the gate and broad* is *the way that leads to destruction, and there are many who go in by it. Because narrow* is *the gate and difficult* is *the way which leads to life, and there are few who find it"* (Matthew 7:13-14).

For state religion, these words of Jesus must be reversed: "Enter by the wide gate," says the state-church, "for the gate is narrow that leads to destruction, and there are only a few who go by it." Everyone born in a country where there is a government-monopoly state-church is expected to "hear and understand" the gospel. The "few" become those who do not submit to the state-church interrelationship for one reason or another. These "few" are the problem people needing to be silenced into submission to the majority religion.

Infant Baptism

Closely on the heels of a state-church arrangement is the need for a mechanism to enter every citizen into a relationship with the church. For this to take place, another doctrine of Jesus must be tweaked—the doctrine that blood, the will of man, and the will of the flesh have no part in man's spiritual "new birth." This threefold denial of human intermediacy in genuine conversion must be reshuffled to allow man to be the authorizing agent in salvation:

He came to His own, and His own did not receive Him. But as many as received Him, to them He gave the right to become children of God, to those who believe in His name: who were born, not of blood, nor of the will of the flesh, nor of the will of man, but of God (John 1:11-13).

Whereas the Gospel of John clearly states that God's children are born "not of blood, nor of the will of the flesh, nor of the will of man," a state-run church necessitates human leverage in the conversion process. Government-approved personnel (priests or pastors) must be deeded with the human authority to make a divine third-party decision on behalf of the spiritual rebirth of others. Enter infant baptism. The following is Article 27 of the 1572 Thirty-Nine Articles of the Church of England related to baptism (with modernized spelling):

XXVII. Of Baptism.

Baptism is not only a sign of profession, and mark of difference, whereby Christian men are discerned from others that be not christened: but it is also a sign of regeneration or new birth, whereby, as by an instrument, they that receive baptism rightly, are grafted into the Church: the promises of the forgiveness of sin, and of our adoption to be the sons of God, by the holy ghost, are visibly signed and sealed: faith is confirmed: and grace increased by virtue of prayer unto God.

The baptism of young children, is in any wise to be retained in the Church, as most agreeable with the institution of Christ.

The reader will note, that for this Protestant church, infant baptism retained some of the Sacramental notions that had evolved within Roman Catholicism. They emphasized human priests and pastors initiating babies into the church by baptism, while offering these babies all the doctrines associated with conversion and justification in the New Testament. These novel notions of third-party baptism developed from the state-church partnership going back to Constantine the Great (fourth century A.D.).

Meanwhile, the biblical verbs related to the Great Commission have received minimal attention in Early Church creeds, Medieval Councils, and Confessions of Faith. The pushback against solely "hearing and believing" for salvation is longstanding and deeply entrenched. Fortunately, Luther revived the need to hear with "Scriptures alone." Yet the pre-Reformation theology has influenced textbooks in systematics, Greek Lexicography, Bible translation, and even original language texts. Amazingly, it was not until the late nineteenth century that Acts 8:37 (exemplifying a verbal response prior to receiving baptism) was removed from "critical edition" Greek texts. Meanwhile, salvation has not changed one iota, "faith still comes by hearing and hearing by the word of God."

Hearing in the Book of Acts

Acts is a book about making the word of God heard and responses to this word as it is heralded. In a narrative section at the end of the first sermon of Peter in Acts 2 Luke used three verbs:

> Now when they heard this they were cut to the heart, and said to Peter and the rest of the apostles, "Brothers, what shall we do?" (Acts 2:37 ESV).

Here are the three verbs:

- Hearing (ἀκούω)

- Being cut (κατανύσσω) to the heart

- Saying (λέγω), "Brothers, what shall we do?"

Upon hearing, the two-edged sword did its work, and some of the listeners were "cut to the heart." Further, they initiated the follow-up question related to receiving salvation, "Men and brothers, what shall we do?" And Peter followed up with his first piece of advice for those who in all ages are cut to the heart by the word of God:

> And Peter said to them, "Repent and be baptized every one of you in the name of Jesus Christ for the forgiveness of your sins, and you will receive the gift of the Holy Spirit. For the promise is for you and for your children and for all who are far off, everyone

whom the Lord our God calls to himself" (Acts 2:38-39 ESV).

And it was all initiated through the preaching of Peter being "heard" (ἀκούω).

Luke used another set of verbs to describe the response of the crowd after they heard the sermon of Stephen in Acts 7:

- Hearing (ἀκούω)

- Being cut (διαπρίω) to the heart

- Gnashing (βρύχω) their teeth at him (Acts 7:54).

It is clear that "hearing" does not always elicit the same response!

The focal point of the 93 New Testament uses of the verb "to hear" and its cognates in Acts is found in Acts 15:7-11. "Hearing" (ἀκούω) appears only once in this passage. But like Romans 10 and Hebrews 4, "hearing" was the spark that burned salvation within the hearts of the Gentile hearers in the home of Cornelius:

> *And after there had been much debate, Peter stood up and said to them, "Brothers, you know that in the early days God made a choice among you, that by my mouth the Gentiles should hear the word of the gospel and believe. And God, who knows the heart, bore witness to them, by giving them the Holy Spirit just as he did to us, and he made no distinction between us and them, having cleansed their hearts by faith. Now, therefore, why are you putting God to the test by placing a yoke on the neck of the disciples that neither our fathers nor we have been able to bear? But we believe that we will be saved through the grace of the Lord Jesus, just as they will"* (Acts 15:7-11 ESV).

In this passage, we find numerous doctrines important to the Protestant Reformation, a passage to which Luther and Calvin were drawn because of Paul's words in Galatians 1:8-9. The doctrines enclosed in Acts 15 are:

- A Necessary Evangelist: "God made a choice among you, that by my mouth"

- By Hearing Alone: "the Gentiles should hear [ἀκούω]"

- By Scriptures Alone: "the word of the gospel"

- By Faith Alone upon Hearing the Word of the Gospel: "and believe"

- The Seal of the Holy Spirit: "And God, who knows the heart, bore witness to them by giving them the Holy Spirit just as he did to us"

- The Cleansing of Hearts in True Salvation: "and he made no distinction between us and them, having cleansed their hearts"

- Purification by Faith Alone: "by faith"

- Salvation Not by Works: "Now, therefore, why are you putting God to the test by placing a yoke on the neck of the disciples that neither our fathers nor we have been able to bear?"

- By Grace Alone through Christ Alone: *"But we believe that we will be saved through the grace of the Lord Jesus, just as [in the same manner as] they will"* (Acts 15:7-11 ESV).

It is amazing to see such a wonderful salvation accomplished for men and so clearly laid forth. A similar outlining can be applied to Romans 3:19-26 to great effect.

The sequence of salvation is initiated when the God-appointed evangelist opens his mouth and begins to verbally declare the word of the gospel. And once the evangelist speaks God's words, then— just like pulling the trigger of a machine gun—it leads to a divinely ordered series of sequential actions. The Book of Acts exposes numerous such salvific series of actions. For example, in Acts 18 we find another sequence of verbs painting God's method of salvation:

> When Silas and Timothy had come from Macedonia, Paul was compelled by the Spirit, and testified to the Jews that Jesus is the Christ. ... Then Crispus, the ruler of the synagogue, believed on the Lord with all his household. And many of the Corinthians, hearing, believed and were baptized (Acts 18:5, 8).

Consider these verbs:

- Compelled (συνέχω)

- Testified (διαμαρτύρομαι)

- Hearing (ἀκούω)

- Believed (πιστεύω)

- Were baptized (βαπτίζω).

After Paul had reasoned in the synagogue, and having persuaded both Jews and Greeks (Acts 18:4), then Silas and Timothy came. This arrival spurred the series of verbs above, used by Luke to canonize Paul's ministry methodology. He was (1) compelled by the Spirit, he then (2) testified about Jesus, this allowed that (3) many of the Corinthians heard, and as it turned out, (4) many of them believed, who were thereupon also (5) water baptized.

Central in these five verbs is the verb "to hear" (ἀκούω). Hearing is the glue between evangelizing and believing. And as we saw at the beginning of this chapter, there are two kinds of hearing, one that does not profit, and one that is mixed with faith. In order to develop this idea, let us consider hearing in Paul.

Hearing in Paul's Writings

Whereas Paul argued for the essential nature of hearing in Romans 10, in other contexts, Paul discussed different types of hearing. There is a type of hearing that does not profit the hearer, this can be called a "carnal" or "fleshly hearing." It is hearing that does not comprehend the spiritual dimensions of what is being said. Much like the early hearing of Nicodemus or the Woman at the Well, while Jesus was making spiritual application, His hearers heard in a carnal sense.

Paul differentiated between a carnal hearing and a hearing of faith in Galatians 3. He spoke of a carnal hearing as related to seeking to obey the letter of the Law. And he spoke of a hearing of faith as providing justification apart from the Law. In Galatians 3:1-5 Paul asked the Galatian Christians at least six rhetorical questions. In so doing, he was challenging the Galatian church to contemplate the core cause of their salvation. The fount of their salvation sprang from "a hearing with faith."

O foolish Galatians! Who has bewitched you that you should not obey [believe] the truth, before whose eyes Jesus Christ was clearly portrayed among you as crucified? This only I want to learn from you: Did you receive the Spirit by the works of the law, or by the hearing of faith? Are you so foolish? Having begun in the Spirit, are you now being made perfect by the flesh? Have you suffered so many things in vain—if indeed it was in vain? Therefore He who supplies the Spirit to you and works miracles among you, does He do it by the works of the law, or by the hearing of faith?—just as Abraham "believed God, and it was accounted to him for righteousness" (Galatians 3:1-6).

By the way, what did Abraham believe as recorded in Genesis 15:6? He believed the word of the Lord: "And behold, the word of the LORD came to him: 'This man shall not be your heir; your very own son shall be your heir'" (Genesis 15:4 ESV). When he heard (ἀκούω) that "word of the LORD," then Moses wrote, "And he believed the LORD, and he counted it to him as righteousness" (Genesis 15:6 ESV).

So, in Galatians 3, Paul was juxtaposing "a hearing of faith" with "the works of the Law." In Hebrews 4:2 was juxtaposed "a hearing mixed with faith" and "a hearing that did not profit them." In 1 Corinthians 1:18 Paul described the message of the cross as "foolishness to those who are perishing," but as the power of God "to us who are being saved." In 2 Corinthians 2:15-16, Paul described the gospel as "the aroma of death" to those who are perishing, but "the aroma of life" to those who are being saved. Oh, the unfathomable designs of God's mercy and grace. Everything He does is right, and all His works shall praise Him.

Other Verbs Directly Related to Hearing (ἀκούω)

The Bible uses several other verbs with the stem "to hear" (ἀκούω). Each of these verbs fills in the doctrinal and methodological importance of hearing.

Refusing to Listen (παρακούω)

An interesting Greek word found in the New Testament several times uses the root word for "to hear" (ἀκούω). The preposition παρά (meaning beside, toward, or against) is added to the beginning of the word—which alters its meaning. The verb, "to refuse to listen" (παρακούω) is found twice in the New Testament related to seeking to restore a brother living in sin:

If he refuses to listen [παρακούω] to them, tell it to the church. And if he refuses to listen [παρακούω] even to the church, let him

183

be to you as a Gentile and a tax collector" (Matthew 18:17 ESV).

Though not used in the context of evangelizing, it is used in the difficult context of seeking to restore a brother. Likewise, sometimes people refuse to listen to the gospel.

Listening Attentively (ἐπακούω and εἰσακούω)

It also happens in witness that certain persons listen attentively. Sometimes prepositions added to the root "to hear" (ἀκούω) intensify its meaning. Two of these are: ἐπακούω and εἰσακούω. The word εἰσακούω is used five times in the New Testament, four times in the context of God hearing prayer and once where man does not listen to God. This last example is found in 1 Corinthians 14:

> In the Law it is written, "By people of strange tongues and by the lips of foreigners will I speak to this people, and even then they will not listen [οὐδέ + εἰσακούω] to me, says the Lord" (1 Corinthians 14:21 ESV, citing Isaiah 28:11-12).

God was said to have listened attentively to men praying, "Zacharias, your prayer has been heard [εἰσακούω]" (Luke 1:13). Yet, as Isaiah noted, God's own people didn't have the same regard to listen to Him as He did listening to them!

But even more stunning, God especially hears us as we call on Him for salvation:

> For he says, "In a favorable time I listened [ἐπακούω] to you, and in a day of salvation I have helped you." Behold, now is the favorable time; behold, now is the day of salvation (2 Corinthians 6:2 ESV, citing Isaiah 49:8).

It appears from these verses, as God's evangelists are faithful in giving the gospel call to all men, God has chosen the perfect time (καιρῷ δεκτῷ) for that gospel call to be sown into the hearts of the elect—"whom we know not except by the event" (paraphrasing John Owen). God Himself inclines His ear from heaven, waiting for His own to respond to that gospel call, so that He can save in the day of salvation.

Hearing to Obey (ὑπακούω)

The verb meaning "harken," "listen to obey," or "hearing to obey" is the Greek verb ὑπακούω. In an unusual way, this verb bridges the gap between a "hearing of faith" and obedience. Often the order of salvation is that we are saved by obeying. However, built into this verb is the need to hear first, to hear attentively, and to obey that which is said.

The word is derived from combining "to hear" (ἀκούω) with the preposition for "under" (ὑπό). The implication is as follows: a hearing with understanding confirmed by obeying what is said. Therefore a "hearing of faith" precedes "obedience of faith."

It is used of inanimate objects, such as the winds and waves obeying the command of Jesus to be still. It is used of demons obeying Jesus as He said, "Come out." It is used of obeying parents and masters. It is used of being "obedient" to righteousness (Romans 6:16-18). But it is also used of "obeying the faith":

> And the word of God continued to increase, and the number of the disciples multiplied greatly in Jerusalem, and a great many of the priests became obedient [ὑπακούω] to the faith (Acts 6:7 ESV).

It is also used of those who "don't obey [μὴ ὑπακούω] the gospel of our Lord Jesus Christ" (2 Thessalonians 1:8).

Evangelicalism is centered on the need to hear the gospel and to believe. Salvation does not come through the Sacraments. Salvation does not come by acts of love, charity, or mercy. Salvation does not find any human activity in its incipient moment, in its mid-point, or in its culmination. Salvation rests solely on the grace of God who gives a hearing of faith to some. The only human element necessary to salvation is a proclaimer of the gospel.

God requires all men to hear and submit to His voice as He speaks through His holy word by His messengers speaking that word:

> Faith comes by hearing, and hearing by the word of God (Romans 10:17).

> And how will they hear without someone preaching? (Romans 10:14 ESV).

God grants a hearing of faith to some, whereas others continue with a carnal hearing. Some have a spiritual hearing. Those on the wide road hear with their temporal ears. The Christian sows the seed of the gospel into the souls of others, and the Holy Spirit cooperates with the gospel, wooing all who are willing to listen by His still small voice, guiding them to a hearing of faith. Two conclusions are clear from this study:

1. It is the Christian's responsibility for all people to hear the gospel

2. It is only God who can give a hearing of faith.

CHAPTER ELEVEN

SOME WERE PERSUADED
—πείθω—

The Greek verb having the broad meaning "to persuade" is πείθω. It is not only interesting as a verb, but its New Testament uses makes it a fascinating verb. We find it uttered from the mouth of an 8- to 10-year-old boy in Acts 23:

> "But do not be persuaded by them, for more than forty of their men are lying in ambush for him, who have bound themselves by an oath neither to eat nor drink till they have killed him. And now they are ready, waiting for your consent" (Acts 23:21 ESV).

"Do not be persuaded by them," the young nephew of Paul pleaded for his uncle's life, having heard of a plot to ambush and kill him.

Paul's Persuading

Three chapters later, we read the most extensive salvation testimony of Paul in the Book of Acts. While Paul is in the middle of telling his story, Festus, the governor of Judea, interrupted Paul. Paul had just mentioned the resurrection of Jesus when Festus spoke to him by name:

> "Paul, you are out of your mind! Your great learning is driving you out of your mind!" (Acts 26:24 ESV).

Right after this comment, Paul focused all his persuasive powers to win over King Agrippa to the Savior:

> But Paul said, "I am not out of my mind, most excellent Festus, but I am speaking true and rational words. For the king knows about these things, and to him I speak boldly. For I am persuaded [πείθω] that none of these things has escaped his notice, for this has not been done in a corner. King Agrippa, do you believe the prophets? I know that you believe" (Acts 26:25-27 ESV).

The king responded to Paul:

> *"In a short time would you persuade [πείϑω] me to be a Christian?"* (Acts 26:28 ESV).

From the mouth of King Agrippa then, we have him say that Paul was seeking to "persuade" (πείθω) him. And it is in this context that we may best understand the powerful use of this mighty verb—that is, in persuading others to believe in Jesus as their Savior and Lord.

Here is a synopsis of the use of this verb *persuade* from the pen of Luke:

1. Luke uses of the verb "persuade" (πείθω) 21 times (Luke, 4 times; Acts, 17 times)

2. Luke describes Paul's use of persuasion in evangelism (cf. Acts 17:4)

3. Acts 26 (above) provides the only example of Paul's use of this verb in direct address in Acts

4. All the other uses of the verb "persuade" (πείθω) in Acts related to Paul's ministry are in Luke's editorial summaries, with the exception of Demetrius' antagonistic use of this verb in Acts 19:26.

Paul's words to King Agrippa provide a prototype of Paul's persuasive speech. First of all, in sharing his testimony in Acts 26:2-23, Paul explained the gospel three times (using Luke 24:46-47 as the rubric). In other words, his testimony was gospel-centered. Second, Paul was respectful throughout his speech, and especially after he was interrupted by Festus. Consider that he addressed Festus as "most noble Festus." His words were not the illogical babblings of a madman. Rather Paul was speaking truth with clarity and lucidity. Third, Paul addressed King Agrippa directly as "the king"—bringing focus to his persuasion. In fact, he used the word "king" four times before he was interrupted, the fourth time including his name, "King Agrippa." Then in his persuasive response to the interruption, Paul twice used the word "king" and the second time he again used Agrippa's proper name, "King Agrippa." Fourth, the prisoner Paul spoke boldly before King Agrippa. His bold speech was found in his use of παρρησιάζομαι ("I speak freely"), as well as in his calling the king to believe, twice using the verb "believe" (πιστεύω) in Acts 26:27. The boldness of Paul was unmistakable!

Perhaps Paul noted something of an open spirit in the eyes or countenance of the king that led him to press home the gospel. Fifth, Paul used a question, "King Agrippa, do you believe the prophets?" There are 1,024 questions in the New Testament. Most of them are in conversational or rhetorical portions. Paul dared to address the king with a direct question, "Do you believe?" The Greek appears even more emphatic, since there is no interrogative pronoun (do, what, why). Whereas in Greek the verb is normally at the end of the sentence, in this sentence, Paul began with the verb "believe": "Believe [you], O King Agrippa, the prophets?" Nor did he use the second person plural, as may be expected—a plural of majesty. Nor did he use the subjunctive mood, "May you believe in the prophets?" or in the optative mood, "Would you believe the prophets?" Rather, Paul was very bold in addressing the king directly in the singular form, in the second person present active, "Do you believe the prophets?"

Paul was incremental in his question. He did not say, "Do you believe in Jesus?" Paul sought to discern if the king had a spiritual hearing to the words of the gospel. So Paul asked him a parallel question related to the prophetic writings of the Old Testament Prophets. This question flowed rather naturally from his prior discourse:

> "To this day I have had the help that comes from God, and so I stand here testifying both to small and great, saying nothing but what the prophets and Moses said would come to pass" (Acts 26:22 ESV).

Sixth, Paul concludes with a comment of affirmation, "I know that you believe." Paul was expectant in his evangelism—expectant that the word of God would reach its mark—expectant that King Agrippa would be gripped to repent and believe.

One must remember that Paul is uttering these words before an audience of perhaps a hundred or more people (Acts 25:23). Luke described the locality as an auditorium filled with the military commanders and prominent men and women of the city:

> So the next day, when Agrippa and Bernice had come with great pomp, and had entered the auditorium with the commanders and the prominent men of the city, at Festus' command Paul was brought in (Acts 25:23).

And yet Holy Spirit boldness allowed the Apostle Paul to focus not on defending himself of false charges against him, but rather on his personal testimony of salvation. And this he did directly and persuasively to the one person in the room who was to judge the matter, King Agrippa. Consider also that King Agrippa, Festus, and Bernice found him innocent of all charges:

> Then the king rose, and the governor and Bernice and those who were sitting with them. And when they had withdrawn, they said to one another, "This man is doing nothing to deserve death or imprisonment." And Agrippa said to Festus, "This man could have been set free if he had not appealed to Caesar" (Acts 26:30-32 ESV).

The king replied to Paul:

> And Agrippa said to Paul, "In a short time would you persuade [πείθω] me to be a Christian?" (Acts 26:28 ESV).

Paul spoke the last recorded public words of the evening:

> And Paul said, "Whether short or long, I would to God that not only you but also all who hear [ἀκούω] me this day might become such as I am—except for these chains" (Acts 26:29 ESV).

Paul's heart desire was for all who heard (ἀκούω) him to be saved. To this end, Paul exerted every effort and all his knowledge of Scripture to persuade others to turn to Christ for salvation. In this amazing context, Luke's pen does not fail to deliver context and content to the verb "persuade" used 54 times in the New Testament.

Πείθω in Acts

The Book of Acts contains 17 uses of the Greek verb for "persuade" (πείθω). Two of those are in Acts 26 as seen above. However, the first three uses of this verb in Acts 5 provides a definitional basis for Luke's use of "persuade" (πείθω) in Acts. These first three uses are found in Acts 5:36-40.

What is interesting about these three uses of "persuade" is that they do not relate to evangelism, the gospel, or the disciples. Rather, they are twice used in the context of the persuasive efforts of the failed false christs, Theudas and Judas. The third use describes the persuasive efforts of Rabbi Gamaliel in his discourse before the Council or Sanhedrin. Here is the discourse and the narrative of Luke:

> But a Pharisee in the council named Gamaliel, a teacher of the law held in honor by all the people, stood up and gave orders to put the men [apostles] outside for a little while. And he said to them, "Men of Israel, take care what you are about to do with these men. For before these days Theudas rose up, claiming to be somebody, and a number of men, about four hundred, joined him. He was killed, and all who followed [πείθω] him were dispersed and came to nothing. After him Judas the Galilean rose up in the days of the census and drew away some of the people after him. He too perished, and all who followed [πείθω] him were scattered. So in the present case I tell you, keep away from these men and let them alone, for if this plan or this undertaking is of man, it will fail; but if it is of God, you will not be able to overthrow them. You might even be found opposing God!" So they took his advice [πείθω], and when they had called in the apostles, they beat them and charged them not to speak in the name of Jesus, and let them go (Acts 5:34-40 ESV).

The astute reader will consider that the word "persuade" is translated as "follow" twice and "took ... advice" once. Why is that? The passive use of the verb is "be persuaded," which can be translated, "be convinced [or] persuaded, believe" or even as "obey"—with the dative of a person or thing in which they put their trust. Hence, the translators of the ESV translated differently. For the sake of evaluative purposes, let us translated the three uses using the verb "persuade":

- Of Theudas (v. 36): *He was killed, and all who followed [πείθω] him were dispersed and came to nothing.*

- Of Judas (v. 37): *He too perished, and all who followed [πείθω] him were scattered.*

- Of Gamaliel (v. 40): *So they took his advice [πείθω], and when they had called in the apostles, they beat them and charged them not to speak in the name of Jesus, and let them go.*

How did Luke use the word persuade (πείθω) in these contexts?

1. Negatively: the verb πείθω was used of the efforts of false teachers seeking to draw away disciples after themselves.

2. Positively: the verb πείθω was used of the positive rhetorical efforts of Gamaliel—although the apostles still received beating; Gamaliel was a noted Pharisee and the Apostle Paul's primary teacher in Jerusalem (Acts 22:3).

3. Exemplified: Luke cited Gamaliel's persuasive efforts (πείθω), so that readers could understand contextually what Luke meant when he used this verb.

So, what does Gamaliel's discourse teach about Luke's intention when he used the verb "persuade"? It was used not only of protagonists, but also of antagonists of the gospel—hence, it does not have an automatically divine or Spirit-filled usage from Luke's pen. But also, when persons are persuaded it will impact their future actions based on the words that persuaded them.

Πείθω In Matthew

All three uses of "persuade" (πείθω) in Matthew are from the crucifixion and resurrection narratives—being used by antagonists of Christ:

- Of the chief priests and elders: *Now the chief priests and the elders persuaded [πείθω] the crowd to ask for Barabbas and destroy Jesus* (Matthew 27:20 ESV).

- Of the mocking crowds: *"He trusts [πείθω] in God; let God deliver him now, if he desires him. For he said, 'I am the Son of God'"* (Matthew 27:43 ESV).

- Of the elders encouraging the soldiers to lie about the resurrection, assuring them that they would pay off the governor: *"And if this comes to the governor's ears, we will satisfy [πείθω] him and keep you out of trouble"* (Matthew 28:14 ESV).

What an interesting and emotive term. It is used twice of the persuasive efforts of the chief priests and elders. Then it is used in the crowing of the crowds against Jesus when he was on the cross dying for the sins of the world.

Interestingly, the Greek Septuagint uses a different Greek word when describing the words that the people would speak against Jesus on the cross. Psalm 22:8 [21:9] has the Greek verb ἐλπίζω (to hope): "He hoped in the Lord, let Him deliver Him..." The verb comes from the Hebrew *galal*, meaning literally "to roll" and with a spiritual meaning "to commit." Consider that King David prophesied in Hebrew what the crowds at the cross would be saying in Greek—1000 years before the event!

However, Matthew records that the crowds used the Greek verb πείθω in their mocking. Matthew's provenance comes after the crucifixion. The Septuagint was a second century B.C. translation. Therefore, Matthew trumps the Septuagint. Spurred on by Satan himself, the mocking crowds slandered Jesus using the strongest verb that they could find to describe His unflinching commitment to His Father's will.

Unpacking Gamaliel's Persuading

In the case of Gamaliel's persuasive technique in the Acts 5 passage cited above, the following are some characteristics of persuasion in the Book of Acts:

1. Gamaliel's words of persuasion are related to a warning: "Men of Israel, take care what you are about to do with these men" (Acts 5:35 ESV).

2. Gamaliel used specific illustrations and named people to buttress his point: Theudas and Judas.

3. Gamaliel used the second person plural four times in his discourse; twice in his introduction, "take care" and "what you are about to do" (Acts 5:35 ESV); and twice in his conclusion, "you will not be able to overthrow them" and "You might even be found opposing God" (Acts 5:39 ESV).

4. Gamaliel explained two ultimatums of their predicament, if they were to oppose the disciples of Christ:

    a. They would be fighting a futile war which they could not win—i.e. "Choose your battles wisely."

b. They may actually find themselves fighting against God—remembering that this account came right after the miraculous jailbreak of Acts 5:19-20.

Gamaliel's "persuading" (πείθω) won the day. The Sanhedrin did, however, go on to have the disciples beaten. Yet Gamaliel's example of persuasion proves helpful as we consider that Luke used this same word of Paul's customary methods in the proclamation of the gospel.

These three uses of the verb "persuade" (πείθω) surrounding Gamaliel's "persuasion" are the first three uses of this verb in Acts. Therefore, it is not unreasonable to consider that these usages provided Luke an opportunity to describe this term in relation to its nine uses in evangelism settings in Acts.

Persuasion in Evangelism

Transferring these same characteristics as noted in the usage of Gamaliel to evangelizing with persuasion, several points can be made. First, to share the gospel in its complete form, the message shared should include a warning. Paul said, "Warning everyone and teaching everyone with all wisdom" (Colossians 1:28 ESV). Surely persuasion is necessary to warn people about the benefits of the gospel and the perils of hell. It follows that a warning implies persuasion to the point of decision. Further, a negative response to warning will either bring persecution or necessitate shaking off the dust from one's feet (Matthew 10:14). Second, although care should be taken in naming names as negative examples for persuasion, it is warranted in Gamaliel's speech, as well as in several examples in 1 and 2 Timothy. Third, the use of "you" may provide persuasion in driving home a point of application. Fourth, New Testament persuasion includes explaining the ultimate results of the hearer's decisions and actions.

And yet, the use of the word "persuade" (πείθω) does not always accompany a "win" for the one persuading. There are two clear cases in Acts where the person or people doing the "persuading" (πείθω) were unsuccessful in their efforts. In Acts 21, Luke and others with him sought to persuade Paul not to go to Jerusalem. They pleaded, begged, or urged (παρακαλέω) Paul not to go. But they gave up when they saw that Paul could not be persuaded:

> And since he would not be persuaded [μή + πείθω], we ceased and said, "Let the will of the Lord be done" (Acts 21:14 ESV).

In this case, the negative particle μή preceded the verb. In Acts 27 two persons were trying to persuade the ship's captain in two different directions. Paul warned the centurion that the voyage would be dangerous:

> "Sirs [Paul said], I perceive that the voyage will be with injury and much loss, not only of the cargo and the ship, but also of our lives" (Acts 27:10 ESV).

The next verse tells us:

> But the centurion paid more attention [πείθω] to the pilot and to the owner of the ship than to what Paul said (Acts 27:11 ESV).

This verse implies that Paul, the pilot, and the ship's owner were all seeking to persuade the centurion about whether or not to take the voyage. In this case, Paul did not win the argument. The centurion was more persuaded by the other two. As the chapter fills out, the trip was hazardous and there was a shipwreck. Yet, because of Paul's presence, all those aboard were miraculously spared alive. Whether win or lose, it is clear from New Testament usage, that merely using persuasion does not always result in the desired response in the hearer.

An interesting parallel to Acts 27:11 is a similar usage of persuade (πείθω) in Acts 28:24. Used in this verse are both the verb "persuade" (πείθω) and the verb "speak" (λέγω). In Acts 27:11, they were not persuaded in "the things spoken by Paul." Whereas in Acts 28:24, "they were persuaded by the things spoken [by Paul]." Acts 28:23-24 stand as the two final uses of the verb "persuade" (πείθω) in the Book of Acts. In this case, Paul is persuading (present-active) and some of the hearers were being persuaded (imperfect-passive):

> So when they had appointed him a day, many came to him at his lodging, to whom he explained and solemnly testified of the kingdom of God, persuading [πείθω] them concerning Jesus from both the Law of Moses and the Prophets, from morning till

> evening. And some were persuaded [πείϑω] by the things which
> were spoken, and some disbelieved (Acts 28:23-24).

Here is a breakdown of Paul's persuasive methodology in Acts 28:

- Paul's method: explaining and solemnly testifying

- Paul's urgency: persuading (πείθω)

- Paul's goal: the rule of God over individual hearts

- Paul's message: Jesus

- Paul's documentary evidence: Law of Moses and the Prophets

- Paul's detail: from morning until evening

- Result: Some were persuaded (πείθω) and some disbelieved (ἀπιστέω).

In this last bullet point, we are reminded of the two options available following a persuasive hearing of the gospel: being persuaded or disbelieving. Hence, Luke ended the Book of Acts with another example of Paul's persuasive (πείθω) gospel-sharing.

The verb *persuade* is also found in the middle of the Book of Acts, where Luke introduced Paul's customary method of evangelism. It was communicated in the context of Paul's preliminary evangelizing ministry in Thessalonica in Acts 17:1-4. This Acts 17 portion provides a parallel to the Acts 28 portion above. But in another sense, it is even more normative and important as regards to understanding Paul's missionary ministry. Luke introduced this "customary method" as a blueprint for interpreting the ministry methodology of Paul in the Book of Acts. It is helpful to evaluate how Paul developed this pattern of ministry, and afterwards, if and why Paul departed from this pattern of ministry:

> Now when they had passed through Amphipolis and Apollonia,
> they came to Thessalonica, where there was a synagogue of the
> Jews. Then Paul, as his custom was, went in to them, and for
> three Sabbaths reasoned with them from the Scriptures,
> explaining and demonstrating that the Christ had to suffer and
> rise again from the dead, and saying, "This Jesus whom I preach
> to you is the Christ." And some of them were persuaded [πείϑω];

*and a great multitude of the devout Greeks, and not a few of the
leading women, joined Paul and Silas* (Acts 17:1-4).

The text reminds us that some were persuaded (πείθω). They were
persuaded after a series of verbs and nouns described Paul's
ministry methodology. Paul first arrived on location (Thessalonica).
Second, he noted that there was a synagogue of the Jews (as
mentioned in Acts 15:21). Therefore, third, some in the city were
aware of Moses and the Old Testament Prophets. Those aware of
Moses and the Prophets in Acts were called Jews and proselytes or
godfearers. Third, we read that Paul followed a customary pattern,
"as his custom (ἔθω/εἴωθα) was." Luke used the evangelism of this
city to introduce us to what became Paul's customary ministry
method. Fourth, he went into the synagogue and for a length of
time discoursed with them on the Scriptures. In this case, the
length of his synagogue evangelism was three Sabbaths. Fifth, what
did he say for these three Sabbaths? He opened up (διανοίγω) the
Scriptures and laid out (παρατίθημι) his arguments. Sixth, his main
argument was that the Christ had to suffer and rise from the dead.
This was the exact gospel mentioned in Christ's Great Commission
in Luke 24:46. Seventh, He declared (καταγγέλλω) unto them, that
the Person who fulfilled these prophesies was Jesus—the Christ.
But his customary method did not end there. Eighth, some were
persuaded (πείθω). And who they were is important to note—they
are listed as including a "great multitude of devout Greeks."

This gospel, as described in Acts 17:2-3 was not just for the
Jews, it was also for the Greeks. It was not effective only for the
Jews, it was effective and impactful for the Greeks also, as noted in
Romans 1 and 1 Corinthians 1. The message of the gospel as
communicated in the Book of Romans was not just for the Jews, it
was also for the Greeks, the learned and the unlearned, the Greeks
and the Barbarians. In 1 Corinthians Paul made it clear that the
same one message was foolishness to the Greeks and a stumbling
block to the Jews, but to us who are being saved, it is the power of
God and the wisdom of God.

Hence, the immense cultural and religious chasm that is
sometimes bemoaned by apologists, missiologists, and evangelists
is not too great that the method of the New Testament will not
penetrate hearts. There is no need to develop a slick presentation

based on cultural anthropology to reach "the Greeks or the barbarians" (Romans 1:14). The same gospel is divinely powerful to reach into and transform the heart of the most learned Greek or the most superstitious barbarian.

Consider that right between Paul's two sermons to the Greeks, both of which were interrupted (Acts 14 and Acts 17), Luke explained that among those who were saved in Thessalonica were Jews and also "devout Greeks" (Acts 17:4). They were all saved with the same message from the Scriptures, just like all people are saved:

> I am under obligation both to Greeks and to barbarians, both to the wise and to the foolish ... For I am not ashamed of the gospel [of Christ], for it is the power of God for salvation to everyone who believes, to the Jew first and also to the Greek (Romans 1:14, 16 ESV).

In the theme sentence of the Book of Romans, Paul expressed the power of the singular gospel to transform people from all walks of life. In keeping with the cosmopolitan nature of first century Rome, Paul's book explained the powerful gospel that could save all of them.

Some apologists and exegetes may feel restricted in using only the Scriptures as their guide. These practitioners adjust the message of the gospel with insights from sociological and anthropological findings. These findings are certainly helpful and necessary, but they ought never change the fundamentals of the gospel.

A favorite ruse of these missiologists is to cite the lack of Old Testament quotations in Paul's Mars Hill Sermon (Acts 17:22-31). This argument from silence leads them to speculate that, for the non-Western mind, true persuasion (πείθω) derives from anthropological insights and comparative religions, and not from Scriptures. This reasoning is sadly fallacious for four reasons:

1. Paul did cite from and alluded to Isaiah 42:5-8 in his Acts 17 Mars Hill message.

2. If Paul did not found his teaching on the Old Testament Scriptures, he would have contradicted his teaching on the power of the gospel in Romans 1 and 1 Corinthians 1-3, and

the authority of the Scriptures in 2 Timothy 3 and Hebrews 4.

3. In Paul's first sermon to the Gentiles in Acts 14:15-17, he also alluded to Exodus 20:11 and Psalm 96:10; this sermon was iconoclastic ("turn from these vain things")—calling on Gentiles to turn from their vain ways and turn to the living God—τὸν Θεὸν τὸν ζῶντα (the God, the Living One).

4. Paul's Mars Hill message was interrupted by hecklers; therefore, it should not be considered illustrative of a complete gospel presentation by Paul (cf. Luke 24:46-47 or Acts 17:2-3); likewise, Paul's sermon in Acts 14 was also interrupted by the crowd's efforts to sacrifice to Paul and Barnabas.

The reader will notice that once the topic of persuasion enters the mix, there is the need to be "wise as a serpent and gentle as a dove" (Matthew 10:16). The addition of human persuasion can lead to poor or improper interpretation as to the content of the message of the gospel. God calls His servants to persuade persons to repent and believe in Jesus following:

- The example of Gamaliel in Acts 5

- The example of Paul with King Agrippa in Acts 26

- The example of Paul with the Jews of Rome in Acts 28

- The ministry pattern of Paul in Acts 17.

God, by His sovereign oversight of all things in history, allows the Christian to use all the powers of his reasoning as he shares the gospel with lost souls. And God opens the hearts of the hearers, using the words of the one evangelizing, especially as they expound upon Jesus from His eternal words. Further, God brings an eternal salvation to the souls of those who "are persuaded." It is a divine mystery that all the praise and glory may belong to God!

CHAPTER TWELVE

CONFESS
—ὁμολογέω—

Confessing is a loaded verb! While the verb ὁμολογέω (to confess) is used 24 times in the New Testament, this verb may be assigned several very distinct meanings. Since the interpretation of this verb is strongly polemic, it may be helpful at the opening of this chapter to consider six different meanings of "to confess." Large swaths of the church have vested interest in narrow meanings that they have attached to this verb, especially when that meaning undergirds the particular means of salvation that they profess:

1. Confessing as Sacramental

   Entering a confessional booth to confess one's sins to a priest, as part of the Sacrament of Penance and Reconciliation

2. Confessing as Liturgical

   Citing or quoting a Confession or Creed, individually or in unison with others; for example, "Let us now confess our faith" (followed the recitation of the Apostle's Creed or the Nicene Creed)

3. Confessing as Conversionistic

   Verbally and publicly declaring one's belief in Christ's atoning work accompanied by an unconditional allegiance to Christ alone for salvation

4. Confessing as Baptistic

   Water baptism following conversion as a confession and testimony to the world of having left the old life of sin and having begun a new life with Christ as Lord

5. Confessing as Reactive Evangelism

Responding positively to a question like, "You are not also *one* of this Man's disciples, are you?" (John 18:17)

6. Confessing as Proactive Evangelism

Taking the initiative to evangelize Christ to others as often as He gives that opportunity.

While some of these views of confess overlap in meaning, others do not. The real tension mounts when a Bible translation purposefully changes the meaning of a verse from one to another of these approaches. Similarly, doctrinal presuppositions can readjust how the verb is understood (in Greek Lexicons), and then how translators view and translate the verb. It must be stated that within the 24 uses of the verb ὁμολογέω (to confess) there are a variety of contexts adding nuance to the meaning of ὁμολογέω. Further, looking at cognate words (words with the same root) increases the number of passages in question and enhances an understanding of its root meaning. The four New Testament cognates associated with ὁμολογέω include:

- Two verbs

  ἐξομολογέω—to confess or profess

  ἀνθομολογέομαι—to return a public declaration, return thanks

- One noun

  ὁμολογία—a confession

- One adverb

  ὁμολογουμένως—undeniably, beyond question, by common confession.

Adding these cognates brings the total New Testament uses to 42 contextual samples. These cognates add color and depth to the verb ὁμολογέω (to confess), providing assistance in understanding its full meaning and power.

Consider, for example, the translation of ὁμολογέω in Hebrews 13:15. The chart below cites only the last phrase of this verse, starting with the words "the fruit." The entire verse reads as follows in the English Standard Version:

> *Through him then let us continually offer up a sacrifice of praise to God, that is, the fruit of lips that acknowledge [ὁμολογέω] his name* (Hebrews 13:15 ESV).

Sample Translations of ὁμολογέω in Hebrews 13:15

KJV (1611, 1769) NAS (1977) NKJ (1982)	RSV (1952) ESV (2016)	Cambridge Basic English (1949)	NLT (2007)	NIV (1984)	ERV (1885)	DRA (1899)	Darby (1884) HCSB (2009)	NIV (2011)
Giving thanks	Acknowledge	Giving witness	Proclaiming allegiance	Confess	Make confession	Confessing to	Confessing	Profess
the fruit of *our* lips giving thanks to his name	the fruit of lips that acknowledge his name	the fruit of lips giving witness to his name	proclaiming our allegiance to his name	the fruit of lips that confess his name	the fruit of lips which make confession to his name	the fruit of lips confessing to his name	*the fruit* of *the* lips confessing his name	the fruit of lips that openly profess his name

Opinions appear to differ over what is really being communicated by the verb ὁμολογέω by God in this verse. Is it discussing proactive evangelism (as in #6 above) or reactive evangelism (#5)? A person's one-time confession of faith (#3)? The reciting of a creedal confession (#2)? Or making a confession before a priest (#1)? Consider that translators may frontload their translation from a variety of angles:

1. The lexical meaning of the word, especially based on contextual usage in the New Testament.

2. The meaning of the text to them or to other scholarly contemporaries.

3. Their preconceived conception of what the original audience may have understood.

4. Their view of the church, salvation, Sacraments, worship, the Great Commission.

THOMAS P. JOHNSTON

5. The "Traditional" interpretation of the text according to their church's teachings.

Truly everyone comes to the Bible with preconceptions. These byproducts of learning and experience are impossible to shed, and can lead to great distress of soul. However, Paul perhaps knowing of this problem, assured Timothy that the mind of Christ is discernible:

> You, however, continue in the things you have learned and become convinced of, knowing from whom you have learned them; and that from childhood you have known the sacred writings which are able to give you the wisdom that leads to salvation through faith which is in Christ Jesus (2 Timothy 3:14-15 NASB).

God directly teaches His people in, with, and by His word by His Spirit. Therefore, all these amazing tapestries of interpretation either portray God speaking to His people by His Spirit through His words, and/or all the gradations of man's sinful, idolatrous, and disastrous logic twisting the words of Scripture. The resulting cacophony of interpretations can sometimes make one's mind spin!

Focusing on the verb ὁμολογέω (to confess), this chapter will compare-and-contrast uses of this verb in the New Testament to distill a core meaning of the word. The goal in determining meaning is centripetal—moving toward the core meaning—and not centrifugal—skirting around the periphery of possible meanings. Having approached a core meaning, that central focus will then be applied to all the New Testament uses of ὁμολογέω, with a special focus on the salvation process—as is proper in a book on Great Commission verbs. It is particularly in the salvation process Christian denominations differ from one another. Because confession (ὁμολογέω) is used in the New Testament within the salvation process, it has drawn a variety of interpretations.

Ὁμολογέω and Friends in the Old Testament

A Pauline quote of the Old Testament initiates the search for the core meaning "confess." It is found used in Philippians 2:11.

> "By myself I have sworn [shaba'; ὄμνυμι]; from my mouth has

gone out in righteousness a word that shall not return: 'To Me every knee shall bow, every tongue shall swear allegiance [shaba'; ἐξομολογέω]'" (Isaiah 45:23 ESV).

In this verse, Isaiah twice used the Hebrew verb *shaba'*, which generally means "to swear." The first use is translated into Greek by the verb ὄμνυμι, which means "to take an oath." The second use, *shaba'*, is translated ἐξομολογέω, which means "to confess outwardly." It is this second translation of the Hebrew "to swear" is picked up in Philippians 2:11. Unto Jesus, wrote Paul, "every tongue will swear allegiance [ἐξομολογέω]." The concept runs parallel to the idea of "pledging allegiance" to the United States flag:

> *I pledge allegiance to the flag of the United States of America and to the Republic for which it stands, one Nation under God, indivisible, with liberty and justice for all.*

In Isaiah, then, God swore (*shaba'*) that unto Him every knee would bow and every tongue take an oath.

In Philippians 2:11, Paul prophesied the fulfillment of that prophecy when one day everyone will submit their allegiance to the name of Christ on bended knee:

> *Therefore God has highly exalted him and bestowed on him the name that is above every name, so that at the name of Jesus every knee should bow, in heaven and on earth and under the earth, and every tongue confess [ἐξομολογέω] that Jesus Christ is Lord, to the glory of God the Father* (Philippians 2:9-11 ESV).

Both Isaiah and Paul in Philippians have the same Greek verb, ἐξομολογέω. In many ways, ἐξομολογέω (to outwardly declare or profess) is almost synonymous to ὁμολογέω (to confess or declare), as shall be noted below. A first lesson is that ἐξομολογέω is something which is done outwardly with the mouth, it is verbal. Secondly, it is also something very serious. At the end of time, closely related to the Great White Throne Judgment, there will be a forced universal kneeling and verbal declaration of submission to the Lord Jesus Christ. This universal declaration will be followed by some being admitted into heaven while many more will be cast into hell.

Confessing Jesus is no joke. For Jesus said:

> *"Everyone therefore who shall confess [ὁμολογέω] Me before men, I will also confess [ὁμολογέω] him before My Father who is in heaven. But whoever shall deny Me before men, I will also deny him before My Father who is in heaven"* (Matthew 10:32-33 NASB).

> *"And I say to you, everyone who confesses [ὁμολογέω] Me before men, the Son of Man shall confess [ὁμολογέω] him also before the angels of God; but he who denies Me before men shall be denied before the angels of God"* (Luke 12:8-9 NASB).

Some modern translations use the verb "acknowledge" here instead of "confess." *Acknowledge* appears to emphasize View #6 above, "Reactive or Passive Evangelism." It seems to soften the implication:

> *"Everyone therefore who shall confess Me before men, I will also confess him before My Father who is in heaven"* (Matthew 10:32 NASB).

Whatever the verb used, for Jesus, confessing or not confessing marked the differentiation between being saved and lost. Christ promised or prophesied that He would reciprocate outward verbal public declaration of Him before men with an outward verbal public declaration of His people before His Father and His holy angels. Mark stated the same thing, without using the word ὁμολογέω (to confess):

> *"For whoever is ashamed of Me and My words in this adulterous and sinful generation, of him the Son of Man also will be ashamed when He comes in the glory of His Father with the holy angels"* (Mark 8:38).

Two potent passages in Deuteronomy confirm the importance of confessing, pledging, or swearing in the name of the Lord:

> *"It is the LORD your God you shall fear. Him you shall serve and by his name you shall swear"* (Deuteronomy 6:13 ESV).

> *"You shall fear the LORD your God. You shall serve him and hold fast to him, and by his name you shall swear"* (Deuteronomy 10:20 ESV).

The context does not appear to describe something like taking an oath on a Bible in the name of the Lord God. Rather, it is more like pledging one's life in marriage. "By His name you shall swear" implies both verbally "pledging allegiance to His name" as well as verbally and outwardly "confessing or professing His name"—that is, "making a public declaration of His name"—which is the heart of evangelism!

Considering Ὁμολογέω in the New Testament

The New Testament provided further clarification for the meaning of the verb ὁμολογέω (to confess). It was used by Jesus in direct address—actually coming out of His mouth—in Matthew 7:23; 10:32; 11:25; and Luke 10:21; and 12:8. It was used by Paul in direct address, Acts 24:14. Further, Jesus prophesied that He would be "confessing" in the future, related to the eternal state of persons in Matthew 7:23; 10:32 and Luke 12:8. Therefore, this word is very important as it relates to assurance of salvation and maintaining a proper fear of the Lord.

However, the binding nature of this word is also very powerful. Because Herod "promised with an oath" he was obliged against his will to serve up the head of John the Baptist on a platter:

> So that he promised [ὁμολογέω] with an oath to give her whatever she might ask (Matthew 14:7 ESV).

Herod had made a public verbal declaration of his intent, from which he could not back down. So also, Judas Iscariot made a public verbal declaration of intent to the chief priests to betray Jesus when the crowds would not be present:

> So he consented [ἐξομολογέω] and sought an opportunity to betray him to them in the absence of a crowd (Luke 22:6 ESV).

Although he later regretted it, Judas had made a public outward verbal declaration by which he was bound. In both sinister scenarios, the verbs ὁμολογέω or ἐξομολογέω were used synonymously to bind Herod and Judas to their pledges.

Ὁμολογέω was also used of a statement in which there could be no equivocation—no wiggle room for retraction. It was twice used of the Apostle John to describe the statement of John the Baptist:

> He confessed [ὁμολογέω], and did not deny, but confessed

[ὁμολογέω], "I am not the Christ" (John 1:20 ESV).

John penned a dual use of the verb ὁμολογέω to indicate that John the Baptist did not even come close to declaring himself to be the Christ. Later John used this same verb of those who did not confess Christ:

> His parents said these things because they feared the Jews, for the Jews had already agreed that if anyone should confess *[ὁμολογέω]* Jesus to be Christ, he was to be put out of the synagogue (John 9:22 ESV).

> Nevertheless even among the rulers many believed in Him, but because of the Pharisees they did not confess *[ὁμολογέω]* Him, lest they should be put out of the synagogue; for they loved the praise of men more than the praise of God (John 12:42-43).

So, both for the parents of the "man born blind" and for many of the "authorities" they avoided "confessing" Christ for motives of religious selfishness. They did not want to be kicked out of the synagogue. So, ὁμολογέω (to confess) was used to describe, on one hand, the necessity of verbally confessing or openly declaring Christ, and, on the other hand, it is used with a negation of those who were unwilling to openly confess or verbally declare their allegiance to Christ. Perhaps these examples clarify the core biblical meaning of this verb.

In Acts 24:14, the Apostle Paul used this verb to describe the belief system that was in his heart:

> "But this I confess *[ὁμολογέω]* to you, that according to the Way, which they call a sect, I worship the God of our fathers, believing everything laid down by the Law and written in the Prophets" (Acts 24:14 ESV).

Paul openly, publicly, and verbally declared what was in his heart. Likewise, Jesus used ἐξομολογέω (to confess, profess) to describe what He already knew in His heart, but wanted those around Him to know:

> In that same hour he rejoiced in the Holy Spirit and said, "I thank *[ἐξομολογέω]* you, Father, Lord of heaven and earth, that you have hidden these things from the wise and understanding and revealed them to little children; yes, Father, for such was your

gracious will" (Luke 10:21; cf. Matthew 11:25).

The Holman Christian Standard translated the verb beginning His prayer as "I praise You, Father, Lord of heaven and earth." Jesus was publicly, outwardly, and verbally declaring the work of God. What Jesus knew in His heart, He wanted to declare with His tongue and voice in the hearing of those present.

And this same significance was a part of Anna's prophetic ministry in Luke 2. She had witnessed Simeon blessing the baby Jesus, and she joined Simeon in declaring and bearing witness of this child:

> *And coming in that instant she gave thanks [ἀνθομολογέομαι] to the Lord, and spoke of Him to all those who looked for redemption in Jerusalem* (Luke 2:38).

Anna confessed "in return" (ἀνθομολογέομαι). She returned verbal public confession of that which God had revealed to her in her heart.

Surely, the word group which God's word has given us by the verb ὁμολογέω and its close relatives draws a picture of what is meant by this important word. Its use paints the picture of a very significant word which has binding power on those who use it. It is used of unequivocal speech. And it speaks of outward, public, and verbal declaration of those things that are in the heart of man. This centripetal meaning can now be applied to the New Testament uses of this verb in other salvation contexts.

Ὁμολογέω in the Salvation Process

The word group ὁμολογέω (to confess) touches on several important components of the salvation process. It is used in relation to the open, verbal, outward, and public declaration of sin. We first find it used of the revival taking place under the ministry of John the Baptist, where people from Jerusalem, all Judea, and the surrounding regions were coming to John to be baptized by him.

> *Then Jerusalem, all Judea, and all the region around the Jordan went out to him and were baptized by him in the Jordan, confessing [ἐξομολογέω] their sins* (Matthew 3:5-6).

These people, humbled by the bold and sincere preaching of John the Baptist, were openly and outwardly "confessing their sins." Hence, we find here an open, verbal, outward, and public declaration. In this case it is not a declaration of Christ. Rather it is a declaration of sins. The same revival reported in Mark 1:5 used the same phrase as Matthew, "confessing [ἐξομολογέω] their sins." This same verb was also used in relation to the revival during the ministry of the Apostle Paul in Ephesus:

> And many who had believed came confessing [ἐξομολογέω] and telling their deeds (Acts 19:18).

The word "deeds" was used in Acts 19 instead of "sins" as in Matthew and Mark. Also, the word for confess (ἐξομολογέω) does not stand alone in Acts 19, but is paired with the verb, "to tell" (ἀναγγέλλω). These humbled people publicly "made known" their deeds.

The significant difference between the preaching of John the Baptist and the preaching of Paul was that Paul proclaimed the cross of Christ. The cross had not yet taken place before John the Baptist was beheaded. Hence, he preached repentance in preparation for the gospel. Paul, however, preached repentance in response to the gospel. Therefore, in Acts 19:18, we find the description, "many who had believed" placed before outward verbal "confession." Belief came before outward confession of sin. After placing their faith in Jesus Christ, they were emboldened to publicly confess their sins. This outward, verbal, and public confession was followed by further proof of relinquishing of those deeds: they burned expensive libraries of books on the magic arts:

> Also, many of those who had practiced magic brought their books together and burned them in the sight of all. And they counted up the value of them, and it totaled fifty thousand pieces of silver (Acts 19:19).

If a working man makes $50 a day, then 50,000 pieces of silver represents about 2.5 million U.S. dollars' worth of books burned in Ephesus (a nice nest egg to start a library)—no wonder a riot was called for by Demetrius the silversmith five verses later!

James the half-brother of Jesus called for the outward, verbal, and public declaration of sin in his epistle:

> Confess [ἐξομολογέω] your trespasses to one another, and pray
> for one another, that you may be healed. The effective, fervent
> prayer of a righteous man avails much (James 5:16).

Whether this confession that is commanded by James is in a large group or in a one-on-one setting, it is a command. The most important concept in this verse may be the "one another." Confession in the body of Christ is not a one-way street, one-to-the-other. Rather it goes both ways, to "one another." No one is above proper confession in the body of Christ. Yes, there are appropriate things to confess in public and there are some things that should only be confessed among trusted peers. In fact, the Bible provides excellent examples of how to tastefully and tactfully confess private matters to avoid embarrassing others, avoiding the placing of evil thoughts in their minds. Yet even so, the "one another" implies that both the discipler and disciplee should be confessing to one another. Both the husband and wife. Both the pastor and the layman. Both the father and the son. Everyone is equal at the foot of the cross! This "one another confession" fosters humble accountability, and also, according to James, it brings true healing.

The confession discussed in 1 John 1:9 runs tangentially to that which is listed above. In 1 John 1:9 the reader is told that he should confess to the One who is "faithful and righteous." This same "faithful and righteous" One is called "an Advocate" in 1 John 2:1, as well as "Jesus Christ, the Righteous One." Jesus is the first and most important person to whom Christians ought to address their confessions. Then comes the need for fostering accountability with peers in the local church, through "one another" confession.

> If we confess [ὁμολογέω] our sins, He is faithful and just to
> forgive us our sins and to cleanse us from all unrighteousness. ...
> My little children, these things I write to you, so that you may not
> sin. And if anyone sins, we have an Advocate with the Father,
> Jesus Christ the righteous (1 John 1:9; 2:1).

In these verses, cleansing from sins is promised to those who confess their sins to Jesus. Further, healing is promised in James when Christians confess their sins one to another.

Ὁμολογέω as Allegiance to Christ

As far as salvation, confession describes the outward, verbal, and public declaration of commitment to Jesus. Confession of Christ acts as a declaration of allegiance to Jesus Christ and Him alone for salvation. The Bible often compares this outward declaration with marriage. In marriage, the couple is engaged, the wedding is planned, friends and family arrive. The real moment they have come for is the bride's and groom's mutual, outward, open, and verbal pledge of loyalty to each other. Once that pledge is made, the couple is pronounced husband and wife.

The New Testament clarifies that this pledge of fealty is to be made to Jesus Christ, the High Priest of our confession:

> Therefore, holy brethren, partakers of the heavenly calling, consider the Apostle and High Priest of our confession [ἡ ὁμολογία], Christ Jesus, who was faithful to Him who appointed Him, as Moses also was faithful in all His house (Hebrews 3:1-2).

The essence of our confession is the Person and work of Jesus Christ—who He is and what He did on the cross! In 1 and 2 John, the Apostle John clarified the "who He is" side of the equation:

> By this you know the Spirit of God: Every spirit that confesses [ὁμολογέω] that Jesus Christ has come in the flesh is of God, and every spirit that does not confess [μὴ ὁμολογέω] that Jesus Christ has come in the flesh is not of God. And this is the spirit of the Antichrist, which you have heard was coming, and is now already in the world (1 John 4:2-3).

> Whoever confesses [ὁμολογέω] that Jesus is the Son of God, God abides in him, and he in God (1 John 4:15).

> For many deceivers have gone out into the world who do not confess [μὴ ὁμολογέω] Jesus Christ as coming in the flesh. This is a deceiver and an antichrist (2 John 7).

John called for some clear specificity as to what and who confessors of Christ were to believe that He truly was. Just as John was unequivocal that John the Baptist did not confess himself to be the Christ, so the Apostle John was clear that believers in Jesus must believe certain things about Jesus Christ:

1. Jesus came in the flesh (1 John 4:2; 2 John 7)

2. Jesus is the Son of God (1 John 4:15).

The implications of these ideas are far-reaching for Protestants who deny the deity of Christ or His Virgin Birth, and for Catholics who make Him something of a sub-deity required to act vicariously through Mary or a bishop in Rome. If the total number of liberal Protestants and mainstream Catholics adherents were combined, then a very large percentage of those who call themselves Christians today may not pass John's muster.

Ὁμολογέω as Verbal Declaration of Christ

While confessing (ὁμολογέω) is a verbal declaration, its link to salvation has a disclaimer. In verbal declaration, one can speak one thing while thinking and doing another. A person may speak something with their lips, but then deny it by their deeds:

> They profess [ὁμολογέω] to know God, but in works they deny Him, being abominable, disobedient, and disqualified for every good work (Titus 1:16).

In this case, consider that NKJV translators chose to translate the verb ὁμολογέω (to confess) as "profess"—an interesting choice for this book on Great Commission verbs. In this situation Paul described the Judaizers who gave heed to "Jewish fables and commandments of men" (Titus 1:14). These Judaizers make open, publicly, verbal declaration of knowing God. Yet by their deeds they denied Him. They were cousins to the Judaizers in Acts 15 who professed to know Christ, and yet added to faith in Christ obedience to all the Laws of Moses. Paul seems to be saying here that faith in Christ for salvation requires faith in Christ alone for salvation—it is primarily a heart-faith and secondarily a verbally communicated faith. Then from the heart and the mouth, the fruits of godly words and righteous deeds necessarily follow. So, if the verb ὁμολογέω means anything, it means outward, open, public, and verbal confession. Yet, such a confession gives glory to Christ alone for salvation and includes deeds in keeping with the confession of the merits of Christ.

Further, as a follow-up to the lack of confession mentioned by Jesus in Matthew 10 and Luke 12, Paul in Hebrews encouraged his readers to hold fast to their confession:

> *Seeing then that we have a great high priest, that hath passed through the heavens, Jesus the Son of God, let us hold fast our profession [ἡ ὁμολογία]* (Hebrews 4:14, Revised Webster's).[1]

> *Let us hold fast the confession [ἡ ὁμολογία] of our hope without wavering, for He who promised is faithful* (Hebrews 10:23).

The possibility lingers that some Christians may emulate the parents of the man born blind in John 9 or the rulers in John 12, and fearing men more than they fear God—and in so doing, let loose of their confession of Jesus.

Likewise, Paul reminded Timothy to confess (ὁμολογέω) the good confession (ἡ ὁμολογία). Paul then called up the example of Jesus who made a good confession before Pontius Pilate—just hours before His death!

> *Fight the good fight of faith, lay hold on eternal life, to which you were also called and have confessed [ὁμολογέω] the good confession [ἡ ὁμολογία] in the presence of many witnesses. I urge you in the sight of God who gives life to all things, and before Christ Jesus who witnessed the good confession [ἡ ὁμολογία] before Pontius Pilate, that you keep this commandment without spot, blameless until our Lord Jesus Christ's appearing* (1 Timothy 6:12-14).

Hence, Timothy needed to be reminded of the confession that he made, so that he would hold fast to it. Paul warns his son in the faith to hold firmly to the confession of Christ. When one's commitment to confession wavers, so one's faith in Jesus also wavers.

For Timothy as for all Christians, just because someone does not live up to their confession does not automatically mean that

---

[1] The English Revised 1833 Webster Update with Pierce's Englishman's Strong's Numbering System. ASCII version Copyright © 1988-1997 by the Online Bible Foundation and Woodside Fellowship of Ontario, Canada. Licensed from the Institute for Creation Research. Used by permission.

the confession they made is invalid. But every Christian needs a Paul to remind them to press on:

> *Therefore do not be ashamed of the testimony of our Lord, nor of me His prisoner, but share with me in the sufferings for the gospel according to the power of God* (2 Timothy 1:8).

Similarly, the possibility of Christians wavering in confessing Christ reminds us that we need to encourage one another to continue in verbally, outwardly, openly, and publicly declaring the gospel of Jesus Christ.

In closing, let's consider Paul's use of the concept of confession as related to salvation in Romans 10. Paul had already established a distinction between faith and works in salvation, making faith the human trigger of salvation based on Genesis 15:6. This faith was manifested both in the heart and out of the mouth. To buttress this point, Paul cited Deuteronomy 30:14, "But the word *is* very near you, in your mouth and in your heart, that you may do it." He wrote:

> *But what does it say? "The word is near you, in your mouth and in your heart" (that is, the word of faith which we preach): that if you confess [ὁμολογέω] with your mouth the Lord Jesus and believe in your heart that God has raised Him from the dead, you will be saved. For with the heart one believes unto righteousness, and with the mouth confession [ὁμολογέω] is made unto salvation* (Romans 10:8-10 ESV).

Paul applied the truth from Deuteronomy 30 by writing a conditional clause, "if you confess." Here he used the verb ὁμολογέω (to confess). This first condition was that the confession be verbal, "if you confess with your mouth." Then the second condition was heartfelt belief, "and believe in your heart." One must consider that it is possible and likely that some follow the first condition without simultaneously holding the second part of the condition. Such were the Judaizers in Titus 1. Such appear to be the seed sown in shallow soil that "believe for a while" (Luke 8:13). These may be the same group who say, "Lord, Lord," while Jesus responds, "I never knew you":

> *"Not everyone who says to Me, 'Lord, Lord,' shall enter the kingdom of heaven, but he who does the will of My Father in*

> heaven. Many will say to Me in that day, 'Lord, Lord, have we not prophesied in Your name, cast out demons in Your name, and done many wonders in Your name?' And then I will declare to them, 'I never knew you; depart from Me, you who practice lawlessness!'" (Matthew 7:21-23).

God calls for verbal confession combined with heartfelt conviction of salvation in and through Jesus and His works alone.

Two conditions remain: verbal confession and heart belief. If those two conditions are met, Paul stated emphatically, "you will be saved" (Romans 10:9). Paul taught a two-condition salvation, outwardly verbal and inner heart conviction. Jesus said, "Out of the abundance of the heart the mouth speaks" (Matthew 12:34). Paul bound up salvation by two cords in Romans 10: verbal confession "with the mouth" and inner belief "in the heart." These two cords remain the human response required of God to acquire the salvation He freely offers.

CHAPTER THIRTEEN

WIN DISCIPLES
—μαθητεύω—

"Follow Me," Jesus said, "and I will make you fishers of men" (Matthew 4:19 ESV). In Mark we find the addition of another verb. "And Jesus said to them, 'Follow me, and I will make you become fishers of men'" (Mark 1:17 ESV). The word for "fishers" in the Greek is not a verb "to fish," but a noun, ἁλιεῖς, meaning "fisherman." Hence, the literal translation of the entire phrase in Mark would read, "Follow after Me, and I will make you become fishermen of men." To reduce redundancy in English, the adjective "after" is removed and the noun "fisherman" is shortened to "fishers." "Follow Me and I will make you become fishers of men." So, for this book on Great Commission verbs, the word for "fishers" is a noun and not a verb.

What then are the verbs in these Matthew 4 and Mark 1 passages? The verb "follow" or "come after" (Δεῦτε ὀπίσω) is found in both texts. This command is then succeeded by verbs respectively explaining what following after Jesus meant. In Matthew 4, Jesus said that if a person was to follow after Him, in return, Jesus would "do" something for them. The verb for "will make" is the simple verb "to do" (ποιέω). Jesus promised that He would make His followers into "fishermen of men." His true followers would not become introverted isolationists. Rather, true followers of Christ would become caring lovers of others—constantly growing in genuine care and concern for those around them. In Mark 1, Jesus added a second verb to this special call. He added the simple verb "to become" (γίνομαι). Jesus would intensify His "soul-work" by pledging to become the personal coach to every one of His followers, helping them to "become fishers of men."

If my experience is typical, becoming a fisher of men was far from my personality type or desire. When I repented of my sin, believing that Jesus died for my sins—that He would forgive me and make me pure if I only asked Him—I felt an inward desire to tell others, but I did not know when, where, or how to do so. So, accompanied by a request for Jesus to be Savior is the request for Him to be personal Mentor and Coach. His word teaches. He uses our experiences, pastors we sit under, and other Christians to build us into followers of Christ. Meanwhile His Holy Spirit prods the believer—"speak of Jesus"—become a "fisher of men"!

"To make" and "to become" are both simple verbs. Jesus committed Himself to His disciples to accomplish a mighty task in their lives—if only they followed after Him! These two simple verbs (do and make) are magnificently rich in understanding how God molds His people into the image of Christ Jesus. These two verbs are only a beginning. This chapter will surf the peaks of New Testament verbs used to draw spiritual pictures of Christ's desire for His followers.

"Taking Men Alive"— ζωγρέω

In the Gospel of Luke, Luke did not include the call to be "fishers of men" as found in Matthew 4 and Mark 1. Instead, Luke 5 tells of another fishing episode. In this account, the reader enters into the daily routine of Peter and Andrew as fishermen. They fished all night and listened to Jesus teach during the day. On a certain day, sometime in the middle of His teaching, Jesus asked Peter if He could borrow his boat to better address the growing crowd. There were so many people, that if Jesus was to get into a boat, perhaps 10-15 feet from the edge of the water, He would be able to more effectively speak to the crowd.

At the end of His teaching, Jesus asked these young fishermen to let out their nets for a catch. Peter was reluctant, perhaps due to the midday heat or perhaps due to the newly cleaned nets ready for another night of fishing. Luke captured Peter's reluctance in his response to Jesus:

> "Master, we toiled all night and took nothing! But at your word I will let down the nets" (Luke 5:5 ESV).

The reluctant Peter let out his nets for a catch, and the Lord of the fish and the sea surprised him with a miraculous and almost comical catch! Peter and Andrew caught so many fish that not only were their nets breaking, but their boat was sinking from all the fish. In fact, Peter and Andrew signaled to their coworkers in another boat to come and help, and both boats began to sink due to the amazing catch of fish!

The boats were overflowing with fish. Peter saw the miraculous catch and "He fell down at Jesus' knees saying, 'Depart from me, for I am a sinful man, O Lord!'" (Luke 5:8 ESV)—in other words, Peter is up to his armpits in fish! The response of Peter is totally unexpected. He did not say, "Good idea, Jesus!" or, "Amen, Jesus, what an amazing catch of fish!" Rather, Peter recognized, maybe for the first time, that Jesus was far more than a mere man. He made a spiritual application of this miracle, recognizing Christ in all His holiness, and likewise himself, with all his sinfulness. Peter likely considered what the demons had already been saying, "You are the Christ, the Son of God" (Luke 4:41). The reluctant obedience of Peter was met by the overabundant grace of God—by the way, is this not always the case?

Jesus followed Peter's verbal and visual humility with a gospel call unique to this passage. As the realization of who Christ was dawned in Peter's mind, Jesus said to Peter:

> "Do not be afraid; from now on you will be catching [ζωγρέω] men" (Luke 5:10 ESV).

We find the words "do not fear" multiple times both in the Old Testament and New Testament. But when Jesus said, "you will be catching men," He used a fascinating verb, the verb ζωγρέω, found ten times in both the Old and New Testaments.

The Greek verb ζωγρέω, meaning "to take men alive," is not a fishing term. It is a military and societal term used twice in the New Testament and eight times in the Old Testament. In the New Testament it is used here in Luke 5 to describe the purpose for which Christ was training His disciples—to take men alive. It is also found in 2 Timothy 2 to describe Satan's activity within those who oppose the gospel.

Both Christ's followers and Satan pursue a similar purpose on this earth. Both seek to "take men alive." Satan seeks to capture persons to accomplish his will, whereas followers of Christ are commissioned to take people alive to submit to the will of God. Here is how Paul used the verb ζωγρέω in 2 Timothy:

> And the Lord's servant must not be quarrelsome but kind to everyone, able to teach, patiently enduring evil, correcting his opponents with gentleness. God may perhaps grant them repentance leading to a knowledge of the truth, and they may come to their senses and escape from the snare of the devil, after being captured [ζωγρέω] by him to do his will (2 Timothy 2:24-26 ESV).

Behind the words "being captured" is the Greek verb ζωγρέω. The Devil seeks to ensnare persons to do his will.

The contextual power of this word is found among its eight uses in the Old Testament. In 2 Chronicles 25:12 we find one of its military uses:

> The men of Judah captured [ζωγρέω] another 10,000 alive and took them to the top of a rock and threw them down from the top of the rock, and they were all dashed to pieces (2 Chronicles 25:12 ESV).

This verse described the victory God gave King Amaziah and the Judeans as they defeated the Edomites. Judah "captured alive" ten thousand enemy soldiers and cast them over a cliff to die. The same verb is used in 2 Samuel 8 to describe King David's treatment of the Moabites after he defeated them in battle:

> And he defeated Moab and he measured them with a line, making them lie down on the ground. Two lines he measured to be put to death, and one full line to be spared [ζωγρέω]. And the Moabites became servants to David and brought tribute (2 Samuel 8:2 ESV).

Two thirds of the captured men were to receive the immediate death penalty and one third was to be spared that fate. The verb used to describe those being spared was ζωγρέω (to "capture alive").

In the Old Testament, however, the most common usage of this term relates to "the ban." Israel was to kill everything that breathed in Canaan due to their horrific sins against God and His laws (Deuteronomy 20:16). Yet, in the war against the Midianites, the Israeli soldiers killed only the males. In astonishment, Moses responded to them twice using the verb ζωγρέω:

> Moses said to them, "Have you let all the women live [ζωγρέω]? Behold, these, on Balaam's advice, caused the people of Israel to act treacherously against the LORD in the incident of Peor, and so the plague came among the congregation of the LORD. Now therefore, kill every male among the little ones, and kill every woman who has known man by lying with him. But all the young girls who have not known man by lying with him keep alive [ζωγρέω] for yourselves" (Numbers 31:15-18 ESV).

The soldiers of Israel had disobeyed God's ban by not killing the Midianite women. It was these women who had tempted the young Israeli men into sexual immorality, following the advice of Balaam—who was to become the predominant example of a false teacher in the Bible. So, Moses modified the ban by allowing the young girls to live, those who had not known a man intimately—these were to be retained as "captured alive" (ζωγρέω).

A parenthetical statement may be in order here. We will see the verb "to thresh" below, wherein the evangelism ministry of the follower of Christ is likened to the separating of the wheat from the chaff. The context of ζωγρέω in the account of Balaam and the Midianite women has the same force. It is, as it were, that the same message is the smell of death to those who are dying and the smell of life to those who are being saved (2 Corinthians 2:15-16).

However, the Old Testament also gives us an example of one woman who was "spared alive" because of her faith—Rahab the Harlot. Rahab ended up being in the family line of Jesus (Matthew 1:5). But even more amazing was the uniqueness of her faith as recorded in Joshua 2. When Joshua sent spies to the city of Jericho, Rahab hid the spies so that they were not caught and killed. But it was while they were on the roof that she bore witness to the spies using the name, Lord Jehovah. She said, "For the LORD your God, he is God in the heavens above and on the earth beneath" (Joshua 2:11 ESV). Then she went on to request that she and all her family be "spared alive" (ζωγρέω) after Israel would conquered the city of Jericho:

> *"Now then, please swear to me by the LORD that, as I have dealt kindly with you, you also will deal kindly with my father's house, and give me a sure sign that you will save alive [ζωγρέω] my father and mother, my brothers and sisters, and all who belong to them, and deliver our lives [souls] from death"* (Joshua 2:12-13 ESV).

Rahab was requesting to be "captured alive" by the armies of Israel, as they conquered the land. Then she clearly used salvific language, "deliver our souls from death."

So, on that amazing afternoon, when Peter took in the miraculous catch of fish, he began to understand the divine nature of Jesus. It was then that Jesus commissioned him, "From now on you will take men alive [ζωγρέω]." This verb used by Jesus had a significant Old Testament context and application. The word implied that life and death issues were at stake. The verb implied a separation between the acceptable and the unacceptable. It implied a ministry revolving around bringing salvation to others. While this call is focused on Peter, it can be generalized to all of Christ's followers. Every disciple of Jesus is commissioned to "take men alive [ζωγρέω]."

The calls to "be made fishers of men" and "take men alive" are only the beginning of the rich metaphors depicting ministry in the New Testament. Jesus and Paul also used agricultural metaphors to symbolize what the Great Commission looks like for the follower of Christ.

"Sowing"—σπείρω

One of the more common agricultural metaphors for the work of the follower of Christ is that of the "sower of seed." Jesus used it in His Parable of the Sower, which is found in Matthew 13, Mark 4, and Luke 8. These next two phrases encapsulate the essence of Jesus' Parable of the Sower:

> *"A sower went out to sow his seed. ... Now the parable is this: The seed is the word of God"* (Luke 8:5, 11 ESV).

This story represents evangelism, follow-up, and discipleship unlike any other portion in the New Testament. It likens the evangelist to a man throwing out seed—almost as if he cannot ascertain what kind of response he will get until the seed literally lands on the ground. The seed is the "word of God"—that is, the literal words of the Bible. These Holy Spirit-inspired words elicit an immediate response wherever and whenever they go forth. In fact, the parable names four responses. It is difficult to improve upon these:

(1) No response, since the seed was snatched and eaten by the birds (Satan)

(2) Immediate reception—with joy, being short-lived, and lacking a necessary root system; the small sprout immediately withers in time of persecution

(3) A promising reception with the initial growth of the seed into a mature plant; however, due to weed-infestation, the plant remains un-reproductive

(4) The reception of the seed into good soil, accompanied by the healthy growth of the plant to the point of bearing much fruit.

Hearing the word is the one common denominator of all the soils, as well as the trigger point to determine their response. Consider the repeated phrase: "are the ones who hear," "when they hear," "when they have heard," and "having heard the word" (Luke 8:12, 13, 14, 15).

Therefore, we have in this parable, aside from the responses which we will discuss in another chapter, the clear calling of the follower of Jesus is to liberally throw out the seed of the word of God into the hearts of those around them. As that word is sown, so, it will supernaturally trigger a response—completely out of the control of the sower. The only task of the sower is to faithfully sow the word of God!

"Reaping"—θερίζω

In John 4, Jesus told His disciples, "One sows and another reaps" (John 4:37 ESV). He preceded this statement with the point, "For here the saying holds true." In actuality, this statement of Jesus is amazingly insightful and powerful. Jesus affirmed that the one who sows the seed of the gospel (the evangelist) is not always the one who leads the person to Christ (another evangelist). Jesus appears to be expounding on two elements in Psalm 126:

> *Those who sow in tears shall reap with shouts of joy! He who goes out weeping, bearing the seed for sowing, shall come home with shouts of joy, bringing his sheaves with him* (Psalm 126:5-6 ESV).

This Psalm teaches that the persistent sower "shall doubtless" return with his sheaves—having reaped the harvest. Jesus, however, adapted the terminology in this Psalm into a two-step process: sowing and reaping. In John 4 this two-step process involves two separate individuals, a sower and a reaper.

Certainly, the sower sows with the prospect of reaping in his mind. And certainly, the reaper reaps knowing that someone had to sow the seed before him, so that he might reap a crop. But Jesus intimated that there are two persons involved. Perhaps He emphasized the two persons and processes for another even more interesting point: the sower and the reaper work simultaneously!

The bigger image that Jesus addressed in John 4 was that of the immediacy of the harvest at the time of sowing the seed. This idea is developed in the following two verses:

> *"Do you not say, 'There are still four months and then comes the harvest'? Behold, I say to you, lift up your eyes and look at the fields, for they are already [ἤδη] white for harvest! And he who reaps receives wages, and gathers fruit for eternal life, that both he who sows and he who reaps may rejoice together"* (John 4:35-36).

Jesus alters the agricultural metaphor of sowing and reaping on one point: chronology. In the timing of God there is no need for four months between sowing and reaping—these are simultaneous events. The prophet Amos said the same thing also using the agricultural metaphor, "The plowman shall overtake the reaper and the treader of grapes him who sows the seed" (Amos 9:13 ESV). Therefore, the sower can sow in expectancy that he can reap a harvest immediately upon sowing, and the reaper can expect to reap immediately because it is very likely that another person has already sown the seed. In either case, there ought to be a holy and bold expectancy in evangelizing due to the supernatural immediacy of the harvest.

On this point, the reader may consider that the punctuation of John 4:35-36 was changed in the Greek text used by the German Bible Society in the late nineteenth century. The "already" (ἤδη) that is part of verse 35 in the KJV and NKJV was placed with verse 36 instead. Hence most English Bibles move the "already" to verse 36 as does the ESV:

> *"Do you not say, 'There are yet four months, then comes the harvest'? Look, I tell you, lift up your eyes, and see that the fields are white for harvest. Already [ἤδη] the one who reaps is receiving wages and gathering fruit for eternal life, so that sower and reaper may rejoice together"* (John 4:35-36 ESV).

While this change may appear minimal at first glance, it does remove one of the few passages in the New Testament that clearly communicates:

1. The simultaneous nature of sowing and reaping

2. God's instantaneous preparation of an immediate harvest

3. Christ's lack of allocating extra time to include human efforts in creating the right environment for harvest

4. The urgency created by an immediate harvest.

As to the power of these four points, perhaps point 3 is deprecating to human nature. Man may want to insert himself into the conversion process, saying, "My role cannot merely be limited to just speaking the gospel. I am far too important!"

Jesus clearly stated that the harvest was fully prepared and "already white for harvest" in John 4:35. Hence, he removed the many ways that man inserts himself into the Great Commission equation. Perhaps this was an underlying reason that Greek scholars chose to alter the sentence punctuation in the late nineteenth century critical edition Greek text?

"Treading"—περκάζω

The Amos passage above brought up another verb related to spiritual labor that is not used in the New Testament. It is the verb "treading":

"Behold, the days are coming," declares the LORD, "when the plowman [ἀλοητός] shall overtake the reaper [τρύγητος] and the treader [περκάζω] of grapes him who sows the seed [ἀποσταλάζω]; the mountains shall drip sweet wine, and all the hills shall flow with it" (Amos 9:13 ESV).

This verse introduces Christian workers as "plowmen" and "reapers," as well as those who "tread" and those who "sow." In the Greek translations of the Hebrew, the first two concepts were translated as nouns: plowman and reaper. In the second two, the translators chose two verbs: treading and sowing. The verb for sowing (ἀποσταλάζω, to "let fall or drop") is a rough synonym to what we just discussed above (σπείρω, to sow). The other verb points to the idea of "treading" (περκάζω).

In the making of wine, there is the need for planting grapevines. Much time is needed for them to mature before the first harvest of grapes. The treading of grapes does not take place for years after the initial grape seed is sown into the ground to start a grapevine! Again, the supernatural realm overturns the chronology necessary for natural processes. In this case, Amos taught that "in that day"—that is, under the New Covenant, the treader of grapes would overtake the sower of seed. An obvious chronological anomaly in a natural sense, but a spiritual reality!

It is also important to note that for the grapes to produce wine they must be crushed. And the crushing is done by the treader. Therefore, God through Amos used a very unusual analogy for spiritual ministry. The work of God accomplished through sharing the gospel is likened to the evangelist crushing the recipient. Consider the work of God:

"For he wounds, but he binds up; he shatters, but his hands heal" (Job 5:18 ESV).

Moreover, the light of the moon will be as the light of the sun, and the light of the sun will be sevenfold, as the light of seven days, in the day when the LORD binds up the brokenness of his people, and heals the wounds inflicted by his blow (Isaiah 30:26 ESV).

God's words must first bruise mankind to bring us to repentance. Through God's power in His word, the bruised party becomes a brokenhearted person, whom the Lord does not despise (Psalm 51:17). God then uses the testimony of His people to share the bruising message of judgment, as well as the healing message of grace. In this light, then, consider the analogy of "threshing."

"Threshing"—ἀλοάω

Paul considered his spiritual work to be likened to a person threshing grain. He used this verb three times in the New Testament, twice in 1 Corinthians 9 and once in 1 Timothy 5. Two of the uses come from the same Old Testament quote:

You shall not muzzle an ox when it is treading [ἀλοάω] out the grain (Deuteronomy 25:4 ESV; cf. 1 Corinthians 9:9; 1 Timothy 5:18).

Moses sandwiched this agricultural command, right after discussing the forty minus one lashes and right before a discussion of passing on the name of a dead brother through substitutionary generation by the next of kin. Paul, for his part, took this agricultural command to apply more to ministers of the gospel than merely to oxen. Consider his two questions: "Is it for oxen that God is concerned? Does He not certainly speak for our sake?" (1 Corinthians 9:9-10 ESV). These rhetorical questions show that Paul considered that this Mosaic law had more to do with Christians ministering the gospel than it did to oxen treading out grain.

So, Paul unsheathed this agricultural metaphor to describe his ministry of evangelizing. Evangelizing for Paul was like crushing the newly shorn stock to separate the wheat from the chaff.

Does he not certainly speak for our sake? It was written for our sake, because the plowman [ἀροτριάω] should plow [ἀροτριάω] in hope and the thresher [ἀλοάω] thresh in hope of sharing in the crop (1 Corinthians 9:10 ESV).

At first glance this analogy may lead the casual reader to merely consider that Paul was speaking of the "hard work" of the ministry. Yet Paul's inspired use of "threshing" as a metaphor for evangelism appears to have a much more consequential meaning. He seemed to be using this metaphor to express the separation between the living and the dead, just as he did in other places:

> For the word of the cross is folly to those who are perishing, but to us who are being saved it is the power of God (1 Corinthians 1:18 ESV).

> For we are the aroma of Christ to God among those who are being saved and among those who are perishing, to one a fragrance from death to death, to the other a fragrance from life to life. Who is sufficient for these things? (2 Corinthians 2:15-16 ESV).

Consider also Paul's three uses of the verb "evangelize" (εὐαγγελίζω) and his one use of the verb "preach" (κηρύσσω) in 1 Corinthians 9. Paul also used the verb to "win" (κερδαίνω) five times and the verb "save" (σῴζω) once. The context clearly depicts treading or threshing as a metaphor for evangelizing.

A winnowing must take place when the gospel goes forth. Evangelizing is threshing. It is treading on the stalks to separate the grain from the chaff. It is hard spiritual labor. Paul then used another verb in his 1 Corinthians 9 comments. This verb is even more poignant than that of treading. Paul spoke of evangelizing as plowing.

"Plowing"—ἀροτριάω

Plowing was also used metaphorically for ministry in the Old Testament. Consider also this poignant usage:

> "Greatly have they afflicted me from my youth, yet they have not prevailed against me. The plowers plowed upon my back; they made long their furrows" (Psalm 129:2-3 ESV).

Plowing was used of the righteous receiving affliction from the wicked in Psalm 129. However, in 1 Corinthians 9, Paul used "plowing" to depict evangelistic ministry. Evangelism is like an evangelist running the conviction of God's word as a plow down the back of a lost person's soul. No wonder the words of the evangelist are like the smell of death to those who are dying! Nevertheless, without the convicting power of the Holy Spirit who convicts of sin, righteousness, and judgment, there is no conviction of sin leading to repentance. Believing without repentance is only superficial. The deeply plowed conviction of sin can lead to belief in the substitutionary work of Jesus who died for sin. This conviction is a marvelous thing. This type of faith is only wrought by the plow doing its preparatory work so that the seed can be dropped deeply into the furrows it leaves behind.

As threshing divides the open people from those that are closed, so plowing cuts deeply into tenderized souls and scrapes hardened hearts. Meanwhile proclaimers of salvation in Jesus are mocked, reviled, and even hated by those who do not submit to the work of the plow upon their heart. Jesus said on many occasions and in a variety of ways, "You will be hated by all for My name's sake" (Matthew 10:22; 24:9; Mark 13:13; Luke 6:22; 21:17; John 15:18; 17:14). The good news is, those tenderized by the plow of God's word reveal their readiness to receive the gospel of salvation. Hence use of the plow is necessary for the evangelist to "bear fruit."

"Bearing" Fruit—φέρω

So, along with sowing, reaping, plowing, and threshing, Jesus spoke of "bearing fruit" as one of the purposes that we exist as His disciples:

> "You did not choose me, but I chose you and appointed you that you should go and bear fruit and that your fruit should abide, so that whatever you ask the Father in my name, he may give it to you" (John 15:16 ESV).

Two causal verbs are used by Jesus to characterize the importance that He places on "bearing fruit": to choose and to appoint. Jesus "chose" His followers and He "appointed" them, for a specific task, to "go" and "bear fruit."

The verb "go" is found in most of the Great Commission passages and in many other commissionings in the Bible. The Christian is called to modify his current life and to add another dimension into it. He is to "go" out of his way. He must make the effort to "go" to others, getting out of his comfort zone, and strive on behalf of Jesus. To what end is he striving? In order to make fruit, fruit that remains.

"Fruit that remains" in John is different from the "fruit of the Spirit" in Galatians. In John 4:36 Jesus called it "fruit for eternal life." He was describing souls. As Dawson Trotman wrote, we are *Born to Reproduce*. Christians are born to multiply the precious seed planted within them. The Parable of the Sower described it as thirty times, sixty times, and a hundred times. All of Christ's followers are to sow the precious seed of the gospel so that it can germinate and bear fruit by multiplying the life of Christ into the lives of others.

"Winning" —κερδαίνω

In an even stronger tone, Paul became competitive when he spoke of winning souls versus living an aimless life. He likened Christian ministry to one running a race, pressing forward toward the prize (1 Corinthians 9:24). He compared evangelizing with boxing, where the boxer does not aimlessly beat the air, but rather punches with purpose (1 Corinthians 9:26). In this athletic context, Paul spoke of his calling as an evangelist to "win" (κερδαίνω) men to Christ.

The verb "win" (κερδαίνω) is found 16 times in the New Testament. A first concentration is found in Jesus' Parable of the Talents in Matthew 25. Here, Jesus used the verb "win" or "gain" to describe the level of return on the investment of the talents to a lord's servants. The one who had received two talents "gained" two more. The one who received five talents "gained" or "won" five more. The one who received one talent buried his talent and gained nothing with it. In this context, the verb "win" or "gain" was used in economic terms.

Win (κερδαίνω) is also used to describe the gaining of people. In Matthew 18, the Christian who first goes directly to his brother who has sinned against him has the chance of "gaining" his brother (Matthew 18:15). It is used in the first three Gospels in a quote by Jesus where He said, "What does it profit a man to gain the whole world and lose his own soul?" (Matthew 16:26; Mark 8:36; and Luke 9:25). Jesus used this verb to contrast economic gain with spiritual-eternal gain, the gaining of one's own soul in a context of being sold out for the gospel and not being ashamed of Jesus. In 1 Peter 3:1, Peter spoke of a chaste wife "winning" her unsaved husband without a word—clearly referencing the salvation of her husband's soul and eternal life. In all these cases, "winning" has a spiritual and eternal significance.

In the case of 1 Corinthians 9:19-22, Paul used the verb "win" to describe his goal in proclaiming Jesus:

- *For though I am free from all, I have made myself a servant to all, that I might win [κερδαίνω] more of them.*

- *To the Jews I became as a Jew, in order to win [κερδαίνω] Jews.*

- *To those under the law I became as one under the law (though not being myself under the law) that I might win [κερδαίνω] those under the law.*

- *To those outside the law I became as one outside the law (not being outside the law of God but under the law of Christ) that I might win [κερδαίνω] those outside the law.*

- *To the weak I became weak, that I might win [κερδαίνω] the weak.*

- *I have become all things to all people, that by all means I might save [σώζω] some* (1 Corinthians 9:19-22 ESV).

Paul had already stated his ministry message in 1 Corinthians 2:2, "For I determined not to know anything among you except Jesus Christ and Him crucified." Then in Chapter 9, Paul stated his ministry goal using the verb "win" (κερδαίνω) five times, "save" (σώζω) once, and "that I might save some." Quite a powerful explanation of Paul's self-understanding of his missional purpose. Verse 22 punctuates the importance that God places on His servants' efforts in working toward the salvation of others! Paul's role was not a corollary to their salvation. Paul entered into God's saving activity by evangelizing them with the gospel.

Consider also Paul's target group that he sought to reach with this one message:

- *That I might win more of them [people]*

- *In order to win Jews*

- *That I might win those who are under the law*

- *That I might win those outside the law*

- *That I might win the weak*

- *That by all means I might save some [people]* (1 Corinthians 9:19-22 ESV).

This same message of the gospel described in Romans and 1 Corinthians was sufficient for "Greeks and barbarians, the wise and the unwise" (Romans 1:14), as well as "Jews and Greeks" (1 Corinthians 2:24). This gospel is also sufficient for all men, the Jew, those under the law, those outside the law, and the weak. It is sufficient to win "some" out of the "more."

Winning and saving therefore describe the end-game or culmination of the evangelizing process. Sowing describes the beginning of the process, reaping the end of sharing the gospel. Treading and threshing describe the nitty-gritty of expounding the reality of sin and the beauty of the Savior. These are internal to gospel ministry. Lastly, there is another term that addresses the end of evangelizing. It is winning disciples.

"Winning Disciples"—μαθητεύω

In several places that we have reviewed so far, the reader of the New Testament encounters verbs wherein the author addressed the end-game of evangelizing. The verbs "win" and "reap" address the result of a positive planting of the gospel in a person's soul. Jesus said, "I have sent you to reap" (John 4:38). He also sends out His servants to "bear fruit that remains" (John 15:16). Paul exerted himself "that I might save some" (1 Corinthians 9:22). All these contexts drive the evangelist to yearn that others may come to know Christ as Savior and Lord. It appears that this same end-game applies to a proper understanding of "make disciples" in Matthew's Great Commission.

The risen Lord, when He uttered the Great Commission as recorded in Matthew, used the primary verb μαθητεύω, "make disciples." The historical-doctrinal-practical impact of the translation of this one verb is so intense that it deserves special attention, being reserved as the last verb in this chapter.

The key verb translated "make disciples" (μαθητεύω) in Matthew 28:19 is found a total of four times in the New Testament, three times in Matthew and once in the Book of Acts. The chart below portrays select translations of this term in English Bibles:

The Four New Testament Uses of Μαθητεύω in Select Translations

Texts	Geneva (1560)	KJV (1611/ 1769)	Young (1862/ 1898)	Darby (1884/ 1890)	ASV (1901)	NKJ (1982)	NIV (1984)	HCSB (2009)	ESV (2011)	John- ston (2017)
Matt 13:52	which is taught	*which is* instruc- ted	having been discipled	discipled	who hath been made a disciple	instruc- ted	who has been instruc- ted	Instruct- ted	who has been trained	being won over
Matt 27:57	who had also him self bene Iesus disciple	was Jesus' disciple	was discipled to Jesus	was a disciple to Jesus	was Jesus' disciple	had also become a disciple of Jesus	had himself become a disciple of Jesus	who himself had also become a disciple of Jesus	who also was a disciple of Jesus	who also had been won as a disciple of Jesus
Matt 28:19	Go there- fore, and teache all nacions	Go ye there- fore, and teach all nations	having gone, then, disciple all the nations	Go there- fore and make disciples of all the nations	Go ye there- fore, and make disciples of all the nations	Go there- fore and make disciples of all the nations	There- fore go and make disciples of all nations	Go, there- fore, and make disciples of all nations	Go there- fore and make disciples of all nations	Go win disciples from all nations
Acts 14: [20]21	And after they preach- ed to that citie & had taught manie	And when they had preach- ed the gospel to that city, and had taught many	Having proc- laimed good news also to that city, and having discipled many	And having announ- ced the glad tidings to that city, and having made many disciples	And when they preach- ed the gospel to that city, and had made many disciples	And when they had preach- ed the gospel to that city and made many disciples	They preach- ed the good news in that city and won a large number of disciples	After they had evan- gelized that town and made many disciples	And when they had preach- ed the gospel to that city and had made many disciples	And when they had evan- gelized that city and won many disciples

233

Several comments about the translation of the verb μαθητεύω (to make disciples). First, the received Latin Vulgate translated μαθητεύω as "teach" (*doceo*) in verse 19, as well as translating διδάσκω as "teach" (*doceo*) in verse 20. Hence, these two concepts became co-mingled. The Latin co-mingling of verse 19 and 20 disadvantages a chronological application of these verses: go (preach the gospel), win disciples, baptizing them, and teaching them. Also, translating μαθητεύω as "teach" benefits denominations who perform infant baptisms to symbolize and actualize Christian conversion, following up on that rite with catechism (teaching).

> And Jesus came and said to them, "All authority in heaven and on earth has been given to me. Go therefore and make disciples of all nations, baptizing them in the name of the Father and of the Son and of the Holy Spirit, teaching them to observe all that I have commanded you. And behold, I am with you always, to the end of the age" (Matthew 28:18-20 ESV).

However, if Jesus was referring to the end of the evangelism process in using the verb μαθητεύω, then He truly meant "winning a disciple." Why so? If the person being baptized—"baptizing them" in Matthew 28:19—refers only to repentant and believing persons. Only those who have personally confessed Christ and verbally expressed their desire to follow Jesus in baptism ought to be baptized (Acts 8:36-37). The verb for "win disciples" (μαθητεύω) in verse 19 therefore must refer to the beginning of salvation, or justification. Whereas the verb "teach" (διδάσκω) in verse 20 refers to the continuation of salvation, that is, sanctification or growing through discipleship.

Further, the most important word to properly interpret μαθητεύω ("win disciples") in Matthew 28:19 may be the demonstrative pronoun "them" (αὐτός). In this verse, "them" is a masculine plural pronoun (αὐτοὺς) which can only refer to *a previously won disciple*. The competing antecedent for "them" is the noun "nations." However, "nations" is a neuter noun. If Jesus had been referring to "nations" by using the pronoun "them," then He would have used the neuter plural of "them" αὐτά, not αὐτοὺς. Moreover, the pronoun αὐτά is found 13 times in Matthew's Gospel, 10 of those uses coming from the lips of Jesus. Therefore,

Jesus was not telling His disciples to indiscriminately baptize *whoever* from "all nations." Rather He commanded His disciples to baptize only those who were won as disciples. Hence, Jesus particularized the harvest by using the verb μαθητεύω ("win disciples"). Misapplying "nations" as the antecedent for the word "them" certainly benefits (1) universalists, (2) infant baptizers, and (3) state-churches. God, however, superintended that the noun "nations" was a neuter word in the Greek language.

Therefore, a proper understanding of Christ's Great Commision in Matthew suggests that "win disciples" (μαθητεύω) speaks of the beginning of faith instead of the continuation or culmination of a life of discipleship. Another use of μαθητεύω in Matthew also commends this interpretation. In Matthew 27:57, Joseph of Arimathea was described as "having become a disciple of Jesus" using the verb μαθητεύω in past completed action (aorist) rather than present continuous action (imperfect). So, Joseph, although he had become a disciple of Jesus, was still only a "secret disciple" of Jesus (John 19:38). His requesting the body of Jesus was akin to publicly identifying with the crucified Savior.

Joseph's spiritual "before and after" were described by the Apostle:

> Nevertheless even among the rulers many believed in Him, but because of the Pharisees they did not confess Him, lest they should be put out of the synagogue; for they loved the praise of men more than the praise of God (John 12:42-43).

Joseph went from being a ruler who loved the "praise of men more," to being a ruler who preferred the "praise of God." He publicly associated with Jesus by giving Him a proper burial. This identification with Christ parallels what takes place in baptism. In baptism, the baptized person publicly identifies with the crucified Christ, just as Joseph did when he requested and performed the burial rite on the body of Jesus.

The authors of the New Testament utilized numerous metaphorical terms to describe the nature of the Great Commission—what it is that Christ has called His followers to accomplish on earth. More than just inform people, Christ wants His followers to win them for Jesus. They are to sow the seed of the gospel, plow the ground of hardened hearts, thresh the wheat from the chaff, and win people to Christ.

Clarifying one's purpose helps clarify how better to serve Christ as He desires. Understanding these verbs can also prepare God's people for the difficulties that they will encounter because of this divine calling to participate in saving the souls of men.

CHAPTER FOURTEEN

BAPTIZING THEM
—βαπτίζω—

With all the controversy around baptism, God has magnificently allowed that there are examples in the New Testament of the use of the verb βαπτίζω (to baptize) in both a natural sense as well as in a religious sense. Before we enter into the spiritual uses of βαπτίζω, let's begin by observing the natural meaning of the verb.

Investigating the Meaning of Βαπτίζω

There are quite a number of words in the New Testament (NT) for washing, bathing, and sprinkling.[1] It is important to note that each biblical author had these and other words at their disposal to illustrate the action that they were describing. Because Christ's use of the verb "to baptize" (βαπτίζω) in His Great Commissions in Matthew and Mark, because of John the Baptist's baptizing (41.7% of cognate uses), and because of baptizing in the Book of Acts (22.5%), the verb βαπτίζω (to baptize) and its cognates became the predominant word for a physical ritual in Christianity.

Jesus used the verb βαπτίζω in Matthew 28:19, as well as in Mark 16:16. Meanwhile, this verb was not recorded in the Great Commissions of Jesus in Luke 24, John 20, or Acts 1. This begs the question, what was Jesus implying when He used the word βαπτίζω in His Great Commissions in Matthew and Mark? Was there an implication based on the literal definition of the term βαπτίζω from which a symbolism emerged for this unique term?

---

[1]For example: ὁ βαπτισμός (dipping, bathing, baptism); τὸ βάπτισμα (that which is dipped); ὁ βαπτιστής (one that dips, a baptizer); βάπτω (to dip); ἐμβάπτω (to dip into); βρέχω (to wet); λούω (to bathe); ἀπολούω (to wash away); τὸ λουτρόν (washing); νίπτω (to wash); ἀπονίπτω (to wash off); πλύνω (to wash); ἀποπλύνω (to wash off or out); ῥαντίζω (to sprinkle); ὁ ῥαντισμός (sprinkling).

It is no secret that different churches baptize differently. Some adhere to water baptism by immersion, others to pouring, and still others to sprinkling. Some baptize infants and others argue that only those able to voice repentance and request baptism should be baptized. There are even examples in the Medieval period of those who practiced baptism without water, focusing uniquely on the baptism of the Holy Spirit. To determine a certain level of specificity in baptism, its New Testament context must be considered.

The Old Testament (OT) uses of the verb βαπτίζω (to dip, baptize) are quite rare (2 uses in OT Canon, 2 in Apocryphal books). However, there are 16 OT uses of the verb βάπτω (to dip). It is first used of "dipping" a hyssop branch into the blood at Passover to sprinkle that blood on the doorposts of a house (Exodus 12:22). Similarly, the same verb is used 7 times in Leviticus related to the blood of sacrifices. Five of these describe the priest dipping his finger into blood for a ceremonial cleansing ritual. In Leviticus 11:32 anything touching a dead person needed to be dipped or placed (βάπτω) in water, being considered unclean until evening.

One interesting OT use of βαπτίζω (to dip, baptize) relates to Naaman dipping himself in the Jordan River seven times:

> So he went down and dipped [βαπτίζω] himself seven times in the Jordan, according to the word of the man of God, and his flesh was restored like the flesh of a little child, and he was clean (2 Kings 5:14 ESV).

Elisha had commanded him to bathe (Greek λούω; Hebrew rachats) in the Jordan seven times (2 Kings 5:10). As the story unfolded, both the Hebrew and the Greek used a different verb to describe what Naaman actually did. He did not bathe himself (Greek λούω; Hebrew rachats) as commanded by Elisha, but he dipped himself (Greek βαπτίζω; Hebrew tabal) into the river seven times. So, in verse 14 the Greek text used a verb other than "to dip" (λούω)—the verb used was "to baptize" (βαπτίζω), a synonym to the verb "to dip."

Naaman dropped himself down under the water of the Jordan River seven times to be cleansed. This one example seems to be the clearest OT precedent for the NT verb βαπτίζω (to dip, baptize). It related to Naaman ceremonially dipping himself for cleansing from the disease of leprosy. Naaman's baptism provides history's first example of self-baptism (aka. *Se-baptism*). Interestingly, as God would have it, Elisha did not perform or observe the rite. He remained at his home and did not even go out to meet Naaman. This curious non-involvement on the part of Elisha infuriated Naaman. Yet, God superintended both the event and its recording, since Naaman's self-baptism became a precedent for the New Testament ordinance of baptism. In the New Testament, the significance shifted from the incurable disease of leprosy to the humanly incurable guilt of sin. New Testament baptism became an outward sign to a watching world of sins having already been cleansed prior to baptism taking place. These sins were already atoned for by blood of Jesus shed on the cross. The cleansing for sins is applied when a person confesses their sins to Jesus and asks Him to forgive them of their sins. Hence, being made a "won disciple" or follower of Jesus they are then qualified to receive water baptism.

This same action of baptism as dipping is exemplified in the New Testament. There is no hint in the New Testament of baptism being anything other than persons going down into the water so that the recipient of baptism is fully immersed or dipped into the water. Where Naaman is the prime example of baptism in the Old Testament, the Ethiopian Eunuch becomes the prime example of baptism in the NT. This example is so rich that it needs to be considered in some detail. As Philip evangelized the Ethiopian Eunuch, using the Isaiah 53 passage that the eunuch himself had already been reading, the narrative abruptly jumps from Philip evangelizing to the eunuch requesting baptism:

> And both Philip and the eunuch went down into the water, and he baptized [βαπτίζω] him. Now when they came up out of the water, the Spirit of the Lord caught Philip away, so that the eunuch saw him no more; and he went on his way rejoicing (Acts 8:38-39).

So, as to the meaning of the word "baptism" (βαπτίζω), as it is used in Acts 8 38-39, we have both the baptizer and the recipient of baptism going "down into the water." Then we have them coming up out of the water. The same "coming up out of the water" was exemplified at the baptism of Jesus:

> When He had been baptized [βαπτίζω], Jesus came up immediately from the water; and behold, the heavens were opened to Him, and He saw the Spirit of God descending like a dove and alighting upon Him (Matthew 3:16).

This action, of going down into the water and coming up out of the water, parallels what was described of Naaman's seven-fold self-baptism in 2 Kings 5.

While there was a spiritual use of the word baptize and baptism, it is interesting to note that the word also has a natural meaning. Both the verb *baptize* (βαπτίζω) and its related noun (ὁ βαπτισμός) are also used in the New Testament in the context of the washing or cleaning of implements for eating:

> When they come *from the marketplace, they do not eat unless they wash [βαπτίζω]. And there are many other things which they have received and hold,* like *the washing [ὁ βαπτισμός] of cups, pitchers, copper vessels, and couches* (Mark 7:4).

> "For laying aside the commandment of God, you hold the tradition of men—the washing [ὁ βαπτισμός] of pitchers and cups, and many other such things you do" (Mark 7:8).

> When the Pharisee saw it, he marveled that He had not first washed [βαπτίζω] before dinner (Luke 11:38).

While these examples do not prove any particular method implied by the term *baptism*, they definitely link the symbolism of baptizing with the washing away of the stain of sin.

Other NT clues to the meaning of baptizing are the descriptions of a significant amount of water being available to baptize. For example, John the Baptist baptized along the Jordan River. So also, the disciples of Jesus baptized where there was available water:

> After this Jesus and his disciples went into the Judean countryside, and he remained there with them and was baptizing [βαπτίζω]. John also was baptizing [βαπτίζω] at Aenon near Salim, because water was plentiful there, and people were coming and being baptized [βαπτίζω] (John 3:22-23 ESV).

> Now when Jesus learned that the Pharisees had heard that Jesus

was making and baptizing more disciples than John (although Jesus himself did not baptize [βαπτίζω], but only his disciples), he left Judea and departed again for Galilee (John 4:1-3 ESV).

These short narratives teach us that the disciples of Jesus (1) were baptizing; (2) were baptizing where there was much water; and (3) were baptizing more disciples than was John. In this context, John the Baptist had said, "He must increase, but I must decrease" (John 3:30).

The order in which the verb is used in Matthew's and Mark's Great Commission provides special clarification as to the recipients of this ordinance. βαπτίζω (to immerse, dip) is not found first in any verbal sequences. Rather the verb follows the commitment verb, whether believing or becoming a disciple.

Βαπτίζω in the Great Commission Order

There is an interesting particularization built into Matthew's Great Commission. It may be that the most important word to properly interpret Matthew's Great Commission is the pronoun "them." The position and parsing of this pronoun provides particular potency. "Them" in Matthew 28:19, "baptizing them," does not modify the first two verbs, "go, make disciples," but to the third verb, "baptizing" (βαπτίζω):

"Go therefore and make disciples of all nations, baptizing [βαπτίζω] them in the name of the Father and of the Son and of the Holy Spirit, teaching them to observe all that I have commanded you. And behold, I am with you always, to the end of the age" (Matthew 28:19-20 ESV).

"Them" in Matthew 28:19 is repeated with a second "them" in verse 20, "teaching them." These pronouns are juxtaposed to the general audience "all the nations" in verse 19. In Matthew's Great Commission there are verbs associated with the universal "all nations," and other verbs associated with the particular "them." The first two verbs of the Great Commission that apply to "all the nations":

- "Go" and

- Work to "Make disciples."

The second two verbal groups relate to disciples who have been made. The term "them" is the particularizing pronoun differentiating that group from the "all nations" in verse 19. The second set of verbs are applied only to "won disciples":

- "Baptizing them"
- "Teaching them to observe."

The third and fourth verbs in Matthew's Great Commission are particularized to the smaller group, those who are made as disciples out of/from all the nations. This group is even more restrained when considering that out of those won as disciples, not all are willing to be baptized. While baptism in the Holy Spirit is accomplished by God for salvation, the physical aspect of "baptizing them" was a commanded action that Christ expected His disciples to obey.

Whereas the verb "make disciples" or "win disciples" is the first level of response to the gospel message, it points to the result of the ministry of the evangelizing disciple, rather than the action of the recipient of the gospel. The second level of response puts the focus on the newly won disciple to be baptized. There seems to be a close link in the New Testament between genuine repentance and belief in Jesus, and a willingness to be baptized as a first step of obedience to Jesus' command.

"Them" in Matthew 28:19 narrows down not only "the nations" but also those who are "won as disciples." As noted in the prior chapter, Joseph of Arimathea had been "won as a disciple" sometime during the ministry of Jesus (Matthew 27:57). He believed in Jesus, but he did so secretly (John 19:38). And he was apparently joined by quite a large group of other believing "rulers" who were likewise "secret" believers:

> Nevertheless even among the rulers many believed in Him, but because of the Pharisees they did not confess Him, lest they should be put out of the synagogue; for they loved the praise of men more than the praise of God (John 12:42-43).

There were "many" among the rulers who had an intellectual or pragmatic belief in Jesus. But these sophisticated rulers did not wish to confess Him before men, lest they be put out of the synagogue. They anticipated pushback from others who did not share their enthusiasm for Christ and His teaching. Likewise, even today, there some who come to faith in Jesus, but are not willing to follow Jesus in obedience to water baptism.

Perhaps this necessary obedience in baptism was exactly the point Jesus was making in His Great Commission in Mark 16:

> And He said to them, "Go into all the world and preach the gospel to every creature. He who believes and is baptized [βαπτίζω] will be saved; but he who does not believe will be condemned" (Mark 16:15-16).

Those who only believe in Jesus and are not willing to be baptized, show that they do not have a proper understanding of what true "believing" implies. They stand condemned. Further, the conjunction "and" in Mark 16:16, between "believes" and "is baptized" marks a chronological or consecutive coordinating conjunction:

- First: "believe"

- Then: "be baptized."

Jesus explained the proper order in which these two verbs must take place—for example, infant baptism reverses that order. Just as a lack of faith condemns, so the presence of true faith saves. True saving faith will lead to a desire for water baptism. Hence, Mark 16:15-16 follows the order and pattern of the verbs in Matthew 28:19-20, while applying a different emphasis.

Some take the "and" in Mark 16:16 to be a correlative conjunction. They consider that believing and being baptized both have equal weight in the sentence—inseparable and equal weight as far as salvation. For example, Alexander Campbell taught this in *The Christian System* (1839):

> But it [baptism] has no abstract efficacy. ... Still to the believing penitent it [baptism] is the means of receiving a formal, distinct, and specific absolution, or release from guilt. Therefore, none but those who have first believed the testimony of God and have repented of their sins, and that have been intelligently immersed into his death, have the full and explicit testimony of God, assuring them of pardon. To such only as are truly penitent, dare

> we say, "Arise and be baptized, and wash away your sins, calling
> upon the name of the Lord"; and to such only can we say with
> assurance, "You are washed, you are justified, you are sanctified
> in the name of the Lord Jesus, and by the Spirit of God."[2]

Campbell aligned the act and fact of dipping in the water of baptism with "absolution from guilt." For him faith alone was not enough for justification to be made complete. He taught counter to Romans 4:3 on this issue:

> For what does the Scripture say? "Abraham believed God, and it
> was accounted to him for righteousness" (Romans 4:3).

Even the Old Testament act of circumcision did not effectuate justification for Abraham. Nor does New Testament baptism effectuate justification or "absolution from guilt" as wrongly taught by Campbell. So, Calvin's borrowing of Old Testament infant circumcision to prove the validity of infant baptism was a moot point (see Calvin's "Against the Anabaptists"). Man is saved by faith alone and only by faith. The entire weight of the Book of Romans rests on "from faith to faith" (Romans 1:17). However, Campbell, applying Mark 16:16 as his fulcrum, taught that water baptism provided for "specific absolution, or release from guilt." Hence, for Campbell, no water baptism by immersion meant no release from guilt. In so doing, Campbell fell prey to Rome's Sacramental notion of regarding the spiritual nature of the water of baptism as was taught by Cyprian, Ambrose, Augustine, Lombard, and Aquinas. Campbell tainted the simplicity of Scriptures alone, faith alone, and grace alone by adding baptism to the mix.

The Holy Spirit, however, sings a different tune in the Book of Acts. The Acts of the Apostles provides many examples of the proper order of verbs: hearing, believing, then baptism. In Acts 18:8 Luke summarized Paul's ministry in Corinth. He wrote, "And many of the Corinthians, hearing, believed and were baptized" (Acts 18:8):

- Hearing

---

[2]Alexander Campbell, *The Christian System*, (Bethany, VA: Forrester and Campbell, 1839), 60.

- Believed and

- Were baptized.

This order registers a doctrinal trademark for the New Testament church. Evangelizing results in "hearing" first, then—in some—"believing" second, and then thirdly, in "baptizing" the willing. In fact, one of the best examples of this same order is the Ethiopian Eunuch in Acts 8.

Βαπτίζω and the Ethiopian Eunuch

Philip's encounter with the Ethiopian Eunuch provides a conceptual and practical precedent for baptism:

- The evangelist responding immediately to the Holy Spirit's call

- God's work in and by His word through the Holy Spirit to humble and convict of sin

- The evangelist being made aware of God's preparation of the contact through hearing him read Scripture

- Evangelizing from one passage of Scripture

- The new believer taking initiative in his own spiritual nurture

- The new believer requesting baptism

- A biblical baptismal dialogue before baptizing someone.

God has overseen that this account is the only New Testament with a dialogue directly related to baptism. In that light, this dialogue is both descriptive and prescriptive. It described what happened in the interchange of Philip with the Ethiopian Eunuch. It also exemplifies important elements of what is necessary prior to baptizing someone.

It is interesting that Jesus, who was to baptize with the Holy Spirit and fire, would also ask His disciples to water baptize persons—in the manner of John the Baptist—once they had become a disciple. Yet, those who submit to the Bible's authority understand that it was Christ's desire that followers of Jesus be water baptized upon conversion. In a way, Jesus using the methodology of John the Baptist highlights the importance of repentance—the focal message of John the Baptist. Through requiring baptism of all His followers, Jesus was highlighting the need for:

- Repentance unto salvation before baptism

- Repentance by the symbol of baptism after salvation.

This ordinance was further confirmed by the many examples of believer's baptism in the Book of Acts. These examples demonstrate the clarity and unity of the Scriptures, wherein the examples in the Book of Acts demonstrate obedience to the commands of Jesus in His Great Commission. Likewise, although the Epistles have much to say about salvation, they have less to say about baptism in comparison to the Gospels and the Acts—which should give pause to those who forge an indelible link between the unconscious mechanism of "infant baptism" and conversion.

After Philip ran up to the eunuch's chariot, he heard him reading from the prophet Isaiah. Philip immediately identified Isaiah 53 as the text he was reading. He began from that Scripture and evangelized him about Jesus. Then the narrative abruptly jumps from Philip evangelizing (εὐαγγελίζω) into the baptismal sequence:

- *Then Philip opened his mouth, and beginning at this Scripture, preached [εὐαγγελίζω] Jesus to him.*

- *Now as they went down the road, they came to some water.*

- *And the eunuch said, "See, here is water. What hinders me from being baptized [βαπτίζω]?"*

- *Then Philip said, "If you believe with all your heart, you may."*

- *And he answered and said, "I believe that Jesus Christ is the Son of God."*

- *So he commanded the chariot to stand still.*

- *And both Philip and the eunuch went down into the water, and he baptized [βαπτίζω] him.*

- *Now when they came up out of the water, the Spirit of the Lord caught Philip away, so that the eunuch saw him no more; and he went on his way rejoicing (Acts 8:35-39).*

This passage is rich with insights—which draws it to be a prime candidate for textual critical issues! We have in this short pericope a great example of "evangelizing [about] Jesus." The conversation begins with three questions that initiate the conversation and the context of the witness of Jesus. It includes the fifth of 15 uses of the verb evangelize (εὐαγγελίζω) in Acts, along with Jesus as the object of the verb. Then, without further development, we find that the recipient of the gospel has been "fully evangelized" (again helping define NT "evangelizing"), as he himself was requesting baptism. Philip the evangelist responded to the eunuch by asking him if he believed with all his heart. Then, we read the only verbal confession prior to baptism in the pages of the NT. It is a verbal confession of Jesus Christ being the "Son of God" (πιστεύω τὸν υἱὸν τοῦ Θεοῦ εἶναι τὸν Ἰησοῦν Χριστόν).

This baptismal interchange appears to be one of the important reasons that Luke included this witnessing encounter in Acts. By doing so, Luke presented an example of baptism for all Christians throughout the history of the church age. This account codifies that the baptismal candidate must first verbally declare allegiance to Jesus Christ. The baptizer, Philip, and the baptismal candidate, the eunuch, both descended into the water together. The baptizer then immersed (βαπτίζω) the candidate in the water. Then they came up out of the water.

There is no question that variants associated with Acts 8:37 merely trumpet the power, practicality, and clarity of this verse. The textual variants associated with this verse displays the controversial nature of believer's baptism since the early centuries of the church, as well as the power of this verse when used to affirm believer's baptism. Baptism was a lightning rod issue for Augustine of Hippo in 382 A.D. antagonism to the Donatists.[3] He

---

[3]"But since no one can doubt that baptism, which is the sacrament of the remission of sins, is possessed even by murderers, who are yet in darkness because the hatred of their brethren is not excluded from their hearts, therefore either no remission of sins is given to them if their baptism is accompanied by no change of heart for the better, or if the sins are remitted, they at once return on them again" (Augustine, *The Seven Books of Augustin, Bishop of Hippo, On Baptism, Against the Donatists*, Book V, Ch. 21—29; in Philip Schaff, ed., *Nicene*

was likely not the first in church history to stumble over what became his *cause célèbre*. It must be noted that many of the oldest Greek codexes, known as the "Four Great Uncials" date to the time of Augustine:

- Codex Alexandrinus (approx. fifth century)

- Codex Ephraemi Rescriptus (approx. fifth century)

- Codex Sinaiticus (approx. fourth century)

- Codex Vaticanus (approx. fourth century).[4]

These dates are from after and during the ministries of:

- Cyprian of Carthage (A.D. 200-258)

- Ambrose of Milan (A.D. 340-397)

- Augustine of Hippo (A.D. 354-430).

All these men held to a Sacramental view of water baptism. A Sacramental view of baptism is not the Evangelical view of baptism, whereby "faith comes by hearing, and hearing by the word of God" (Romans 10:17). In a Sacramental view of baptism, the conversion signified by water baptism is operated by the Holy Spirit working in, with, and by the physical substance of the blessed water of baptism, when rightly administered. The writings of Augustine against the Donatists on baptism, as well as his reliance upon his predecessors Cyprian and Ambrose on this issue, demonstrate that the churches in the fourth, fifth, and sixth centuries were not without division over baptism. Hence, it makes sense that New Testament manuscripts of that era also reflect the polemics of their day.

The entirety of Acts 8:37, exactly as found in the New King James translation, remains intact in the "old Greek" *Greek Orthodox Bible* in my possession titled Ἡ Ἁγία Γραθή (Athens, 2004). The removal of Acts 8:37 is a rather late phenomenon. It took place after late nineteenth century Western scholars began accepting the priority readings of the "Four Great Uncials" above

---

and Post-Nicene Fathers, vol. 4 [Christian Literature, 1887; Peabody, MA: Hendrickson, 2004], 474).

[4]Dates are based on "paleographic dating."

the thousands of other extant Greek manuscripts coined the "Majority Text." With slight circular reasoning, manuscripts are added to the Majority Text group because of their distinctive readings, such as that they include portions like Acts 8:37.

Due to the polemic nature of baptism and because there is no state-church in the United States, varying views of baptism have also emerged. Four views will be displayed for consideration: Thirty-Nine Articles of the Church of England (1572), Wesley's Book of Discipline (1784), Westminster Confession (1646), and the Baptist Faith and Message (2000).

Select Views of Baptism

A study of the doctrinal basis upon which different churches operate clearly communicates what each denomination felt was important as they drew up their confessions. In this section, we will only consider four groups due to space limitations.

Thirty-Nine Articles of the Church of England (1572)

The *Forty-Two Articles* of the Church of England were originally drawn up by Archbishop of Canterbury Thomas Cramner in 1553 during the reign of the Protestant King Edward VI. During the reign of Elizabeth I, Archbishop of Canterbury Matthew Parker revised the Forty-Two Articles into Thirty-Nine. The *Thirty-Nine Articles* are defining statements in forming the doctrinal basis for the Church of England. Article 27 of the *Thirty-Nine Articles* addressed baptism:

> BAPTISM is not only a sign of profession, and mark of difference, whereby Christian men are discerned from others that be not christened, but it is also a sign of Regeneration or new Birth, whereby, as by an instrument, they that receive Baptism rightly are grafted into the Church; the promises of forgiveness of sin, and of our adoption to be the sons of God by the Holy Ghost, are visibly signed and sealed; Faith is confirmed, and Grace increased by virtue of prayer unto God. The Baptism of young Children is in

any wise to be retained in the Church, as most agreeable with the institution of Christ.[5]

Of interest for the purposes of this study, the reader will consider that:

1. Most of the blessings of conversion are bestowed upon the infant receiving baptism who is:

    a. Fully unconscious of the repentance or faith being exerted for him and transferred to him by a third-party

    b. Unable to personally repent of his sins or to verbally confess them, as was exemplified in John the Baptist's ministry

    c. Unaware of the blessings of salvation that he is presumed to be receiving by third-party proxy.

2. The infant is incapable of following the example of the Ethiopian Eunuch, because he is:

    a. Unable to request baptism

    b. Unable to verbally profess faith in Jesus Christ.

3. All the blessings of conversion through baptism are being actuated by a third-party prayer over the water soon to be used in baptism, that it may bestow the graces it signifies

4. In the 1553 *Forty-Two Articles* and the 1572 *Thirty-Nine Articles*, the respective archbishops of Canterbury also felt it necessary to include a sentence encouraging the retention of the practice of the "Baptism of young children."

Wesley's *Book of Discipline* (1784)

The evangelist John Wesley drew up some articles of religion for the growing group of Methodist adherents. In so doing, he revised the Thirty-Nine Articles of the Church of England. His omissions on the issue of baptism are quickly evident to the discerning reader:

---

[5]"The Thirty-Nine Articles of Religion of the Church of England Published 1571"; in Philip Schaff, ed., *The Creeds of Christendom*, vol. 3 (Harper and Row, 1931; Grand Rapids: Baker, 1998), 504-04.

XVII. Of Baptism. Baptism is not only a sign of profession, and a mark of difference, whereby christians are distinguished from others that are not baptized; but it is also a sign of regeneration, or the new birth. The baptism of young children is to be retained in the church.[6]

Westminster Confession (1646)

The Westminster Confession was requested by the English Parliament. It was authored in 1646 and published in 1647. The Westminster Confession has since that time become a faith standard for many Presbyterian groups. While still adhering to infant baptism, and while still retaining a Sacramental view of the water of baptism, the Westminster Confession made two clarifications on baptism, which appear to correspond to the New Testament witness:

Although it be a great sin to contemn or neglect this ordinance, yet grace and salvation are not so inseparably annexed unto it as that no person can be regenerated or saved without it, or that all that are baptized are undoubtedly regenerated.[7]

In this one sentence, the Westminster Divines provided two retractions to the absolute Sacramental view of baptism:

- *Grace and salvation are not so inseparably annexed unto it as that no person can be regenerated or saved without it*

- *All who are baptized are not undoubtedly regenerated [by it].*

The Westminster Divines showed their submission to the text of Scripture by these two concessions. The "Thief on the Cross" provides the sure example of one who was saved without baptism:

And He said to him, "Truly I say to you, today you shall be with Me in Paradise" (Luke 23:43 NASB).

---

[6]"Methodist Articles of Religion"; in Philip Schaff, ed., *The Creeds of Christendom*, vol. 3 (Harper and Row, 1931; Grand Rapids: Baker, 1998), 811.

[7]"The Westminster Confession of Faith (1646)"; in James T. Dennison, Jr., *Reformed Confessions of the 16th and 17th Centuries in English Translation: Volume 4, 1600-1693* (Grand Rapids: Reformation Heritage, 2014), 267.

Likewise, the New Testament provides an example of one who believed and was baptized, but was not saved. That is, Simon the Sorcerer in Acts 8. In Acts 8:12-13 Luke twice used examples of the sequence of verbs mentioned above:

> But when they believed Philip as he preached the things concerning the kingdom of God and the name of Jesus Christ, both men and women were baptized. Then Simon himself also believed; and when he was baptized he continued with Philip, and was amazed, seeing the miracles and signs which were done (Acts 8:12-13).

The two verbal sequences are:

- Verse 12: [Men and women] believed … were baptized;

- Verse 13: [Simon himself] believed … was baptized.

At first glance, Simon appears to be a neutral participant among those mentioned in verse 12, since the same verbs were used. However, the second sequence as applied to Simon is singled out for a reason. His true spiritual nature was soon to reveal itself based on Peter's admonition. Simon lusted for the power to give the Holy Spirit to the point of offering money to Peter and John to receive this power. The verdict on Simon's lack of genuine regeneration was given from the mouth of Peter.[8] Luke in Acts 8 warned his readers that some self-seeking unbelievers will feign faith in Christ and be baptized. Once in the church they would seek to ravage the flock of God (Acts 20:29-30). Luke, then, right after dealing with Simon the Sorcerer in Acts 8, guided his readers as to the means of proper baptism through the example of the Ethiopian Eunuch.

Baptist Faith and Message (2000)

The 2000 Baptist Faith and Message provides an excellent summary of the Bible's teaching on water baptism. It was drawn up by Southern Baptist pastors and scholars committed to believer's baptism:

---

[8]See Chapters 8 and 9 on Peter's words to Simon.

> *Christian baptism is the immersion of a believer in water in the name of the Father, the Son, and the Holy Spirit. It is an act of obedience symbolizing the believer's faith in a crucified, buried, and risen Saviour, the believer's death to sin, the burial of the old life, and the resurrection to walk in newness of life in Christ Jesus. It is a testimony to his faith in the final resurrection of the dead. Being a church ordinance, it is prerequisite to the privileges of church membership and to the Lord's Supper.*[9]

The reader will note that according to this statement of faith, the act of baptism is considered symbolic, not Sacramental. It does not operate conversion, but necessitates faith prior to receiving it. This author conceives in baptism as described in the Baptist Faith and Message 2000.

Baptism has produced significant discord and disarray in the history of the churches. Yet God has provided a sufficient witness for Himself on the issue of baptism. Pragmatism and false teachings have crept into various church patterns of worship and creedal documents. The word of God provides a final and authoritative constitution from which to properly understand and practice baptism. Only born-again believers in Jesus, who can give verbal witness of their belief in Jesus, and who request baptism, ought to be baptized. Furthermore, Jesus Himself codified the importance of water baptism by Himself being baptized and by including it in two of His five Great Commission passages.

---

[9]Southern Baptist Convention, *The Baptist Faith and Message* (Nashville: Lifeway, 2000), 14.

CHAPTER FIFTEEN

TEACH THEM TO OBEY
—διδάσκω + τηρέω—

When Jesus first sent out His disciples, He said, "Go!" Next, as stated in Mark's Great Commission, is the command to "preach the gospel." A result of "preaching the gospel" is that some hearers become disciples. Hence, in Matthew, as noted in a prior chapter, disciples are commissioned to "win disciples out of/from all the nations." It is at the point of winning disciples that a distinction is made in the text. Whereas the call to "win disciples" is a call to universal evangelism, the call to baptize is a particular call. The grammatical marker for this particularization is the word "them." The first "them" in Matthew's Great Commission refers to those who become disciples and request baptism. It refers only to won disciples among those for whom the efforts to "win disciples" proves fruitful. The second "them" builds on this first "them." The second "them" designates what is to be done with disciples who are won and baptized. They are to be taught to obey all the commands of Christ.

The Great Commission of Jesus in the Book of Matthew is where we find "teaching them to observe all that I have commanded you" (Matthew 28:20). A principle of Bible interpretation is to consider the context of a command (the Book of Matthew), and to seek to examine this command first from that context before branching out into other Scripture. This principle led me to study the commands of Jesus. The fruits of this study make up significant portions of this chapter and the next.

The verb "teach" (διδάσκω) used by Christ in His Great Commission in Matthew has a long precedent in the Bible. After introducing the King of Israel to the boundaries of his country in Deuteronomy 2-3, Moses began to emphasize the importance of his teaching ministry:

> *"And now, O Israel, listen to the statutes and the rules that I am teaching you, and do them, that you may live, and go in and take possession of the land that the LORD, the God of your fathers, is giving you"* (Deuteronomy 4:1 ESV).

Moses used the piel stem of Hebrew verb *lamad* ("to teach") ten times in Deuteronomy, nine of which were translated as διδάσκω ("to teach") in the Greek Septuagint. Teaching was perhaps the most important part of Moses' commissioning from God:

> *"Make them known to your children and your children's children—how on the day that you stood before the LORD your God at Horeb, the LORD said to me, 'Gather the people to me, that I may let them hear my words, so that they may learn to fear me all the days that they live on the earth, and that they may teach their children so.' … And he declared to you his covenant, which he commanded you to perform, that is, the Ten Commandments, and he wrote them on two tablets of stone. And the LORD commanded me at that time to teach you statutes and rules, that you might do them in the land that you are going over to possess"* (Deuteronomy 4:9-10, 13-14 ESV).

Also in Deuteronomy, Moses commanded fathers to "inculcate" God's words into their children using a Hebrew verb *shanan* found only once in the Hebrew Scriptures in the piel stem:

> *You shall teach them diligently to your children, and shall talk of them when you sit in your house, and when you walk by the way, and when you lie down, and when you rise* (Deuteronomy 6:7 ESV).

The Hebrew for "inculcate" (here translated "teach diligently") was translated into Greek as προβιβάζω ("to prompt, push forward"). "Teaching" alone did not seem to have enough depth of meaning for God. He chose the Hebrew verb *shanan* to augment the concept of "teach" (*lamad*) to focus on the final product. Used eight times, the qal stem of *shanan* means "to whet, sharpen" (Deuteronomy 32:41; Psalm 45:6). It appears then, that in its full meaning, *shanan* describes "to teach to sharpen or shape"—to teach to "rightly divide the word of truth" (2 Timothy 2:15). God encouraged fathers to use His words to shape the lives of their children.

In His Great Commission, Jesus passed that same teaching mantle to all His disciples. "teaching them to observe all that I have commanded you" (Matthew 28:20 ESV). In our next chapter we will consider the words "all that I have commanded you." In this chapter we are focusing on "teaching to observe."

The Greek verb behind the English "observe" is a very simple verb. It is τηρέω which means "to keep, keep watch, guard, observe." There is an intensity wrapped up in this verb. Teaching to observe is more than mere philosophical head knowledge. Jesus was encouraging His disciples to "inculcate" His commands into His future disciples—they were to learn to keep them. Like spiritual fathers to their spiritual children, they were to aim for life-change as they taught Christ's disciples all of His commands.

Three questions come to the fore when considering Christ's command to "teach them to observe." First, why teach only "them"? Second, what does it mean to "teach to obey"? And third, how do we "teach them to obey"? These three points provide the main points for the remainder of this chapter.

Why Teach Only "Them"?

This final command in Matthew's Great Commission passage is confined to apply only to "them." It does not apply to the "all nations" as did the command to "make disciples." Why was this command particularized by Jesus Christ?

There is one lesson of the New Testament that seems to have been lost to the history of the churches. It is the need for conversion to Christ before attempting to progress in the spiritual disciplines. There are major swathes of the church that have taught that instantaneous conversion is either unnecessary or a misunderstanding of the grace of God. Rather to them the "way of obedience" consists of a life of continual conversion. Those who adhere to this point-of-view are often those who subscribe to infant baptism. Since for them infant baptism marks regeneration, the only thing that remains for the regenerate infant is to submit to the commands of Christ.

The Puritan Richard Baxter explained the need for distinction here:

THOMAS P. JOHNSTON

> *The work of conversion, of repentance from dead works, and of faith in Christ must be taught first and in a frequent and thorough manner. The stewards of God's household must give to each their portion in their season. We must never go beyond the capacities of our people, nor should we teach Christian maturity to those who have not yet learned the first lesson.*[1]

Before moving through Christ's command to win a disciple, and before moving through His command to baptize them, it is necessary to be sure that they are a won disciple. The evangelist must not move beyond repentance from dead works and belief in the finished work of Christ until that lesson has been fully ingested and its promises procured.

It appears to be a very dangerous precedent to feed a spiritually dead person an array of commands to fulfill when they lack the Holy Spirit's assistance to understand (1) why they are doing those commands; and (2) what obedience to those commands will accomplish for them. It can only lead them to feelings of helplessness or to the pride of self-righteousness. If they do not have the Holy Spirit's presence, which is received only at conversion and regeneration, then how can they understand the need to sacrificially share the gospel, read and memorize the Bible, or love their neighbor as themselves? These become duties fulfilled for a demanding God, rather than actions of gratitude to a loving God. The unsaved may easily misunderstand that by doing certain Christian duties they are thereby presenting themselves as acceptable to God in their own efforts. They will seek to establish a righteousness of their own, and will not submit to righteousness through faith in Jesus Christ.

> *What shall we say then? That Gentiles, who did not pursue righteousness, have attained to righteousness, even the righteousness of faith; but Israel, pursuing the law of righteousness, has not attained to the law of righteousness. Why? Because they did not seek it by faith, but as it were, by the works of the law. For they stumbled at that stumbling stone. As it is written: "Behold, I lay in Zion a stumbling stone and rock of*

---

[1]Richard Baxter, *The Reformed Pastor: A Pattern for Personal Growth and Ministry*, ed. by James M. Houston (Portland: Multnomah, 1982), 15.

*offense, and whoever believes on Him will not be put to shame."
Brethren, my heart's desire and prayer to God for Israel is that
they may be saved. For I bear them witness that they have a zeal
for God, but not according to knowledge. For they being ignorant
of God's righteousness, and seeking to establish their own
righteousness, have not submitted to the righteousness of God.
For Christ is the end of the law for righteousness to everyone who
believes* (Romans 9:30-10:4).

It is a difficult balance to maintain, remaining subject to spiritual disciplines, not for any self-glorification or self-exaltation, but only out of humble gratitude for a Savior who has already "paid it all."

Similarly, Jesus in His teaching distinguished between those who had ears to hear, and by comparison, those who did not. One of the trademarks of Jesus' teaching in parables was His restraint toward those who could not understand and His openness to those who could understand His parables. "He called out, 'He who has ears to hear, let him hear'" (Luke 8:8 ESV). Not everyone has ears to hear. Nor does everyone have ears to properly understand why they should practice spiritual disciplines.

Personal spiritual disciplines are for the "spiritual"—those who are alive in Christ and alive to Christ—those who have been born again and are filled with the Holy Spirit. These are the "them" who need to be taught to observe all things whatsoever Christ commanded.

What Does It Mean to "Teach to Obey"?

There are many modes and methods of teaching and there are many subjects that need to be taught. Jesus, however, in His Great Commission in Matthew narrowed the curriculum for His disciples. Their primary commission was not to teach the Old Testament, the Law, the Prophets, and the Writings, as important as these are. Neither was their primary commission to teach a biography of the life of Jesus, as important as it is to understand the life and times of Christ. They were not even to teach all that Jesus said. Jesus narrowed the focus in their teaching. They were to laser in on the commands of Christ.

Nor were they to teach the commands of Christ in an aloof, detached, or disengaged way. They were to teach other disciples how to obey the commands of Christ. They were called as active, joyful, and engaged participants to train other disciples to observe the same commands of Christ that they were observing. These disciples were to move well beyond knowledge to hands-on practice. In Matthew's Great Commission, the disciples were commissioned to be practitioners teaching practitioners—anything less than teaching practical truth misses the mark and lies outside of Christ's Great Commission in Matthew.

This author can exclaim from experience that it is much simpler to teach cognitive truth. Teaching cognitive truth often has few lifestyle implications. Cognitive truth can be classified as theory and neatly arranged in the rainbow of a truth spectrum. Cognitive truth can be weighed by the teacher in the light of other theories of truth. He can pass on his cognitive perspective to the wonder of unlearned novitiates who are amazed at his broad grasp of the many theories of truth.

But Jesus demanded a clean break from Athens and its theories of truth. He moved well beyond Alexandria with its famed library. Like a swirling tornado, the touchdown of the wind funnel finds its most potent velocity at obedience of all the commands of Christ. **As a matter of fact, obeying the very commands of Christ has preceded and accompanied** *every* **revival of the Christian religion in** *every* **land throughout** *all* **the history of the churches.** Obedience of all the commands of Christ, prayer included but not exclusively prayer, have accompanied all true works of God. This fact is consistent with Christ's Great Commission to "teach them to obey."

There needs to be practical application of teaching all that Christ has commanded. It needs to be constantly and consistently practical truth, wedded with motivation and infused with impulse to obey. Gone are the theories of interpretation and higher critical approaches to the Bible—important as these may be for a better application of true obedience to the message of the Bible. Hello to the straightforward humble submission to the plain meaning of the text.

Paul told young Timothy to remember that he had learned truths directly from God Himself:

> You, however, continue in the things you have learned and become convinced of, knowing from whom you have learned them; and that from childhood you have known the sacred writings which are able to give you the wisdom that leads to salvation through faith which is in Christ Jesus (2 Timothy 3:14-15 NASB).

The teacher of the young disciple needs to get out of the way, and allow the learner to sit at the feet of Jesus, hearing His voice, learning directly from Him, and falling in love with Him.

This practical teaching is difficult. It is easy to lean too heavily one way or the other. Scripture always properly balances knowledge and love, grace and truth.

> And the Word became flesh and dwelt among us, and we have seen his glory, glory as of the only Son from the Father, full of grace and truth. (John bore witness about him, and cried out, "This was he of whom I said, 'He who comes after me ranks before me, because he was before me.'") For from his fullness we have all received, grace upon grace. For the law was given through Moses; grace and truth came through Jesus Christ (John 1:14-17 ESV).

Jesus exemplified grace and truth kissing each other: "Steadfast love and faithfulness meet; righteousness and peace kiss each other" (Psalm 85:10 ESV). Paul admonished the same to the self-important Corinthian believers, "Knowledge makes arrogant, but love edifies" (1 Corinthians 8:1 NASB).

There must be a balance of grace and truth—all grace and all truth—not half grace and half truth. It is in the proper balance of knowledge and mercy that the Holy Spirit comes down. When teaching and obedience are in a humble equilibrium, then the presence of Jesus descends and He confirms His presence, "Lo, I am with you always, even to the end of the age" (Matthew 28:20).

How Do We "Teach Them to Obey"?

The example of Christ with His disciples is a phenomenal training ground for lessons in "teaching them to observe all that I have commanded you" (Matthew 28:20 ESV). Books have been written on this topic that have gleaned important truths from

Jesus, such as A. B. Bruce's *The Training of the Twelve* (1872), Robert Coleman's *The Master Plan of Evangelism* (1963), Bill Hull's *Jesus Christ Disciple Maker* (1984), Francis Chan's *Multiply* (2012), and David Platt's *Radical* (2013). Likewise, this section seeks to elicit some practical points of implementation from the text of Scripture related to teaching disciples to obey all that Christ has commanded them. Considered will be the two verbs *establish* and *exhort*, seeking instructional specificity, five stages in training, levels of discipleship, and churches as Bible colleges. Two verbs that come up several times in the NT in terms of follow-up and discipleship are *establishing* and *exhorting*.

Establish and Exhort

There are two pairs of verbs used to describe the evangelism and follow-up ministry of Paul in Acts 14:

- Evangelize (εὐαγγελίζω) and win disciples (μαθητεύω)
- Establish (ἐπιστηρίζω) and exhort (παρακαλέω)

The first pair has already been noted in prior chapters of this book. Their presence in Acts 14:21 provides a grammatical megaphone drawing the reader to focus attention on the second pair:

> When they had preached the gospel [εὐαγγελίζω] to that city and had made many disciples [μαθητεύω], they returned to Lystra and to Iconium and to Antioch, strengthening [ἐπιστηρίζω] the souls of the disciples, encouraging [παρακαλέω] them to continue in the faith, and saying that through many tribulations we must enter the kingdom of God (Acts 14:21-22 ESV).

Consider the two groups of people who are recipients of the ministry of Paul and Barnabas in these verses. The first verbal pair—evangelize (εὐαγγελίζω) and win disciples (μαθητεύω)—were directed to those "in that city." This matches the recipients of the "make/win disciples" in Matthew 28:19 unto "all the nations." However, once disciples were made, then the second set of verbs was set in motion to describe the ministry of Paul and Barnabas to newly won disciples—strengthen (ἐπιστηρίζω) and exhort (παρακαλέω). The first set of verbs is for the multitudes. The second set of verbs is "for disciples only," corresponding to "teaching them to observe" in Matthew 28:20.

The reader will note that baptism is not mentioned in this summary statement in Acts 14. It appears that Luke's purpose in recording this first missionary journey of Paul was to introduce his early evangelism strategy and not the totality of his ministry methodology. Remembering that Paul's strategy seems to have evolved until he "developed a custom" by the time he traveled to Thessalonica in Acts 17:1-4. Even so, baptism continued to be important in the ministry of Paul, as indicated by the fact that he himself baptized some church members in Corinth (1 Corinthians 1:14-16), and as is noted in his ministry in Acts 18:8:

And many of the Corinthians:

1. *Hearing*

2. *Believed and*

3. *Were baptized* (Acts 18:8).

A study of the second verbal pair for follow-up elicits some interesting facets. The verb to strengthen (ἐπιστηρίζω) above is a cognate to the verb to establish (στηρίζω). It likens establishing someone in the faith as in driving a pole into the ground to build a pole barn. The only way that the barn will hold up to winds and storms is because the poles holding up the barn have been firmly driven into the ground. When Paul sent Timothy to Thessalonica, he sent him with the express purpose of establishing (στηρίζω) them and comforting (παρακαλέω) them (1 Thessalonians 3:2). The new believer must be firmly established in Christ and in His words. The second verb translated "comfort" is the same verb translated "exhort" in Acts 14:22. To describe Timothy's commissioned ministry, Paul used the identical verb (παρακαλέω) found in Acts 14:22. The other verb differs only by way the addition of prepositional prefix ἐπί to render the word more emphatic:

Upon [ἐπί] + Establish [στηρίζω]

= Establish Upon or Strengthen [ἐπιστηρίζω].

The second verb in this pair, translated "comfort" or "exhort," is the verb παρακαλέω (parakaleo). From this word is transliterated the name *Paraclete*—as found in some English Bibles—to describe the role of the Holy Spirit. This name is given to the Holy Spirit in John Chapters 14-16. So, Paul's ministry to the churches in the region of Pisidia included giving strength (ἐπιστηρίζω)—to firm up. It also included exhortation or comfort (παρακαλέω). Παρακαλέω (to comfort, exhort) is used 108 times in the NT. Παρακαλέω literally means to "call to one's side":

Παρά (beside) + καλέω (call) = "call to one's side" (παρακαλέω)

It is translated in a variety of ways depending on the context. Sometimes it is translated to "call," "summon" (Acts 28:20). Other times it is translated to "implore" or "beg" (Acts 16:9). It is also translated "exhort," "urge," "encourage" (Acts 27:33). And it is translated "comfort," "cheer," or "encourage" (2 Corinthians 1:4).

Interestingly, παρακαλέω was used in Psalm 23 of God's gentle guiding in the lives of His people using a rod and a staff, "Your rod and your staff, they comfort (παρακαλέω) me" (Psalm 23:4 ESV). Παρακαλέω (translated from the Hebrew *nacham*) gathers the two sides of this amazing verb (παρακαλέω): (1) the rod of correction; and (2) the staff for leaning upon. Hence this verb covers a range of meaning from implore, exhort, encourage, to comfort.

Παρακαλέω is used 7 times in follow-up situations in the Book of Acts. The verb ἐπιστηρίζω (to strengthen) is used only 4 times in the NT, all of which are in follow-up situations in Acts. The pair is used in reverse order in Acts 15:32 to describe the affirmation of the ministry of Judas and Silas for the church in Antioch after the Jerusalem gathering and statement:

And Judas and Silas, who were themselves prophets, encouraged [παρακαλέω] and strengthened [ἐπιστηρίζω] the brothers with many words (Acts 15:32 ESV).

Consider also the other two solo uses of "to strengthen" (ἐπιστηρίζω) for follow-up in Acts:

And he went through Syria and Cilicia, strengthening [ἐπιστηρίζω] the churches (Acts 15:41 ESV).

And having spent some time there, he departed and passed successively through the Galatian region and Phrygia, strengthening [ἐπιστηρίζω] all the disciples (Acts 18:23 NASB).

Notice the recipients of the "strengthening." In Acts 14 it was "the disciples," in Acts 15:32 it was "the brothers," in Acts 15:41 it was "the churches," and in Acts 18:23 it was again "all the disciples." Clearly, this ministry of follow-up was only directed to those who were won as disciples and baptized, exactly as Christ had commanded as recorded in the Great Commission in Matthew.

In similar manner, God had commanded Moses to encourage and strengthen Joshua, preparing him to be the next leader of the people of Israel:

> "But charge Joshua, and encourage [παρακαλέω] and strengthen [κατισχύω] him, for he shall go over at the head of this people, and he shall put them in possession of the land that you shall see" (Deuteronomy 3:28 ESV).

The dual verbs come out in Deuteronomy. Moses was to "encourage" (παρακαλέω) Joshua, and to "strengthen" (κατισχύω) him. Likewise, the disciples of Jesus are called to train other disciples to faithfully obey the voice of God.

Seeking Instructional Specificity

Curricular guidelines are not easy to find in the New Testament. First, where the Gospels were only prophetic related to the death and resurrection of Jesus (that is the heart message of the Gospel), the post-resurrection teaching of Jesus, the Book of Acts, the Book of Romans, and 1 Corinthians 15 are imminently clear. Second, where the New Testament does not provide a point-by-point training manual for follow-up, discipleship, spiritual disciplines, and cross-cultural ministry equipping, Christians have been sure to fill the void. There are hundreds of manuals and methodologies. God has given sufficient information, then He has allowed His people to provide culturally relevant approaches to ministry, in like manner to the command, "Sing a new song" (Psalm 33:3; 40:3; 96:1; 98:1; 144:9; 149:1). The Holy Spirit has guided and illuminated those He indwells to press forward into new methods and new models of ministry to meet the new challenges encountered by each generation—ever-mindful that new challenges are just reinterpretations of old challenges.

Lest the reader be disappointed in the lack of tangible application in how to "teach them to obey," Acts 18 provides an interesting petri dish as it relates to the training and ministry of Priscilla and Aquila. As to their level of training, by the end of the chapter, we note that Priscilla and Aquila were sufficiently trained to instruct Apollos in doctrinal matters regarding the death and resurrection of Jesus:

> Now a certain Jew named Apollos, an Alexandrian by birth, an eloquent man, came to Ephesus; and he was mighty in the Scriptures. This man had been instructed in the way of the Lord; and being fervent in spirit, he was speaking and teaching accurately the things concerning Jesus, being acquainted only with the baptism of John; and he began to speak out boldly in the synagogue. But when Priscilla and Aquila heard him, they took him aside and explained to him the way of God more accurately (Acts 18:24-26 NASB).

Consider then this couple, Priscilla and Aquila, who were qualified to instruct the eloquent Alexandrian Apollos. How did they receive such training? We begin the chapter with them being referred to as "Jews" come from Italy. The title "Jew" implies that they were not brethren, disciples, Christians, or among "those who believed through grace" (Acts 18:27). Paul was a tentmaker with Aquila, and he occupied his ministry time with reasoning in the synagogue in Corinth (Acts 18:4).

The next time we read of Priscilla and Aquila, they were traveling companions with Paul on a trip to Jerusalem, and apparently listed among the "brethren." Although how they became so is not explained.

> After this, Paul stayed many days longer and then took leave of the brothers and set sail for Syria, and with him Priscilla and Aquila. At Cenchreae he had cut his hair, for he was under a vow (Acts 18:18 ESV).

Later, in Romans 16:3, Priscilla and Aquila are named as fellow-workers of Paul, as well as house church leaders in 1 Corinthians 16:19. Yet in Acts 18 we learn nothing more about Priscilla and Aquila. We do not hear about their salvation, nor of Paul's work-related evangelism methodology. We do not read of

Priscilla's or Aquila's baptism, nor of their being received into the church. We do not read of their discipleship training, their spiritual disciplines, nor of their missionary curriculum for going on a mission trip with Paul. We know that they were not saved at the beginning of Acts 18, and that by the end of the chapter they were qualified to give instruction to Apollos. It is actually quite amazing what we do not learn in this chapter.

What can we learn from Luke's silence? Inspired by the Holy Spirit, Luke did not feel it necessary to provide all these details. He allowed that assumptions could be made based on the context. Perhaps by the Holy Spirit, God gives a level of freedom for gospel presentations to be developed that meet the religious and cultural norms of each society. Likewise, there is freedom, under the absolute authority of the Scriptures, to develop curricula to train and disciple new believers to grow in the Lord. Just as "Sing a new song" is often repeated, so pastoral and missionary training manuals need to be produced by each generation for each generation. The divine restraint and constraint remains true, "Back to the Bible"—whatever the program developed might be called, Jesus demanded that it submit to His predetermined parameters, "Teaching them to observe all that I have commanded you" (Matthew 28:20). That said, there are some clues for important elements to discipleship training.

Five Stages in Training

For men to learn how to fish, they need to walk with a fisherman. They need to see a fisherman at work. They need to learn to throw out the net and actually fish. They need to be trained. "Teaching to obey" necessitates training in practical ministry. And practical ministry training with respect to Matthew's Great Commission revolves around five stages or lessons:

1. Training to "Go"
2. Training to "Preach the gospel"
3. Training to "Win a disciple"
4. Training to "Baptize"
5. Training to "Teach to obey."

Disciples will not "go out" themselves unless they are led out and shown what it is to "go out." They literally need to "go out," just as Jesus sent out His disciples in:

- Matthew 9-10
- Mark 6
- Luke 9
- Luke 10.

In Matthew 9 it clearly noted that Jesus had just exemplified going out before sending them out, and then He continued to go out after sending them out:

And Jesus went throughout all the cities and villages, teaching in their synagogues and proclaiming the gospel of the kingdom and healing every disease and every affliction (Matthew 9:35 ESV).

When Jesus had finished instructing his twelve disciples, he went on from there to teach and preach in their cities (Matthew 11:1 ESV).

Jesus sent out His disciples to do what He Himself was willing to do and what He had already shown them by example. Christ exemplified preaching the gospel, before He sent them out to preach. Christ modelled winning disciples—before He sent them out to win disciples. Christ taught His disciples to baptize. Christ modelled everything that He wanted His disciples to do—which is the very reason the Gospels are great sourcebooks for discipleship training. The Book of Acts builds on the foundation of the Gospels. These NT narrative books provide a sufficient and efficient resource to train every believer to fully and effectively obey each of these stages of Christ's Great Commission. One thing exemplified in these books is the many levels of discipleship ministry.

Levels of Discipleship

Effective follow-up and discipleship includes multiple layers of interaction between believers. Jesus had many levels of relationship, as was experienced by His disciples and those who followed them:

- Jesus spoke to great multitudes in parables (Luke 8:4)

- Jesus addressed 500+ (1 Corinthians 15:6)

- There were also the 120 disciples after the ascension (Acts 1:15)

- Jesus sent out the 70 others (Luke 10:1)

- Jesus called the 12 disciples unto Himself (Luke 6:13) to whom He explained the parables (Luke 8:9-10)

- Jesus chose three disciples to join Him on the Mount of Transfiguration (Luke 9:28)

- And lastly, Jesus had His one disciple whom He loved and who leaned on His breast (John 13:23, 25; 21:20).

These seven distinct levels of relationship characterized the levels of discipleship within the ministry of Jesus. For maximum effectiveness, it would seem that the disciple-maker should keep in mind these levels to maintain a full-bodied ministry of discipleship. There is a need for one-on-one discipleship. Small groups and home groups are important. There is need for various levels of fellowship, as well as for large group worship. Then there is the ministry to the multitudes who do not know Christ. Jesus continued to reach out to lost folks until the hour that He died. All these levels of relationship play a role in "teaching them to obey." It is not a matter of one being "better" than the other. Rather, each level of interrelationship is necessary and each has its place.

Churches as Bible Colleges

In a most striking command to the king of Israel, God commanded that the new king make it his first priority—upon succession to the throne—to handwrite his own copy of the Book of Deuteronomy. The proud new king may have thought, "Who needs that?" And thereby, he would seal his fate as an "evil king." For he would have ignored a commandment that God told him was to be his first priority:

> And when he sits on the throne of his kingdom, he shall write for himself in a book a copy of this law, approved by the Levitical priests. And it shall be with him, and he shall read in it all the days of his life, that he may learn to fear the LORD his God by keeping all the words of this law and these statutes, and doing

them, that his heart may not be lifted up above his brothers, and that he may not turn aside from the commandment, either to the right hand or to the left, so that he may continue long in his kingdom, he and his children, in Israel (Deuteronomy 17:18-20 ESV).

By this command, God was inviting the new king into a personal relationship with Him. He was introducing Himself to the king. And, as was the case for Hezekiah and Josiah, when they read the Law of the Lord they were humbled by it.

While handwriting the Bible may appear painstaking and uninteresting, it proves itself to be a phenomenal methodology for communing with the Lord and learning from Him. The most important element that the disciple-maker can communicate to those he is mentoring is priority of hearing and submitting to the word of God.

In a similar way, Jesus affirmed the importance of His very words as the foundation for all of life:

"Everyone then who hears these words of mine and does them will be like a wise man who built his house on the rock. And the rain fell, and the floods came, and the winds blew and beat on that house, but it did not fall, because it had been founded on the rock. And everyone who hears these words of mine and does not do them will be like a foolish man who built his house on the sand. And the rain fell, and the floods came, and the winds blew and beat against that house, and it fell, and great was the fall of it" (Matthew 7:24-27 ESV).

These words are life and vitality. They provide strength in the storms of life. Peter told Jesus after the discouragement of 5,000 disciples leaving Jesus, "Lord, to whom shall we go? You have the words of eternal life" (John 6:68).

The challenge for the disciple-maker is building the lives of those he mentors upon the rock of the words of Christ. As noted in the beginning of this chapter, Christ commanded that His very commands be the bedrock of all discipleship training. How can this be made practical?

One amazing example in the Book of Acts is the Apostle Paul's ministry in the city of Ephesus. We must assume that Paul was providing all of church history an example of fully applying the principles of the Great Commission within this city. And he did so by reasoning, deliberating, or disputing daily in the school of Tyrannus. We do not read of his two-year curriculum. But we read of its impact. Would it not be amazing if every local church could be a microcosm of Paul's ministry in Ephesus?

> And he entered the synagogue and for three months spoke boldly, reasoning and persuading them about the kingdom of God. But when some became stubborn and continued in unbelief, speaking evil of the Way before the congregation, he withdrew from them and took the disciples with him, reasoning daily in the hall of Tyrannus. This continued for two years, so that all the residents of Asia heard the word of the Lord, both Jews and Greeks (Acts 19:8-10 ESV).

Perhaps churches are so oriented to organizing worship and hearing from their pastor, that they have forgotten "teaching them to observe all that I have commanded you" (Matthew 28:20 ESV). While the Old Testament Temple was to include singing and praise, worship was not a huge part of the New Testament record for church gatherings. Prayer was. "For My house shall be called a house of prayer for the peoples" (Isaiah 56:7 ESV; cf. Luke 19:46). Among the four pillars of the local church are:

- The Apostles' doctrine
- Fellowship
- The breaking of bread, and
- Prayer (Acts 2:42).

Just as important as was prayer, so was training the disciples in the practice of the word of God. This emphasis on the practical teaching of the Bible parallels today's Bible school model.

In Acts 19 Paul was forced to "shake the dust" from his feet and leave the synagogue in Ephesus. He moved the assembly of followers of Christ into the School of Tyrannus. Then in that location he began to teach them daily. Again, we do not find the curriculum he used, nor his daily teaching schedule, nor if he had levels of classes or language classes. The Bible is beautifully silent on those points. However, we do have the practical result of his teaching. Paul was teaching those who gathered "to observe all that Christ had commanded you" (Matthew 28:20 ESV). And in two years, "all the residents of [the province of] Asia heard the word of the Lord, both Jews and Greeks" (Acts 19:10 ESV). Because of this first century Bible School, the entire province of Asia was evangelized one time through!

Full circle here. The teaching in the school of Tyrannus was not to seekers nor was it evangelistic. Paul taught disciples to make disciples following the command of Christ. And they went out and fulfilled the first step in disciple-making—they shared the gospel with all who lived in the province of Asia. The outcome is proof of the content of training. Paul did not teach mere philosophical knowledge, he taught his hearers to obey. They were biblical pragmatists, and they completed the task of reaching their entire province in two years!

"Teaching them to observe all that I have commanded you" (Matthew 28:20 ESV).

CHAPTER SIXTEEN

ALL THAT I HAVE COMMANDED YOU
—πᾶς + ἐντέλλομαι + σύ—

Jesus, the Lord of all the universe, limited the discipleship content for all of church history to those things that He had specifically commanded His disciples. As the Lord of all the universe, He clearly has authority to place such a boundary on what is taught to His people in His Church. Consider that the command to teach "all that I have commanded you" (Matthew 28:20) was meant for:

- Every language group in the world

- Every religious and worldview grouping

- Every cultural and ethnic construct

- Every philosophical approach.

The spiritual needs of every human being on earth, no matter what their language, religious, or cultural extraction was to be met by the study of all that Christ commanded His disciples.

Further, by His supreme authority, Christ exacted immense weight to His Great Commission commands. Because of Christ's authority, those who obey His commands nurture powerful conviction of spirit. So also, the powerful imperatives of Jesus provoke contention from false teachers and false prophets. Differing doctrinal presuppositions inject significant variants as to how these commands are to be obeyed. One is confronted with the issue of perspective and question framing. There exist many systems of core beliefs in Christianity. Approaches to topics in training new adherents rest on a system's view of salvation and spiritual growth. This chapter approaches discipleship from a conversionistic, Evangelical, and Baptist point-of-view:

- By conversionistic is meant the necessity of Christian conversion unto salvation with one's own volition, during one's lifetime.

- By Evangelical is meant an active commitment to declaring the gospel to the unsaved that they may hear and be saved.

- By Baptist is meant that the ordinance of baptism is to be observed only for those who first ask for it, and give clear verbal testimony of their conversion to Christ.

As noted in prior chapters, the best way to interpret and apply the Great Commission in Matthew is to look at its multiple verbs chronologically. Hence, prior to giving His Great Commission, Jesus Christ explained that He had the supreme jurisdiction and plenary authority to give binding commandments to all His followers from every language group and over the entire face of the planet earth for all remaining history. This sovereign authority was confirmed by His declaration in Matthew 28:18:

> And Jesus came and said to them, "All authority in heaven and on earth has been given to me" (Matthew 28:18 ESV).

Of all the people in the world who have ever lived or ever will live, only Christ had and has the unique position and power to make such a declaration. As He uttered these words, they became compulsory to every living creature until time is no more. Hence, the commands that follow in verses 19-20 receive affirmation and validity by the truth proposition of verse 18. From this first chronological element, and moving through the other commands, our chapter lands at its theme, "All that I have commanded you."

As disciples of Christ go out, in obedience to the "Go" in Matthew's Great Commission, their stated goal was to "make/win disciples." They were called to share the gospel of Jesus Christ in such a way that disciples of Jesus would result from their going out. The necessity for preaching the gospel to make disciples is evident from the context of Matthew's Gospel, as well as other commands throughout the New Testament. Christ did not need to repeat it here; it to be presumed as part of the logical sequence, an ellipsis.

> "And as you go, preach" (Matthew 10:7).

Therefore, following the preaching of the gospel, and once a disciple is "won" to Christ, then the next chronological step was for that disciple to be baptized in the name of the Father, and the Son, and the Holy Spirit. This obedience to the command, "baptizing them," made the newly won disciple a part of the "them." This important "them" was then used again in the next verse:

"Teaching them to observe all that I have commanded you" (Matthew 28:20 ESV).

Continuing after believer's baptism, the next command was to be "taught to obey all things that Christ has commanded us."

A thorough study of all the commands of Jesus is more complex than may be considered at first glance. In the Book of Matthew there are 365 verbs that are in the imperative mood. Of these a total of 256 come from the lips of Jesus. Sixty-two of these 256 are the word "behold" which is the imperative of the verb "to see" (ὁράω). If these are subtracted then there are 194 imperatives from the lips of Jesus in the Book of Matthew alone. Now, some of these imperatives are not meant to be obeyed, such as "arise and walk" (Matthew 9:5). Jesus, however, specified the commands addressed to "you," meaning to His disciples, "that I have commanded—you."

This restriction of Jesus drops the number of imperatives to those that are contextually universal in nature. If only the general commands of Christ are counted, then the number drops to approximately 173 commands of Christ. Some verbs that are commands are not in the imperative mood. The verbs "go," "baptize," and "teach" in Matthew's Great Commission are participles:[1] "go" is an aorist[2] participle; and "baptize" and "teach" are present participles. It follows then that Christ's commands in Matthew are not all written in the imperative mood. This potentially increases the actual number of verbal commands of Christ. On top of this we have the commands in Mark, Luke, and

---

[1]Participles in English generally end with "-ing," for example "going," "baptizing," "teaching."

[2]The aorist tense is the inflectional form of a verb denoting simple occurrence. In Greek it implies point-in-time (punctiliar) action.

John, as well as other commands of Christ cited by Paul that are not found in the Gospels. A statistical analysis of the commands of Christ proves rather complex.

Instead of looking uniquely at the imperatives in the Book of Matthew, and comparing the exact number and ratio of Greek tenses in Christ's commands, we will seek to consider the spirit of His words. Christ desired humble obedience of His words:

> *"Everyone then who hears these words of mine and does them will be like a wise man who built his house on the rock. And the rain fell, and the floods came, and the winds blew and beat on that house, but it did not fall, because it had been founded on the rock"* (Matthew 7:24-25 ESV).

The implication of obedience is a humble submission to the rulership of Christ in every area of life. For, even as plants mature and develop, so Christians ought to grow and develop. As they grow in the grace and knowledge of the Lord (2 Peter 3:18), so they also grow in obedience to the commands of Christ. Further in each season of life some commands become more prominent than others as followers of Christ grow in Christlikeness.

By way of introduction, George Patterson, formative in the development of Theological Education by Extension (TEE), provided a helpful synopsis of the seven basic commands of Christ:

- *Repent and Believe: Mark 1:15*

- *Be Baptized (and continue in the new life it initiates): Matt 28:9-10; Acts 2:38; Rom 6:1-11*

- *Love God and neighbor in a practical way, Matt 22:37-40 [John 13:34, in first edition]*

- *Celebrate the Lord's Supper: Luke 22:17-20*

- *Pray: Matt 6:5-15 [John 16:34, in first edition]*

- *Give: Matthew 16:19-21; Luke 6:38*

- *Disciple others [Witness, in first edition]: Matthew 28:18-20.*[3]

These provide a summary of the many commands of Christ found in the Gospels. The reader may note that some of these commands are likewise considered as separate chapters in this book on Great Commission verbs.

Clarity in understanding the content for mentoring is necessary. Likewise, methodologies of training are taught and exemplified in the New Testament. The description of Jesus' ministry in the Four Gospels and the example of the church leaders in the Book of Acts and the Epistles provided Christ's disciples sufficient and authoritative methodologies of how they themselves might disciple others.

The underlying issue of this chapter is to consider the proper "content" for Christian mentorship. Is there a "Regulative Principle" to assist in developing a curriculum for discipleship training? While specific passages do not directly recommend curriculum, can lesson series for discipleship training and mentoring be derived from Scripture? What should a church be teaching its people? The simple and complex answer from Christ in Matthew's Great Commission is: "all that I have commanded you." The impact of these few words will be fleshed out in this chapter, ordered by three questions:

1. What is the interrelationship between the commands of Christ and the example of Christ?

2. In light of Christ's restraint of content to His commands, what is the purpose and place of the Book of Acts and of the New Testament Epistles?

3. How may the commands of Christ best be summarized and communicated?

Using these broad points as a guide, each question will be considered. What difference is there, if any, between the commands of Christ and the example of Christ?

---

[3]George Patterson, "The Spontaneous Multiplication of Churches"; in Ralph D. Winter and Steven C. Hawthorne, *Perspectives on the World Christian Movement: A Reader,* 3rd ed. (Pasadena, CA: William Carey, 1999), 601.

The Commands of Christ
Versus The Example of Christ

In Medieval Christianity there brewed a battle over methodology and terminology. Some desired to follow the example of Christ, thinking to find salvation merely from following His lifestyle. For them, discipleship training found it purest form as the "Imitation of Christ" (*imitatio Christi*). Several leaders from this group even claimed that they had experienced the sufferings of Christ through a phenomenon called, the "Stigmata"—having blood ooze from their hands, feet, and brow in a type of mystical union with the sufferings of Christ on the cross.

Another group preferred the concept of the "imitation of the Apostles" (*imitatio apostolorum*). Their desire was to imitate the Apostles, somewhat following the command of Paul who wrote:

Imitate me, just as I also imitate *Christ* (1 Corinthians 11:1).

However, their imitation was largely confined to rigid obedience of the lifestyle of the Apostles, such as following the commands listed in Matthew 10:9-10:

"Acquire no gold or silver or copper for your belts, no bag for your journey, or two tunics or sandals or a staff, for the laborer deserves his food" (Matthew 10:9-10 ESV).

At first glance these verses seem to buttress the Benedictine "Vow of Voluntary Poverty"—one of the thee foundational vows of Western Monasticism. However, further examination demonstrates that Christ revised this command on the night before He died:

And he said to them, "When I sent you out with no moneybag or knapsack or sandals, did you lack anything?" They said, "Nothing." He said to them, "But now let the one who has a moneybag take it, and likewise a knapsack. And let the one who has no sword sell his cloak and buy one" (Luke 22:35-36 ESV).

Christ clearly changed the command found in Matthew 10:9-10, Mark 6:8, and Luke 9:3; 10:4. Now followers of Christ are under the authority of His words, "but now," as found in Luke 22:36.

A third group, among many others, followed a view titled, "Apostolic Life" (*conversatio apostolic*). The Medieval Cathars adhered to this approach, which appears to approximate contemporary evangelicalism. In this view, the disciples of Jesus, and especially church leaders, were to follow the pattern of ministry set forth in the Bible, with a special focus on the Book of Acts.

Numerous other terms and distinctions have emerged over the years. These examples should be sufficient to show that there have been important differences over obedience to the Great Commission throughout the history of the churches. This issue distills down to several questions:

- What is to be retained and passed on from the life of Christ?

- If His example is to be imitated, what part of His example, everything or were some of the things He did signs that He was the Messiah?

- And if His commandments, which ones?

Fortunately, Christ Himself eloquently answered the first question in His Great Commission in Matthew. It was the commands of Christ that were to remain the Central Interpretive Motif of all discipleship training in the churches, and not His example. Yes, Christ did leave us an example. But the example He left was not plenary. Each context limited the extent of Christ's example to a specific aspect of His life and ministry. Consider for example the following passages:

> "If I then, your Lord and Teacher, have washed your feet, you also ought to wash one another's feet. For I have given you an example, that you also should do just as I have done to you" (John 13:14-15 ESV).

> But I received mercy for this reason, that in me, as the foremost, Jesus Christ might display his perfect patience as an example to those who were to believe in him for eternal life (1 Timothy 1:16 ESV).

> For what credit is there if, when you sin and are harshly treated, you endure it with patience? But if when you do what is right and

> *suffer* for it *you patiently endure it, this* finds *favor with God. For you have been called for this purpose, since Christ also suffered for you, leaving you an example for you to follow in His steps* (1 Peter 2:20-21 NASB).

In John 13, Jesus was an example of a servant leader. In 1 Timothy 6, Christ was an example to Paul of perfect patience. In 1 Peter 2, the example of Christ was focused on how He handled suffering. So each time that the New Testament encourages us to follow the "example" of Christ, the extent of His example is limited by the biblical context.

There are some things in Christ's example that are not meant to be repeated. For example, His death on the cross. It is not necessary to build a cross and to hang oneself upon it to imitate Christ. The New Testament states that His death on the cross was a one-time event—not needing to be repeated:

> *For Christ also died for sins once for all,* the *just for* the *unjust, in order that He might bring us to God, having been put to death in the flesh, but made alive in the spirit* (1 Peter 3:18 NASB).

So also, all the miracles of Christ were done for a specific purpose, they were meant to display that Jesus was in fact the Christ. Prophecy after prophecy foretold that the Messiah would do miracles as proof of His Messianic office. Although Christ continues to use the miraculous among His people when He wills it, these signs need not be repeated either:

> *Then the eyes of the blind shall be opened, and the ears of the deaf unstopped; then shall the lame man leap like a deer, and the tongue of the mute sing for joy. For waters break forth in the wilderness, and streams in the desert* (Isaiah 35:5-6 ESV).

So, Jesus affirmed the uniqueness of His role to the disciples of John the Baptist when they asked Him if He was the Messiah:

> *Now when John heard in prison about the deeds of the Christ, he sent word by his disciples and said to him, "Are you the one who is to come, or shall we look for another?" And Jesus answered them, "Go and tell John what you hear and see: the blind receive their sight and the lame walk, lepers are cleansed and the deaf hear, and the dead are raised up, and the poor have good news preached to them. And blessed is the one who is not offended by*

me" (Matthew 11:2-6 ESV).

No one else in history needs to prove that he is the Messiah. That position is not vacant—Jesus is on His throne. He has not vacated His office, nor will He ever vacate His office. Just as Stephen saw Him, Jesus Christ is right now standing at the right hand of God in full authority (Acts 7:56).

Even so, the miracles of Jesus did not "wow" the crowds in His day—nor did the miracles provide an infallible preparatory grace for the reception of the gospel. The crowds were still offended by His teaching—after all, they did hang Him on a cross! Hence, if Christ's truly divine and miraculous miracles did not change the souls of those who experienced them, why should a Christian think that his human workings of miracles, acts of kindness, friendship, or even persuasive apologetic arguments ought to transform people's souls?

> *Jesus answered them, "I have shown you many good works from the Father; for which of them are you going to stone me?" The Jews answered him, "It is not for a good work that we are going to stone you but for blasphemy, because you, being a man, make yourself God"* (John 10:32-33 ESV).

If Jesus' working of miracles did not render His audience receptive, it only follows that a Christian's working of miracles will not *sine qua non* be "powerful unto salvation" for the spiritual receptivity of others. The trigger for receptivity is not human friendship or good works—although being friendly and kind are definitely a plus! There is a living instrument at the Christian's disposal that is "the power of God to salvation," and that is the gospel of Christ:

> *For I am not ashamed of the gospel of Christ, for it is the power of God to salvation for everyone who believes, for the Jew first and also for the Greek* (Romans 1:16).

Nor did Christ command His disciples to:

1. "Teach all that I have shown you,"

2. "Do all the things that I have done in front of you," nor

3. "Try to imitate My miracles to impress the crowds."

Jesus placed a boundary line around the content of discipleship training, segmenting many things out. Not included in imitating Christ are:

- His miraculous birth
- The dove coming down at His baptism
- Voices from heaven affirming who He was
- The Transfiguration experience
- The obligation to work miracles like His
- His death and resurrection.

Included in imitation as noted above are:

- Washing one another's feet like Jesus (John 13:14-15)
- Displaying patience like Jesus (1 Timothy 1:16)
- Endure suffering for righteousness like Jesus (1 Peter 2:20-21).

Rather than focusing on the theatrical or exhilarating elements of Christ's life, Christians are to focus directly and only on that which led Him to be crucified—His teachings—and even less than His teachings, only a part of His teachings—His commands. That is, disciples of Christ are to focus their attention upon the need to appropriate and act upon His teachings.

No Wiggle Room!

Nor ought the obedient disciple pick and choose what is to be taught in the teachings of Christ. The disciple cannot say:

- "I will leave out this command of Christ"
- "These sets of commands are unimportant, I will focus on these few here"
- "This one command is so important that I can ignore all the rest."

Jesus said the content for discipleship training was to include "all that I have commanded you."

Christ, foreknowing the treachery of men's hearts (John 2:24-25), and having experienced Satan's Scripture twisting when He was tempted (Matthew 4:6), knew that man is prone to "pick and choose" commands to his liking. This self-determined selection is called "Question Framing." Question framing is done by asking a question in such a way as to predetermine its answer. Jesus did not want His followers to frame the question of their discipleship training—He Himself has already framed it!

> "Teaching them to observe all that I have commanded you" (Matthew 28:20 ESV).

Jesus, the only One who has authority in heaven and on earth, framed every question that He felt was necessary to discuss, exactly how He wanted it framed—in His word. Therefore, the Gospels specifically, and the entire Bible more broadly, discloses:

1. The issues to discuss

2. The terminology by which to discuss those issues

3. The context from which, by which, and in which the issues are to be discussed.

This purposeful question framing was devised and set to print by the supreme King of all kings and Lord of all lords! The obedient disciple of the Savior would do well not to seek to wiggle out of His path by adding to His words or subtracting from His words.

From Theory to Practice

So, when Christ used the words "that I have commanded you," He focused discipleship training on His teaching ministry, and in particular on His ministry of exhortation. The essence of a commandment is applying truth in such a way that it may be acted upon. A command is clear, concise, and doable. Jesus did not sound an unclear trumpet:

> Again, if the trumpet does not sound a clear call, who will get ready for battle? (1 Corinthians 14:8 NIV).

Jesus asked His disciples to move beyond informing to warning. Informing implies giving content, warning suggests applying the content so that it can be obeyed. A warning marks out the resulting path if people disregard the warning. Paul included in a list of verbs the end goal, which was *to warn*. He was following the command of Christ by moving from mere teaching to urging obedience of the commandments of Christ:

> *Him we proclaim, warning everyone and teaching everyone with all wisdom, that we may present everyone mature in Christ. For this I toil, struggling with all his energy that he powerfully works within me* (Colossians 1:28-29 ESV).

In perfect accord with Christ's words, "to teach them to observe all that I have commanded you," Paul borrowed the concept of warning from God's commissioning of Ezekiel to his prophetic ministry (Ezekiel 3:16-21).

Hence, the content for discipleship training is a verb and not a noun, "all things I have commanded you." The verb in this case is ἐντέλλομαι (to command). Although nouns are great and necessary, the primary content of discipleship training is a verb. In fact, the entire phrase includes three verbs:

1. To Teach (διδάσκω) them

2. To observe (τηρέω) all things

3. I have commanded (ἐντέλλομαι) you.

The meat of discipleship content is found in the third verb, ἐντέλλομαι (to command)—for which Jesus serves as the subject of the verb. Likewise, discipleship content is to relate directly to what Jesus taught and commanded—His teaching is central. Only what Jesus taught, and all that Jesus taught. Perhaps this boundary around discipleship is why "Red Letter" editions of the Bible exist. If that is the reason for red letter editions of the Bible, then "Amen" for red letter editions of the Bible!

Jesus Retains His Absolute Lordship

Further, Jesus remains the subject of the verb. He has not transferred His commanding authority or office to anyone else. As clearly stated in Matthew 28:18, only Jesus Christ has the authority to command. Nor has He deeded this authority to any person or group of persons. Christ tells His obedient disciples, "teach all that I have commanded you." He still retains occupancy of His office.

Even Paul was hesitant to render a commandment on anything that Christ Himself had not already delineated. In his first epistle to the Corinthians he provided an excellent hermeneutical principle—the need to take heed lest we go "beyond what is written":

> "For who has understood the mind of the Lord so as to instruct him?" But we have the mind of Christ (1 Corinthians 2:16 ESV, citing Isaiah 40:13).

> And again, "The Lord knows the thoughts of the wise, that they are futile" (1 Corinthians 3:20 ESV, citing Psalm 94:11).

> I have applied all these things to myself and Apollos for your benefit, brothers, that you may learn by us not to go beyond what is written, that none of you may be puffed up in favor of one against another (1 Corinthians 4:6 ESV).

The preposition translated "beyond" is the preposition ὑπέρ, meaning "above." Consider the arrogance of some scholars or commentators who place themselves "above" the Scriptures—that they might instruct God! David warned of this "great transgression" in Psalm 19:

> Who can discern his errors? Declare me innocent from hidden faults. Keep back your servant also from presumptuous sins; let them not have dominion over me! Then I shall be blameless, and innocent of great transgression (Psalm 19:12-13 ESV).

In 1 Corinthians, Paul applied the very hermeneutical principle that he had just taught the Corinthian believers—some of whom appeared to go "beyond what is written" in their evangelism and teaching ministry. When the Apostle Paul gave a command, he was quick to cite its original source:

> To the married I give this charge (not I, but the Lord): the wife should not separate from her husband (1 Corinthians 7:10 ESV).

> To the rest I say (I, not the Lord) that if any brother has a wife who is an unbeliever, and she consents to live with him, he should not divorce her (1 Corinthians 7:12 ESV).

> Now concerning the betrothed, I have no command from the Lord, but I give my judgment as one who by the Lord's mercy is

trustworthy (1 Corinthians 7:25 ESV).

For I received from the Lord what I also delivered to you, that the Lord Jesus on the night when he was betrayed took bread (1 Corinthians 11:23 ESV).

In the Law it is written, "By people of strange tongues and by the lips of foreigners will I speak to this people, and even then they will not listen to me, says the Lord (1 Corinthians 14:21 ESV, citing Isaiah 28:11-12).

If anyone thinks that he is a prophet, or spiritual, he should acknowledge that the things I am writing to you are a command of the Lord (1 Corinthians 14:37 ESV).

In his caution to avoid exceeding "what is written" (1 Corinthians 4:6), Paul provided all obedient disciples of Christ in the history of the churches an example. As an Apostle and follower of Christ, Paul was also under obligation to adhere to Christ's command to teach "all that I have commanded you." As a warning in the Bible, Jeroboam, king of Israel, chose to go "beyond what is written" for political expediency, as recorded in 1 Kings 12:25-33. He devised and funded the making of two golden calves for the people of Israel to worship to keep them from going to Jerusalem to worship the Lord God, as God had commanded them to do. God spoke His great displeasure at the sin of Jeroboam:

After this thing Jeroboam did not turn from his evil way, but made priests for the high places again from among all the people. Any who would, he ordained to be priests of the high places. And this thing became sin to the house of Jeroboam, so as to cut it off and to destroy it from the face of the earth (1 Kings 13:33-34 ESV).

Therefore, a healthy fence is erected around the content for discipleship training, "nothing beyond what is written!" Christ commanded that the content for discipleship training is all Jesus taught and only what Jesus taught. So then, if it is all about Jesus and only about Jesus and His commands, then what is the role of the Book of Acts and the epistles in the New Testament as far as normative divine revelation?

What Is the Place of the Book of Acts
And of the New Testament Epistles?

Christ placed Himself as the central focus of all of discipleship training by His statement, "teaching them to observe all that I commanded you." Further, as to His Person, work, and words, Jesus was, is, and will be throughout eternity the central focus of praise (Revelation 5). Only He has been given the Name above every name, that "at the name of Jesus every knee should bow" (Philippians 2:9-11). So, every part of divine revelation must point to Christ if He is the Center of it all. Every part of salvation emanates from Christ. Hence, the question is not, what is the internal authority of the books of the Old and New Testaments? The question is, how does the Lord Jesus Christ by His teaching and His example lend authority to the books of the Old and New Testaments?

Building from the issue of authority, as related to Christ's commandments being the central focus of discipleship training, what do the commands of Christ teach about the Old Testament? Because this limitation comes from Matthew's Great Commission, these questions will be answered beginning from Matthew's record of Jesus. While the other inspired biographies of Jesus provide richness and depth to God's self-revelation in Christ, the lock was found in Matthew, and so the key ought to be found there too. And in fact, Matthew's Gospel does provide the key to unlock the boundary that Christ established in Matthew.

Jesus on the Law, the Prophets, and the Writings

First of all, Christ lent His divine authority to every part of the received Hebrew Old Testament: the Law, the Prophets, and the Writings. Of the Law and the Prophets, Christ said:

> "Do not think that I have come to abolish the Law or the Prophets; I have not come to abolish them but to fulfill them. For truly, I say to you, until heaven and earth pass away, not an iota, not a dot, will pass from the Law until all is accomplished" (Matthew 5:17-18 ESV).

> "So whatever you wish that others would do to you, do also to them, for this is the Law and the Prophets" (Matthew 7:12 ESV).

287

Jesus cited the Book of Deuteronomy (the fifth book of the Law) in response to all three temptations of Satan in Matthew 4, citing Deuteronomy 8:3; 6:16; and 6:13, respectively. Jesus affirmed the Prophets by quoting them as authoritative. Whereas Matthew's pen affirmed the prophet Isaiah in Matthew 3:3; 4:14; 8:17; and 12:17, and Jesus Himself affirmed Isaiah in Matthew 13:14 and 15:7:

> *"Indeed, in their case the prophecy of Isaiah is fulfilled that says: 'You will indeed hear but never understand, and you will indeed see but never perceive.' For this people's heart has grown dull, and with their ears they can barely hear, and their eyes they have closed, lest they should see with their eyes and hear with their ears and understand with their heart and turn, and I would heal them"* (Matthew 13:14-15 ESV, citing Isaiah 6:9-10).

> *"You hypocrites! Well did Isaiah prophesy of you, when he said: 'This people honors me with their lips, but their heart is far from me; in vain do they worship me, teaching as doctrines the commandments of men'"* (Matthew 15:7-9 ESV, citing Isaiah 29:13).

Jesus explained the spirit of the Law rather than the letter of the Law in Matthew 5. On another occasion, when the Pharisees came to test Jesus, He interpreted, explained, and then applied the writings of Moses, as if He knew the true mind of the author:

> *They said to him, "Why then did Moses command one to give a certificate of divorce and to send her away?" He said to them, "Because of your hardness of heart Moses allowed you to divorce your wives, but from the beginning it was not so. And I say to you: whoever divorces his wife, except for sexual immorality, and marries another, commits adultery"* (Matthew 19:7-9 ESV).

Jesus had an intimate knowledge of Moses' writings, applying it to living people (Deuteronomy 5:3). His command of the Scriptures and His knowledge of the mind of the authors shows Him to be the true author of Scripture. It was this divine touch upon the words of the Law, Prophets, and Writings that gave them their eternal quality, as was the case with His own words.

> *Forever, O LORD, your word is firmly fixed in the heavens* (Psalm 119:89 ESV).

Long have I known from your testimonies that you have founded them forever (Psalm 119:152 ESV).

The sum of your word is truth, and every one of your righteous rules endures forever (Psalm 119:160 ESV).

"Heaven and earth will pass away, but my words will not pass away" (Matthew 24:35 ESV).

Further, Matthew was meticulous in relating the number of prophecies that Jesus was fulfilling, citing repeatedly, "This was to fulfill what the Lord had spoken by the prophet." This fact is borne out by a study of Matthew's 43 uses of the word "prophet." Matthew also cited:

- Micah in Matthew 2:5

- Hosea in Matthew 2:15

- Jeremiah in Matthew 2:18 and 27:9

- Zechariah in Matthew 21:4.

Jesus Himself affirmed Jonah in Matthew 12:39-41 and 16:4.

As regards to the third part of the Hebrew Canon, that is, the Writings:

- Jesus called the Psalmist Asaph a prophet in Matthew 13:35, citing Psalm 78:2.

- Jesus cited Daniel 11:31; 12:11 in Matthew 24:15.

- And in Matthew 12:42 Jesus cited the Queen of Sheba's visit to Solomon which is discussed in 1 Kings 10 and 2 Chronicles 9.

The allusions to the Law from creation to the death of Moses are too many to cite, as is the case with a breadth of allusions from the Prophets and the Writings. For example, many of the principles taught in Matthew's Beatitudes (Matthew 5:3-10) are either direct quotes or allusions from Psalm 37 and numerous other portions of the Old Testament.

Jesus on the Acts and the Epistles

Second, Christ spoke of the need for further revelation, while limiting it to first century Apostolic authority. He alluded to His resurrection appearances in two commands in Matthew:

> *"But after I am raised up, I will go before you to Galilee"* (Matthew 26:32 ESV).

> Then Jesus said to them, *"Do not be afraid; go and tell my brothers to go to Galilee, and there they will see me"* (Matthew 28:10 ESV).

In John 16, in the Upper Room Discourse, on the night before He died, Jesus explained to His disciples that He still had "many things" (πολλὰ) to say to them. But out of concern for them He did not tell them, since they had not yet received the Holy Spirit:

> *"I have many more things to say to you, but you cannot bear them now"* (John 16:12 NASB).

The "many things" that Jesus had to say were reserved for John 20-21, Luke 24, His appearances in Acts 1, as well as His special appearances to the Apostle Paul, as noted in 1 Corinthians 15:8 and alluded to in 2 Corinthians 12:1-6. Further, the Holy Spirit was to give them remembrance and understanding of what Jesus had earlier said and done:

> *"But the Helper, the Holy Spirit, whom the Father will send in my name, he will teach you all things and bring to your remembrance all that I have said to you"* (John 14:26 ESV).

> *"When the Spirit of truth comes, he will guide you into all the truth, for he will not speak on his own authority, but whatever he hears he will speak, and he will declare to you the things that are to come. He will glorify me, for he will take what is mine and declare it to you"* (John 16:13-14 ESV).

From these verses comes the concept of "Apostolic Authority." Only the Apostles, or those who had received specific apostolic sanction, had the authority to author authoritative New Testament writings. John went on to explain the editorial specificity by which the authors of the Gospels had to refrain themselves in writing, being that there was so much material available on the life of Jesus:

> This is the disciple who is bearing witness about these things, and who has written these things, and we know that his testimony is true. Now there are also many other things that Jesus did. Were every one of them to be written, I suppose that the world itself could not contain the books that would be written (John 21:24-25 ESV).

The Gospel writers had to refrain themselves from saying everything. Rather, being moved by the Holy Spirit, they wrote only that which was pertinent to their specific purpose in writing.

Nevertheless, even though God has included the Old Testament, the Book of Acts, and the Epistles within the Bible, Christ's commands remain front and central. This limitation pleases Jesus, who Himself spoke Matthew's Great Commission. Notwithstanding the need for further revelation beyond the Gospels, even so, Christ has confined His discipleship training strategy to include all and only His commands.

Toward Summarizing the "Commands of Christ"

As was noted earlier, there are 173 imperatives of Christ in the Book of Matthew, if one drops out the 62 "beholds" and the 21 imperatives that are given in specific instances, such as "Rise up and walk." Also, as noted above, the commands of Christ are not all in the imperative mood. For example, Christ's spoken Great Commission in Matthew includes nine total verbs and only two imperatives, one of which is "behold" in verse 20. Hence, the only imperative in Matthew's Great Commission is "win disciples" (μαθητεύσατε from μαθητεύω) in verse 19.

When analyzing the imperatives in Matthew, the highest concentration of imperatives fall on the three major sermons of Jesus. These three discourses are:

1. Matthew 5-7, The Sermon on the Mount

2. Matthew 10, The Sermon on Mission

3. Matthew 24-25, The Olivet Discourse.

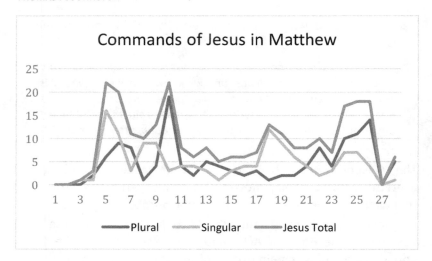

Each of these sermons also contains different foci of the commands of Christ. The chart above delineates the singular and plural imperatives of Jesus in the Book of Matthew chapter-by-chapter. The reader will note that the sermons of Jesus contain concentrations of the commands which are to form the backbone for Christian discipleship training.

The three highest "peaks" of concentrations are the three sermons indicated on the chart (see chart on next page). Where the Sermon on the Mount and the Olivet Discourse emphasized singular commands, the Sermon on Mission used a higher percentage of plural commands. Moreover, each of these three sermons speaks to three missional themes developed in the Book of Matthew:

1. The Moral Theme

2. The Missional Theme

3. The Eschatological Theme.

The final portion of this chapter will therefore seek to clarify what is meant by "all that I have commanded you," in these three categories. We begin with the Moral Theme of the Sermon on the Mount in Matthew 5-7.

The Moral Theme

The first theme is the moral category. This moral dimension corresponds to the preparatory preaching of John the Baptist to "Repent" (Matthew 3:2). Jesus used this same word in His first plural command, "Repent" in Matthew 4:17. The context for the preaching of repentance stems from the fact that all of humanity has transgressed the righteous Law of God. Here stands the Moral Argument—by which every man is justly condemned as a guilty sinner before a righteous God. Jesus very aggressively wielded the sword of the Law of God in the Sermon on the Mount, particularly in Matthew 5 where He uttered six plural commands and 16 singular commands. He laid bare the motives of men's hearts. For those ready to repent at the Moral Argument, they were then taught to cry out to God, using the Lord's Prayer as a guide with its seven imperatives (or in the jussive, seven supplications).

In Matthew 5:20 Jesus explained how narrow was the narrow way:

> "For I tell you, unless your righteousness exceeds that of the scribes and Pharisees, you will never enter the kingdom of heaven" (Matthew 5:20 ESV).

Matthew 5:48 ought to humble even the most self-righteous and self-exalting heart:

> "You therefore must be perfect, as your heavenly Father is perfect" (Matthew 5:48 ESV).

A heart humbled by Jesus' teaching in Matthew 5 then proceeds to Jesus' explanation of prayer. In analyzing the seven requests of the Lord's Prayer, the first three petitions ask God to do His will on earth. The last three solicit God's help in following His commandments—almost like a Sinner's Prayer. The middle request, which is the center of a chiasm, begs for necessary daily spiritual feeding, "Give us today our bread for today" (Matthew 6:11). As Jesus was teaching them to pray, He was simultaneously giving them spiritual food. The Sermon on the Mount was their spiritual feeding. Spiritual food is the word of God and visa-versa. The words of Christ are the very Rock upon which the obedient listener builds his life (Matthew 7:24-27).

Now, the verb "believe" is used 11 times in Matthew, but never as a command. For example, the first time it is used is in Matthew 8:13 after the command, "Go": "Go your way; and as you have believed." In Mark, however, the command "believe" follows immediately after the command to "repent." "Repent and believe in the gospel" (Mark 1:15). So Matthew appears to bear down on the theme "Repent" in Jesus' Sermon on the Mount by showing all of mankind that they cannot achieve the perfection of God, and to hunger and yearn after the teaching that only He can give. Then, after the Sermon on the Mount, Jesus began to use the verb "believe" as He spoke with people (Matthew 8:13).

The Missional Theme

The second theme is missional—evangelistic. This missional category is found in Jesus' Sermon on Mission in Matthew 10. Jesus started calling His disciples to mission in Matthew 4:19. Here we find the second plural command of Jesus, "Follow Me, and I will make you fishers of men." Jesus' Great Commission in Matthew 28:19-20 completes His development of this theme in Matthew. And between these two bookends, Matthew recorded the longest "Sermon on Mission" of the first three Gospels. There are three parallels to this sermon in Mark 6 and Luke 9 and 10, as well as scattered in several other places.

Jesus' Sermon on Mission is quite a shocking sermon. It does not explain the message to be preached, but rather focuses on the reception or lack of reception of the message. This sermon has long fascinated this author. The sermon includes 19 plural commands of Christ and 3 singular commands. As far as commands, we find 14.3% (or 1/7) of Matthew's plural commands of Jesus concentrated in this chapter. The first grouping of commands consists of a series of seven concepts on mission:

1. "Go" (Matthew 10:6)

2. "Preach" (Matthew 10:7)

3. "Heal," "cleanse," "raise," "give" (Matthew 10:8)

4. "Inquire," "stay" (Matthew 10:11)

5. "Greet" (Matthew 10:12)

6. "Let it come," "let it return" (Matthew 10:13)

7. "Shake off" (Matthew 10:14).

The seasoned pioneer missionary cannot improve on these sets of commands. They form the foundation for Matthew's evangelistic missionary activity. They are powerful and effective if followed. The next command opens a long warning section in this sermon:

> *"Behold, I am sending you out as sheep in the midst of wolves, so be wise as serpents and innocent as doves"* (Matthew 10:16 ESV).

Immediately after explaining what to do when cities do or do not receive the evangelistic message, then Jesus entered His first teaching portion. Here He explained persecution for the sake of His name. He described His disciples as vulnerable sheep among ravenous wolves. Then followed the two commands:

1. Be wise—wise as serpents

2. Be innocent (or harmless or gentle)—innocent as doves.

Jesus warned of harsh hatred and fierce persecution because of the preaching of the gospel. Hatred from the authorities. Hatred from family members. Discord within family systems. Then He gave a cluster of four commands on fearing:

> *"Therefore do not fear them, for there is nothing covered that will not be revealed, and hidden that will not be known. What I tell you in the darkness, speak in the light; and what you hear whispered in your ear, proclaim upon the housetops. And do not fear those who kill the body, but are unable to kill the soul; but rather fear Him who is able to destroy both soul and body in hell. Are not two sparrows sold for a cent? And yet not one of them will fall to the ground apart from your Father. But the very hairs of your head are all numbered. Therefore do not fear; you are of more value than many sparrows"* (Matthew 10:26-31 NASB).

Three times we find "have no fear," "do not fear," and "fear not"; one time "fear." There is nothing like the death-grip of the fear of man to keep an evangelist's mouth closed:

> *And the Lord said to Paul in the night by a vision, "Do not be afraid any longer, but go on speaking and do not be silent; for I am with you, and no man will attack you in order to harm you,*

for I have many people in this city" (Acts 18:9-10 NASB).

The first accomplishment of fear to is close one's lips. The fearful become silent and do not speak. God commanded Paul as he planned his escape, "Speak and do not keep silent." The promised persecution in Matthew 10 should prepare the unsuspecting disciple. In a similar context, Jesus told His disciples in John 16:

> *"These things I have spoken to you, that you may be kept from stumbling. They will make you outcasts from the synagogue, but an hour is coming for everyone who kills you to think that he is offering service to God. And these things they will do, because they have not known the Father, or Me. But these things I have spoken to you, that when their hour comes, you may remember that I told you of them. And these things I did not say to you at the beginning, because I was with you"* (John 16:1-4 NASB).

Jesus likewise explained the reality of persecution in the Upper Room Discourse in John 14-16, on the night He was betrayed.

The sub-category of Christ's Commands, the missional theme, corresponds to central points that the Apostle Paul shared with Timothy in 2 Timothy: persecution, perseverance, boldness in being a verbal witness for Christ. All these themes were important among the commands of Jesus, as they were to the Apostle Paul.

The Eschatological Theme

The third concentration of commands of Christ is found in the Olivet Discourse. This message of Christ concerns the "End Times." The theological word for "End Times" is eschatology. This eschatological emphasis also began very early in the preaching of both John the Baptist and Jesus. Both John and Jesus said, "Repent for the kingdom of God is at hand." The "kingdom" or "rule of God" was coming quickly—so quickly that you could reach out and touch it. It was "at hand." Now this coming "rule of God" speaks of two kinds of rule:

1. The individual rule of God in individual hearts by repenting and believing the gospel

2. The End Time rule of God when, "The kingdom of the world has become *the kingdom* of our Lord, and of His Christ; and He will reign forever and ever" (Revelation 11:15 NASB).

The impact of the individual rule of Christ is fleshed out in various passages throughout Matthew. The beginning of the end, that is, the Eschatological rule of Christ, is developed in Jesus' Olivet Discourse in Matthew 24-25. In this sermon, we find 21 plural commands and 14 singular commands of Christ. This represents a very high concentration of commands. If therefore the obedient disciple of Christ adheres to teaching "all that I have commanded you," a part of that teaching will include training the new disciples to be ready for the Second Coming of Christ.

Among the 21 commands in the Olivet Discourse, two concepts stand out. First is the cerebral and emotive element. Jesus commanded His disciples to be careful, take care, and watch out:

- *"Take heed [βλέπω] that no one deceives you"* (Matthew 24:4)

- *"See [ὁράω] that you are not troubled [μή + θροέω]"* (Matthew 24:6)

- *"Understand [νοέω]"* (Matthew 24:15)

- *"Know [γινώσκω] that summer is near"* (Matthew 24:32)

- *"Know [γινώσκω] that it is near—at the doors!"* (Matthew 24:33).

There is a necessary urgency that Christ communicates in these commands. He requires watchfulness of His disciples. The follower of Christ is to avoid sloth and negligence. Christ begs His servants to be alert and vigilant.

In the middle of Matthew 24 there is an interesting cluster of four "beholds" (ἰδού) found in four verses:

"Then if anyone says to you, 'Look, here is the Christ!' or 'There!' do not believe it. For false christs and false prophets will rise and show great signs and wonders to deceive, if possible, even the elect. See, I have told you beforehand. Therefore if they say to you, 'Look, He is in the desert!' do not go out; or 'Look, He is in the inner rooms!' do not believe it" (Matthew 24:23-26).

Because of the reality of false teachers, the obedient disciple-maker must protect new believers by teaching the warnings of Christ that make up a part of His commandments. Later Paul shared a similar warning when he spoke to the Ephesian elders in Miletus:

> "Therefore take heed to yourselves and to all the flock, among which the Holy Spirit has made you overseers, to shepherd the church of God which He purchased with His own blood. For I know this, that after my departure savage wolves will come in among you, not sparing the flock. Also from among yourselves men will rise up, speaking perverse things, to draw away the disciples after themselves. Therefore watch, and remember that for three years I did not cease to warn everyone night and day with tears. So now, brethren, I commend you to God and to the word of His grace, which is able to build you up and give you an inheritance among all those who are sanctified" (Acts 20:28-32).

The salty Apostle, looking forward through the eyes of Scripture and experience, could feel the savage wolves nipping at his heels. Those who would twist the truth could not wait to come in to lay waste the flock of God. The imperatives of the Olivet Discourse beg to be used in discipleship training. The urgency of an End Times focus is part of the healthy spiritual diet of a growing disciple. Consider that Jesus did not request going beyond His words. The focus must be His commands, not the End Times particularities of human thought, as important as they may be.

- Jesus did not say, "Make sure you have all the details of My Second Coming clear"

- He did not say, "Give special attention to the 70 weeks in Daniel"

- Rather, Jesus said, "Teach them to observe all that I have commanded you."

Of necessity in working through the text of Scripture with the new disciple, is a special emphasis on the commands of Christ. It is so easy to get sidetracked into "useless wranglings" (1 Timothy 6:5; cf. Romans 14:1). Jesus specifically commanded that His commands be taught first and foremost, of which the End Times is a significant portion in Matthew's Gospel.

So, whereas Jesus gave His followers a variety of commands. They were to "Go." They were to "Win disciples." They were to "Baptize them in the name of the Father and of the Son and of the

Holy Spirit." Then He gave them commandment that they should be taught to observe something. The accreditation committee up in heaven sent down some instructional guidelines. The curriculum from the Committee of One is to consist of "all that I have commanded you."

In analyzing the imperatival clusters of Christ in the Book of Matthew, three significant topics come to the fore:

1. Moral teaching—from which leads to a heart of repentance and faith

2. Missional Teaching—which leads to watchful and proactive missional efforts among the churches of Christ

3. End Times Teaching—which results in a Bride ready for the return of her Husband.

These three prove foundational for a Great Commission discipleship curriculum.

In all discipleship training, Christ has limited its course content to His commands. His commands are not burdensome. His yoke is easy and His burden is light. He explained the tactics of the Pharisees who loved to lay burdens on others in Matthew 23:4. On the other hand, Christ's Great Commission commands provide a roadmap and a worldview for proper discipleship training. "All things whatsoever I have commanded you":

1. Frames the question of Christian spiritual education

2. Provides Christian spiritual growth its Central Interpretive Motif

3. Shapes best practices for obedience to Christ's Great Commission.

CHAPTER SEVENTEEN

BE CAREFUL HOW YOU BUILD
—βλέπω + πῶς + οἰκοδομέω—

There is a very interesting hypostatic union involved in building on the foundation of Christ. Christ clearly stated that He would build His own "Gathering" or "Assembly" (ἡ ἐκκλησία) of the elect. Jesus said, "I will build [οἰκοδομέω] My church" (Matthew 16:18). The word order is quite interesting in this verse. The possessive pronoun "My" precedes the noun church, which is out of the ordinary. In this case, the emphasis is not "church," but rather Christ's possession. Much like Acts 20:28, "shepherd the church of God which He purchased with His own blood" (NASB).

Apostle Paul used the same verbal root to describe building on the foundation of Christ: "But let each one take care (βλέπω) how he builds (ἐποικοδομέω) on it." Paul, however, was not referencing Christ's efforts in building, but rather man's efforts in building on the foundation of Christ:

> According to the grace of God given to me, like a skilled master builder I laid a foundation, and someone else is building upon it. Let each one take care [βλέπω] how [πῶς] he builds [ἐποικοδομέω] upon it (1 Corinthians 3:10 ESV).

First, the key word for this second group of builders is "how" (πῶς). Christ is clearly interested in the "how" (πῶς)—that is the *praxis*—how we build. Second, Christ's concern for "how" should lead the Christian to "take heed" or "watch out." The Christian should work with extra diligence under the watchful eyes of the crucified Savior. Third, he is to "build" for the Lord's construction company, of whom Christ Jesus is the Chief Architect and General Contractor. He is no maverick who works for Christ. He is to build using His divine building code.

In this case "build upon" (ἐποικοδομέω = ἐπί + οἰκοδομέω) is a contraction of the preposition ἐπί = ἐπ' (meaning "upon") with οἰκοδομέω (to build), the verb used by Jesus in Matthew 16:18. The combination of the teaching of both these passages displays that there is a mysterious cooperation between Christ and man in gathering and grouping persons into assemblies of God's saints.

Paul warns followers of Christ that there is accountability for "how" building on the foundation of Christ is completed. Accountability also implies activity, either positive or negative activity. God has sovereignly purposed that man's activity in building on the foundation of Christ is not mere empty duty—an empty shell game or vain pursuit. God has literally invited His people to cooperate with Him in assembling His elect ones in space and time. He has given us a seat at His table, put a sword and trowel in our hand, and He told us to "Get to work!"

The focus of this chapter will not be on Christ building His church, but rather on man's side of the hypostatic union. In this book on Great Commission verbs, the emphasis is not on what Christ has done and does—preeminent as that is, but rather on the "how" of the duties that Christ has contracted man to fulfill. For according to Paul, men are to "take care how" when building on the foundation of Christ. The command to "take care how" assumes that men need exert their intellectual and volitional abilities with care and caution to see that they are properly building on the foundation laid by Christ. "Take care how" implies the possibility and likelihood of divergent methodologies: good and bad! One builds one way, another builds another way—the differences are captured in the "how."

Christ cares about the "how." The "how" is not neutral. In fact, it is the undercurrent of this entire book. Christ has communicated His policies and procedures for the "how." Christ's "how" is always better than man's "how" in every way:

> *"For my thoughts are not your thoughts, neither are your ways my ways, declares the LORD. For as the heavens are higher than the earth, so are my ways higher than your ways and my thoughts than your thoughts"* (Isaiah 55:8-9 ESV).

Arrogant man must humble himself to understand that God's ways are always higher and always better than his ways. This same applies to Christ, because of His deity. Likewise, the Bible's ways are always higher than man's principles and procedures—always! Christ did not leave His desired methodology in a vacuous state to rest upon the whims and dreams of mankind. Rather Christ has clearly communicated in His word principles and procedures for properly accomplishing His work.

When Jesus said, "I will build My church," in Matthew 16:8, He was inviting His army of followers throughout the history of the churches to join with Him in extending His rule in the individual hearts of men. The eternal all-powerful Son of God was reaching out to all His blood-bought faithful to join Him in the battle for the souls of men.

> "And I tell you, you are Peter, and on this rock I will build my church, and the gates of hell shall not prevail against it" (Matthew 16:18 ESV).

In the same breath by which He promised to build His church, Jesus described the front door of that deadly foe against which all followers of Christ must resist and overcome—"the gates of hell." For, just as Christ is the gate unto eternal life and is literally "the door of the sheep" (John 10:7), so also there is another door. That is the door of Hell. Hell has an entrance point, a gate. This gate to Hell stands wide open:

> Therefore my people go into exile for lack of knowledge; their honored men go hungry, and their multitude is parched with thirst. Therefore Sheol has enlarged its appetite and opened its mouth beyond measure, and the nobility of Jerusalem and her multitude will go down, her revelers and he who exults in her (Isaiah 5:13-14 ESV).

"Therefore Sheol has enlarged its appetite and opened its mouth beyond measure." According to this somber prophecy, the gates leading into Hell were opened so wide that Isaiah saw God's chosen people descending into it. "Therefore my people," wrote Isaiah. Truly in this prophecy, Isaiah described the intense spiritual battle in which he himself was involved in his day. This same prophecy was recorded for out benefit:

> Now all these things happened to them as examples, and they were written for our admonition, upon whom the ends of the ages have come (1 Corinthians 10:11).

Leaders of Christ's little flock ought to take great heed.

Consider Isaiah's identified problem: dignitaries or leaders were spiritually starving. Nor did they nor could they quench the spiritual thirst of the multitudes of God's people. Meagre rations from the pulpits and spiritual destitution in the pews. Consider therefore the sorry result: "Sheol has enlarged its appetite and opened its mouth beyond measure."

Did not Christ foresee this eventuality in His letter to the church of Thyatira:

> "But I have this against you, that you tolerate the woman Jezebel, who calls herself a prophetess, and she teaches and leads My bond-servants astray, so that they commit acts of immorality and eat things sacrificed to idols" (Revelation 2:20 NASB).

Christ was fully aware of the battles that would face His flock. He Himself gave His disciples warning over and over again. These cautions included His many "bewares" and "take heeds," especially as found in His Olivet Discourse (Matthew 24-25):

> And Jesus answered and said to them: "Take heed that no one deceives you. For many will come in My name, saying, 'I am the Christ,' and will deceive many" (Matthew 24:4-5).

> "And then many will be offended, will betray one another, and will hate one another. Then many false prophets will rise up and deceive many. And because lawlessness will abound, the love" (Matthew 24:10-13).

> "Then if anyone says to you, 'Look, here is the Christ!' or 'There!' do not believe it. For false christs and false prophets will rise and show great signs and wonders to deceive, if possible, even the elect. See, I have told you beforehand. Therefore if they say to you, 'Look, He is in the desert!' do not go out; or 'Look, He is in the inner rooms!' do not believe it" (Matthew 24:23-26).

To these stern warnings, Paul also added many more. For example, Paul prophesied of the future church to the Ephesian elders in his last sermon to them:

> "For I know this, that after my departure savage wolves will come in among you, not sparing the flock. Also from among yourselves men will rise up, speaking perverse [διαστρέφω, twisted] things, to draw away the disciples after themselves" (Acts 20:29-30).

So, even while Christ was "building His church," using faithful servants like the Apostle Paul, savage wolves were clawing and salivating in the background, just waiting for their opportunity to come forward and devour the flock of God. These men would speak "twisted" (διαστρέφω) truths. They would render crooked "the straight ways of the Lord" (Acts 13:10)—using the words of the Bible and twisting them like Satan (Genesis 3:1). These wolves have corrupt/twisted (διαστρέφω) minds (1 Timothy 6:5). They speak corrupt/ruinous (καταφθείρω) truths (2 Timothy 3:8). Of these men, Jude lamented in his epistle, as did Peter in 2 Peter 2. In fact, every New Testament author described and warned of false prophets and their false teachings.

With these men in mind, Christ, the Supreme Ruler of heaven and earth, provided a sufficient, efficient, and triumphant road map for His churches. Christ would build His church no matter how many would be swallowed up by the "gates of hell." Christ promised the on-time completion of His providential work, which He would one day render "not having spot or wrinkle or any such thing" (Ephesians 5:27). The One with "the nail-scarred hands in heaven" promised to accompany His people on earth, knowing that they would also bear the scars of spiritual battles on their bodies:

> *"If the world hates you, you know that it hated Me before it hated you"* (John 15:18).

> *I, Paul, write this greeting with my own hand. Remember my chains. Grace be with you* (Colossians 4:18 ESV).

> *And indeed, all who desire to live godly in Christ Jesus will be persecuted. But evil men and impostors will proceed from bad to worse, deceiving and being deceived* (2 Timothy 3:12-13 NASB).

The One who gave the Great Commission also bears its battle scars. No scarring any Christian experiences will ever exceed or supersede what Jesus experienced to buy the world's salvation!

Congregationalize!

Knowing of this spiritual battle, Christ sent out His disciples to evangelize and congregationalize. They were not merely to lead persons to Christ, they were to gather them into assemblies within which they could learn and grow. Jesus' own words "teaching them to observe" assumes and implies ongoing interaction between teacher and learner, between Jesus' disciples and their newly made disciples. Teaching and learning necessitate linguistic commonality. The teacher and the learner need to communicate in a language they both know and understand—this may seem self-evident, but let the reader consider that there are 1,705 languages and dialects in the world.

"Teaching to observe" also necessitates the ongoing lifestyle dynamic of relational closeness. Built into Matthew 28:20 is the need to congregationalize in proximal geographic regions where regular (even daily) gatherings among followers of Christ are possible. Matthew's Great Commission strongly implies the need for the multiplication of assemblies of disciples meeting in a common place with a common language—local church fellowships!

Further, Christ provided insights in "building His church" within the New Testament. The entire Bible is a manual for church planting and development. In the remainder of this chapter are noted some insights provided in the Bible for the particular benefit of gathering and nurturing Christ's people.

Types of Churches

As His disciples formed gatherings of baptized people, Christ foreknew the troubles that they would face in the years to come. He left a "Procedural Manual" to detect and discern all the issues churches would encounter. One concentrated New Testament portion, addressed to every churches that existed and would exist, was penned by His "beloved disciple"—John. In Revelation 2-3 Christ chose to address seven different churches, churches that co-existed in the first century:

1. Ephesus (Revelation 2:1-7)

   2. Smyrna (Revelation 2:8-11)

      3. Pergamum (Revelation 2:12-17)

         4. Thyatira (Revelation 2:18-29)

      5. Sardis (Revelation 3:1-6)

   6. Philadelphia (Revelation 3:7-13)

7. Laodicea (Revelation 3:14-22).

It appears that Christ was developing a church typology to describe all church types for future generations. Using sufficient descriptors, Jesus prescribed a plan of action for each church to help them encounter the issues and struggles they would face. Christ's church planting and church revitalization secrets are encoded into these chapters. The draw of Revelation 2-3 for this book is that they include numerous direct commands from Christ, hence, following Matthew's Great Commission, "teaching them to observe all that I have commanded you" (Matthew 28:20 ESV).

While looking at these seven churches chronologically is common, this normally leads the reader to conclude that his contemporary church is always typified as the last church, the "Church of Laodicea." Alternatively, looking at these seven churches through chiastic structure analysis opens new avenues of interpretation. A "chiasm" designates an organizational methodology in which points and counter-points are placed in opposing intervals of the outline, pointing and focusing on the center point. The reasons that chiasm may prove helpful for examining the seven churches in Revelation are:

- The odd number of churches (seven churches)—leaving the possibility for considering that Jesus was using chiasm

- Churches #2 and #6 are the only churches that have no warning given to them—these are chiastic markers, being respectively second from the beginning of the seven and second from the end

- Interlocking patterns in churches #3, #4, and #5: these churches form an intermingling downward progression through recurring themes developed in these churches.

When considering the seven churches in Revelation 2-3 as chiasm, the focus shifts from the last church (Laodicea) to the middle of the seven, the fourth church—the corrupt Church of Thyatira.

> *"He who has an ear, let him hear what the Spirit says to the churches"* (Revelation 2:29 NASB).

Like peering into a radiant diamond, looking at these seven churches as a chiasm elicits new patterns of interrelationship. As every facet of the diamond has its own hue and shade, reflecting and refracting light from various angles, so churches today can learn lessons from these seven churches. The risen Christ called on churches and church leaders to regularly assess their ministries in light of their spiritual battle against the "gates of hell." Paul said, "Let each one take care how he builds."

The first and last church appear to be polar opposites. Ephesus was doctrinally pure, but had lost its first love. The church in Laodicea appeared arrogant and spiritually blind. Jesus opened and closed the chiasm with these opposing church characteristics. Neither churches in Smyrna or Philadelphia received a warning from Christ. Rather Jesus encouraged them to persevere. The chiasm finds its sharpest focus in churches #3, #4, and #5:

> #3: *"You hold fast My name, and did not deny My faith. … You have there some who hold the teaching of Balaam. … Thus you also have some who in the same way hold the teaching of the Nicolaitans."*

> #4: *"You tolerate the woman Jezebel, who calls herself a prophetess, and she teaches and leads My bond-servants astray, so that they commit acts of immorality and eat things sacrificed to idols. … But I say to you, the rest who are in Thyatira, who do not hold this teaching."*

> #5: *"You have a name that you are alive, but you are dead. Wake up, and strengthen the things that remain, which were about to die. … But you have a few people in Sardis who have not soiled their garments"* (Revelation 2:13-15, 20, 24; 3:1-2, 4 NASB).

Consider this pattern showing the increase of false teachers and false teaching permeating the churches:

1. "You hold fast My name"
   "You have there some who hold the teaching of Balaam"

2. "You tolerate the woman Jezebel, who ... teaches and leads My bond-servants astray"
   "But I say to you, the rest ... who do not hold this teaching"

3. "You have a name that you are alive, but you are dead"
   "But you have a few people ... who have not soiled their garments."

The clear pattern of false teaching began as a minority position in the Pergamum church. However, within the Thyatira church structure, the false prophetess Jezebel held a leadership position. She had already drawn away many disciples after herself, as Paul had prophesied in Acts 20:29-30. The church in Thyatira is the watershed church, wherein false teaching gains prominence, and those who hold to the truth are shunned. Jesus' judgment of the fifth church, the church in Sardis, was, "You are dead" (Revelation 3:1). Using these three churches as types in the center of His chiasm, Christ composed a divine rubric for the spiritual analysis of all New Testament churches. Jesus revealed the spiritual downgrade of local churches in Revelation 2-3 because it already existed in the first century—as it has in every century of the church. Paul warned to "let each one take care how he builds on it."

Building on the power of this warning, Paul taught about congregationalizing from two perspectives in his epistles. He taught from a leadership point-of-view, and he taught from the viewpoint of the church body. Each of these perspectives contains interesting verbs giving insight into the "how to" of Christ's Great Commission.

From the Leader's Perspective

The identified issue facing the church in Corinth was division based on personality cults. The members of the church in Corinth were differentiated into at least four subgroups: Paul, Apollos, Cephas (or Peter), and Christ. Paul picked up on this spirit of division by using the first two of the four to make an important point. In 1 Corinthians 3:6-10, Paul used a synthetic parallel to differentiate his ministry with that of Apollos. Using parallelism, Paul discussed planting (φυτεύω), watering (ποτίζω), and building upon (ἐποικοδομέω). Consider that the issues at hand were differences in "how to" do ministry. By the way, as noted in prior chapters, massive divergences exist between church groupings over things like, "how to" evangelize, "how to" lead someone to Christ, "how to" baptize, "how to" do the Lord's Supper, etc. These methodological differences historically and theologically lead to different church names, as well as variance in doctrinal formulations. The point is that these differences are legitimate and they continue until our day. How did Paul answer divergent views of ministry?

First, in 1 Corinthians Paul laid a common doctrinal foundation, especially related to the gospel evangelized in 1 Corinthians 15. In his Book of Galatians Paul addressed different approaches to evangelism due to difference in doctrinal positions.

Second, in 1 Corinthians Paul focused on God who works, not man who works:

> I planted, Apollos watered, but God gave the growth. So neither he who plants nor he who waters is anything, but only God who gives the growth (1 Corinthians 3:6-7 ESV).

The spiritually working disciple can become prideful in the fruits of his labor, and he and his followers can begin to consider that he is "something." Paul puts the working Christian in his place by stating that he is not "anything." Rather, it is all about God.

Third, Paul reminded his readers that fellow-workers in the harvest are "one." They are on the same team working toward the same goal.

> He who plants and he who waters are one, and each will receive his wages according to his labor (1 Corinthians 3:8 ESV).

The laborers in Christ's harvest are working toward the same goal. They are "one."

Fourth, Paul warned the Corinthian schismatics that their individual labor would not be judged as a group project. Rather, each individual worker would be judged individually for his labor. In the phrase, "each will receive his wages according to his labor," Paul used two individualistic adjectives: each (ἕκαστος) and his own (ἴδιος). Obedience to God's commands would be judged by God individually, not as a group effort. The disciple cannot blame others. He is given the Bible as a blueprint, and he will be rewarded according to his labor.

From a methodological point-of-view, Paul highlighted that he "planted" (φυτεύω) the gospel in Corinth. We read of his pioneer efforts in Acts 18. In his ministry in Corinth a house church had begun at the house of Justus, next door to the synagogue. Crispus, the rule of the synagogue believed and was baptized. We find that Paul ministered in that city for 18 months according to Acts 18:11. He was the pioneer "church planter." Later Apollos began to minister in Corinth as described in Acts 19:1. Paul described Apollos' ministry as one of "watering" (ποτίζω). Apollos built upon the pioneering work of Paul, emphasizing "teaching them to obey all that I have commanded you" (Matthew 28:20 ESV).

- Paul's ministry was: Evangelism first—Discipleship second

- Apollos' ministry was: Discipleship first—Evangelism second.

There was the rub: Is the local church primarily a vehicle for evangelism or discipleship. This rub was found in the early twentieth century, as it is in every generation of Christ's church:

> It is not wise to say that soul winning is the main thing or that soul building is the main thing. They are Siamese twins of God's gospel, going hand in hand, and they ought to keep up with each other.... And this leads me to say that the main thing in the Kingdom of God is the evangelistic spirit, the martial note and conquest tread.[1]

So Paul had to address the soul-winning and soul-building contingents to solicit their cooperation.

This same issue appears to be a primary difference between the evangelist and the pastor. Paul was the church planting

---

[1]L. R. Scarborough, *Recruits for World Conquest* (New York: Revell, 1914), 58.

evangelist in Corinth, and Apollos served as their pastor (shepherd). Consider that these two distinct leadership roles were found listed in Ephesians 4:11:

> And He Himself gave some to be apostles, some prophets, some evangelists, and some pastors and teachers (Ephesians 4:11).

Both Paul and Apollos were "working the work of God." Their different roles to the ministry were considered "one." There stands no competition between evangelism and discipleship. They are co-equal and co-important in Christ's Great Commission. Far from eclipsing man's work in these two different phases of a local church lifecycle, God worked through these men to give the increase: "God gave the growth."

> I planted, Apollos watered, but God gave the growth (1 Corinthians 3:6 ESV).

Paul and Apollos were standard-bearers of God's sovereign division of labor. In His economy of His church, all are not called to be evangelists, all are not called to be pastors, and all are not called to be teachers. True, these ministries overlap and each one necessitates participation in the other. However, Christ, who sovereignly oversees the lordship of His church and the giving of the gifts, bestows individuals with the role that He deems best for them and for His Bride, the Church.

Evangelism and Discipleship Balanced in Ezekiel 3

A very interesting Old Testament passage used the exact same verbs for the ministry of the prophet to the wicked (evangelism) and to the righteous (discipleship). The parallelism in this passage is pointed and powerful. Following the Lord's calling of Ezekiel as a watchman, He described four scenarios for Ezekiel.

> "If I say to the wicked, 'You shall surely die,' and you give him no warning [διαστέλλω], nor speak to warn [λαλέω + διαστέλλω] the wicked from his wicked way, in order to save his life, that wicked person shall die for his iniquity, but his blood I will require at your hand. But if you warn the wicked [διαστέλλω], and he does not turn from his wickedness, or from his wicked way, he shall die for his iniquity, but you will have delivered your soul. Again, if a righteous person turns from his righteousness and

commits injustice, and I lay a stumbling block before him, he shall die. Because you have not warned [διαστέλλω] him, he shall die for his sin, and his righteous deeds that he has done shall not be remembered, but his blood I will require at your hand. But if you warn [διαστέλλω] the righteous person not to sin, and he does not sin, he shall surely live, because he took warning, and you will have delivered your soul" (Ezekiel 3:18-21 ESV).

Four scenarios are manifest:

1. God warned the wicked—Ezekiel did not—Ezekiel became bloodguilty

2. God warned the wicked—Ezekiel also warned him—Ezekiel saved himself

3. God warned the righteous—Ezekiel did not do so—Ezekiel was bloodguilty

4. God warned the righteous—Ezekiel also warned him—Ezekiel saved himself.

In each of the four scenarios the same verb was used—to warn (διαστέλλω). In the case of the wicked and the righteous, the responsibility of the prophet of the Lord was "to warn." If the person took warning, they delivered themselves, if they did not take warning, they died in their iniquity. As far as God's messenger, if the prophet warned the wicked or the righteous, he was released from his responsibility. Yet if he did not warn those to whom he was sent, whether wicked or righteous, "his blood I will require at your hand."

In like manner in 1 Corinthians 3, both he who plants and he who waters are responsible for their part. The ministry of one was primarily to warn the "wicked" (evangelism). The ministry of the other was primarily to warn the "righteous" (discipleship). Paul's ministry of planting the gospel seed in the souls of "wicked" men was one of evangelism. Barnabas worked with those whom Paul had evangelized and led in repentance and faith in Christ. Barnabas' ministry of "watering" consisted of "warning" the righteous that they should not sin. As in Ezekiel 3, God used the same verbs and set the same criteria for judgment for both warning the wicked and warning the righteous.

In Exodus 32, Moses described Aaron's sin as a leader in that he did not "restrain" the people—he did not warn them so that they would not sin:

> *Now when Moses saw that the people were unrestrained (for Aaron had not restrained them, to their shame among their enemies) (Exodus 32:25).*

Even today, it is for God's leaders to help restrain their people from licentious living.

In summary, in Christ's Great Commission there is a responsibility to the wicked, that is, to evangelize them, and there is a responsibility to the righteous, that is, to "teach them to observe." Both are important, both are co-equal, and both must remain in a cooperative balance. Christ provided His people a lesson from the pen of Paul so that they would not divide into the two camps: "Evangelism First" or "Discipleship First."

From the Congregation's Perspective

Paul, who himself experienced three shipwrecks and spent 24 hours floating on the sea, being driven by the winds and waves, spoke of immature Christians being "tossed to and fro" and "carried about by every wind of doctrine" (Ephesians 4:14 ESV). These ungrounded disciples were easily caught in the "trickery of men," with their "cunning craftiness" and "deceitful plotting" (Ephesians 4:14 NKJ). Paul called these young believers and members of newly formed churches "children." They were like the unwarned righteous in Ezekiel 3.

Youthful Over-Optimism

In their newly found faith, young Christians can mimic the same optimism of Paul testified in Jerusalem:

> *"So I said, 'Lord, they know that in every synagogue I imprisoned and beat those who believe on You. And when the blood of Your martyr Stephen was shed, I also was standing by consenting to his death, and guarding the clothes of those who were killing him'"* (Acts 22:19-20).

The Lord countered the newly converted Saul of Tarsus:

"Depart, for I will send you far from here to the Gentiles" (Acts 22:21).

Astonishingly, the response of the crowd to whom Paul shared his testimony displayed that God's earlier warning to Paul was in fact valid—even years later:

And they listened to him until this word, and then they raised their voices and said, "Away with such a fellow *from the earth, for he is not fit to live!"* (Acts 22:22).

The death penalty for him! Not only was Paul preaching Jesus Christ, but he had gone to do so among the Gentiles!

Surely these new disciples do not understand the extent of the spiritual battle they face as part of their salvation. This teaching was reserved by Jesus for the Upper Room. Jesus held back promised persecution from His disciples until His last night with them:

"And these things I did not say to you at the beginning, because I was with you" (John 16:4 NASB).

God gave to Paul what he needed as he had ability to receive it. So, Christ gives to His people what they need at the proper time. Along with feeding His followers as they grow and develop, Christ has made a point of giving the proper leadership to each congregation at the proper time.

Church Leadership Gifts

The crucified, risen, and glorified Christ left the best example of leadership training. He chose, called, trained, commissioned, and supervised a group of men, who were to provide spiritual depth and maturity to the next generation of churches. These men would establish in writing the unalterable rock of His words and pass them on to the next generation.

Even so, Christ continues to designate, train, and deploy His leaders in the right way and at the right time throughout the history of the churches. Christ has done it. He has done a masterful job of it. These past 2,000 years have gone exactly according to His perfect plan—He is in total control!

As can be expected, true leadership training for the up-building the church begins and ends with Christ:

> But grace was given to each one of us according to the measure of Christ's gift. Therefore it says, "When he ascended on high he led a host of captives, and he gave gifts to men." (In saying, "He ascended," what does it mean but that he had also descended into the lower regions, the earth? He who descended is the one who also ascended far above all the heavens, that he might fill all things.) And he gave the apostles, the prophets, the evangelists, the shepherds and teachers, to equip the saints for the work of ministry, for building up the body of Christ, until we all attain to the unity of the faith and of the knowledge of the Son of God, to mature manhood, to the measure of the stature of the fullness of Christ, so that we may no longer be children, tossed to and fro by the waves and carried about by every wind of doctrine, by human cunning, by craftiness in deceitful schemes. Rather, speaking the truth in love, we are to grow up in every way into him who is the head, into Christ, from whom the whole body, joined and held together by every joint with which it is equipped, when each part is working properly, makes the body grow so that it builds itself up in love (Ephesians 4:7-16 ESV).

Paul described Christ's plan to delegate His work through five leadership roles to establish His Bride in the knowledge of the Son of God. Paul set up his comments by introducing Christ's orchestrating function, citing portions of Psalm 68 and Deuteronomy 30. Christ was the Premiere Focus of this portion of Scripture, although its purpose was to discuss the role of men in the church. Paul went to pains to keep men from usurping Christ's sovereign role and rule in His church. Christ remains the Alpha and the Omega of His church.

To introduce Christ's spiritual gift of leaders for His churches, Paul began with a quote of Psalm 68 which discusses God in the third person, the Lord in the third person, and then abruptly moves into the second person:

> You ascended on high, leading a host of captives in your train and receiving gifts among men, even among the rebellious, that the LORD God may dwell there (Psalm 68:18 ESV).

Paul applied this prophecy to Jesus, who ascended (ἀναβαίνω) into the heavens and also descended (καταβαίνω) into the lowest parts of the earth. Paul used these same verbs to describe the transcendent Christ's gift of salvation in Romans 10:6-7. Christ by His death and resurrection earned the ultimate authority, even as Moses used these verbs in Deuteronomy 30:11-14. Paul explained the human side of salvation in Romans 10. Whereas, in Ephesians 4 Paul used these verbs to affirm Christ's sovereign protection of His sheep. He would indeed provide spiritual leaders to prepare and protect His flock for their spiritual battle (Jeremiah 23:4). These leaders were described by five roles: Apostles, Prophets, Evangelists, Shepherds, and Teachers.

The ultimate purpose of these five leadership gifts was to protect the spiritual integrity of all future churches. These gifts would allow that all future gatherings of disciples would grow in love for Christ, rather than shrink into false teaching. Whether churches have men called by these titles or not, only by their presence in the midst of any congregation are they assured the promised results of Ephesians 4:12-16. It was only by the pen of the Apostles that we received the "commands of Christ" (Matthew 28:20) that have guided and nurtured Christians for over 2,000 years. These literal "words of Christ" are the rock described in Matthew 7:24-25. The divine authority radiating from this rock validates the authority of the Old Testament, the Book of Acts, and the New Testament Epistles. This rock of the words of Christ, as transcribed by His Apostles, continues to be under constant attack from the seemingly unending efforts of "deceitful plotting," "cunning craftiness," and "the trickery of men." God, however, will keep them and preserve them from this generation forever (Psalm 12:7).

Building from this unalterable foundation of the words of the Apostles, the other leaders take their place:

- Prophets warn

- Evangelists evangelize

- Pastors shepherd

- Teachers "teach them to observe all that I have commanded you" (Matthew 28:20 ESV).

Through these leaders rightfully following His words, Christ is truly present in, with, and among His people. Christ and the salvation that He wrought remains the focal point of everything.

Consider these amazing verbs in Ephesians 4:12-16:

- Evangelists gather (ὁ καταρτισμός) the elect together through their evangelism (v. 12)

- Pastors edify (ἡ οἰκοδομὴν) them (v. 12)

- Teachers truth-speak (ἀληθεύω), equipping the saints (v. 15)

- By these gifted leaders Christ grows (αὐξάνω) His body (v. 15)

- Christ joins them together (συναρμολογέω) (v. 16)

- He knits together (συμβιβάζω) as members of His body (v. 16).

It is Christ at work. It's from Him, for Him, through Him, and by Him.

Perhaps the important thing is for man to get out of the way. Let Christ be the Master Architect and Master Builder of His church, and may man submit to His complete authority, follow His directives. For Christ to be the Lord of His church, His people must obey all that He has commanded them. Leaders must take care not to drift "to the right or to the left" (Proverbs 4:27).

Proper Fellowship in the Local Church

Intersecting with Christ's gift of leaders is the New Testament "one another" commands. Those delineated as "them" in Matthew's Great Commission are called to obey the 62 "one another" commands. For example, 1 Peter 4:19 includes one of these "one another" commands:

Show hospitality to one another [ἀλλήλων] without grumbling (1 Peter 4:9 ESV).

In this verse, we find a reciprocal adverb ἀλλήλων translated by the English adverbial phrase "one another." Whereas there are 99 total

New Testament uses of ἀλλήλων ("one another"), 62 of these modify commands dealing with relationships within the local church. In these 62 commands, Christ manifested His desire for relationships within the church.

These "one another" commands address the special relational dynamic to be found in a local church body. While it is physically impossible for someone in the twentieth century to "be hospitable" to someone who lived 500 years ago, not so for someone living today. While it may be impossible to "be hospitable" to someone who resides 1,500 miles away, not so for someone who lives in our hometown. While it may be difficult or impossible for us to communicate with someone of an unknown tongue, not so for someone who speaks our own language. "Hospitality," as commanded in 1 Peter 4:9, requires geographical proximity, temporal proximity, and a fair level of linguistic commonality—hence, a "local" church.

Five "one another" commands in Galatians 5 are:

For you were called to freedom, brethren; only do not turn your freedom into an opportunity for the flesh, but through love serve one another [ἀλλήλων] (Galatians 5:13 NASB).

But if you bite and devour one another [ἀλλήλων], take care lest you be consumed by one another [ἀλλήλων] (Galatians 5:15 NASB).

Let us not become boastful, challenging one another [ἀλλήλων], envying one another [ἀλλήλων] (Galatians 5:26 NASB).

Using these five "one another" commands, Paul admonished the Galatian house churches to resolve their relational sins.

The command to "love one another" is the most prominent of the 62 "one another" commands. It is found 12 times in the New Testament. Three of them were spoken by Jesus in two verses in John 13:

"A new commandment I give to you, that you love one another [ἀλλήλων]: just as I have loved you, you also are to love one another [ἀλλήλων]. By this all people will know that you are my disciples, if you have love for one another [ἀλλήλων]" (John 13:34-35 ESV).

Jesus prophesied that He would give discernment to a watching world. The manner of love His disciples had for one another (ἀλλήλων) would display their relationship with Christ. Where the word of God rules, Christ rules. Christ rules His people by His words. When Christ's words rule, there He pours out His perfect love. This love is a foretaste of the joys of heaven, bearing witness to a watching world of something that they do not have. Seeing this love in action convicts them, tortures them, and renders them jealous. They cannot mimic this love—though they may try—it's not possible for them. Because this love comes only from God Himself:

> And hope does not put us to shame, because God's love has been poured into our hearts through the Holy Spirit who has been given to us (Romans 5:5 ESV).

It was into this loving fellowship of Jesus' disciples that Paul foresaw the rampaging of savage wolves and self-seeking men. In every stage of the Great Commission there is a battle for the souls of men.

A full assessment of all 62 "one another" commands is beyond the scope of this chapter. May the interested reader consider these commands of Christ, as they commend the behaviors that please Him within the church family.

Let Each One Take Care

Christ has no place for mavericks in His church. He calls for faithful men—rock solid and unashamedly focused upon His words. Some may seek to mix the teachings of Christ with worldly teaching. Others may garner approval in the eyes of the world. They may consider that increased worldly credibility will improve their overall impact on the world. The dangerous result of seeking the world's acclaim may in fact be watered-down truth and a watered-down faith. The salt can lose its savor. The sword can lose its edge. In a context of evangelizing, Paul wrote of his ultimate desire to please only God:

> For am I now seeking the favor of men, or of God? Or am I striving to please men? If I were still trying to please men, I would not be a bond-servant of Christ (Galatians 1:10 NASB).

With his characteristic clarity, Paul called out the Galatian church for watering down the gospel to please men. For, although the true gospel can never lose its power, Paul wrote elsewhere of diminishing the power of the gospel through supposed wisdom of words:

> For Christ did not send me to baptize, but to evangelize—not with clever words, so that the cross of Christ will not be emptied of its effect (1 Corinthians 1:17 HCSB).

Paul stated that using the wisdom of words would result in the gospel being "emptied of its effect"—or as translated another way: "made void." There are ways of evangelizing that will actually reduce the impact of the gospel—which is inherently, "the power of God to salvation" (Romans 1:16).

God admonished the false teachers in the time of Jeremiah of the dangers of mixing and blending their finite notions with God's eternal words. The result was that the people "forgot" (Hebrew *shakach*) the name of the Lord:

> "I have heard what the prophets have said who prophesy lies in my name, saying, 'I have dreamed, I have dreamed!' How long shall there be lies in the heart of the prophets who prophesy lies, and who prophesy the deceit of their own heart, who think to make my people forget my name by their dreams that they tell one another, even as their fathers forgot [shakach] my name for Baal?" (Jeremiah 23:25-27 ESV).

Much like voiding the power of the gospel through "wisdom of words," Jeremiah explained that the ministry of the false prophets led God's people to forget His name!

It is a dangerous thing to mix the tincture of human teaching to the words of God—whatever the reasoning given for its supposed necessity. A muddied pool and a polluted well are unhelpful (Proverbs 25:26). Paul preached Christ crucified, "to the Jews as stumbling block and to the Greeks foolishness." He did not attempt to please the Greeks with the wisdom of words nor to please the Jews with signs. He commended the simple preaching of Christ and His cross:

> But to those who are called, both Jews and Greeks, Christ the power of God and the wisdom of God (1 Corinthians 1:24 ESV).

321

This book now returns to its original premise. God has given His people the message of salvation. He has shown them a method of propagating that gospel. His word provides the "Regulative Principle" for New Testament church forms, and it provides patterns for Christian evangelism and mentorship. It is dangerous to be a maverick in Christ's kingdom. The unsuspecting Christian leader may think, "Perhaps the world hated Jesus, but it does not need to hate me." Jesus warned His disciples to turn away their eyes from seeking the world's acclaim:

> *"If the world hates you, know that it has hated me before* it hated *you. If you were of the world, the world would love you as its own; but because you are not of the world, but I chose you out of the world, therefore the world hates you"* (John 15:18-19).

"Let each one take care how he builds upon it" (1 Corinthians 3:10 ESV). God is interested in the "how" of ministry as well as the "what" of ministry.

This book ends returning to the emphasis of chapter one. Like a stallion in the starting gates waiting to run a race, God's living words wait in hopeful expectation to exert their life-giving power within this fallen world. These words alone are uniquely shaped to transform the human soul from death to life. They are prepared, expectant, and fully able to accomplish every good work of God. All that is needed are men and women willing to believe and use God's eternal sword.

Remain faithful to God's word in message and practice. Rediscover and relish the God-ordained methods of ministry communicated through the commands of Jesus and teaching of His Apostles. Learn from the infinite treasures lodged in His Great Commission verbs. An incredible storehouse of truth waits to be unlocked and investigated.